Percy Bysshe Shelley, Richard Herne Shepherd

Prose Works From the Original Editions

Edited, Prefaced and Annotated

Percy Bysshe Shelley, Richard Herne Shepherd

Prose Works From the Original Editions
Edited, Prefaced and Annotated

ISBN/EAN: 9783744685931

Printed in Europe, USA, Canada, Australia, Japan

Cover: Foto ©Thomas Meinert / pixelio.de

More available books at **www.hansebooks.com**

PERCY BYSSHE SHELLEY

From the Portrait by AMELIA B. CURRAN, *painted at Rome in* 1819

THE PROSE WORKS

OF

PERCY BYSSHE SHELLEY

REPRINTED FROM THE ORIGINAL EDITIONS

AND EDITED BY

RICHARD HERNE SHEPHERD

FINE-PAPER EDITION

IN TWO VOLUMES—VOL. II

WITH A FRONTISPIECE

LONDON

CHATTO & WINDUS

1912

CONTENTS.

CONTENTS.

A DEFENCE OF POETRY.

CCORDING to one mode of regarding those two. classes of mental action, which are called reason and imagination, the former may be considered as mind contemplating the relations borne by one thought to another, however produced; and the latter, as mind acting upon those thoughts so as to colour them with its own light, and composing from them, as from elements, other thoughts, each containing within itself the principle of its own integrity. The one is the τὸ ϛ ποιεῖν, or the principle of synthesis, and has for its object those forms which are common to universal nature and existence itself; the other is the τὸ λογιζειν, or principle of analysis, and its action regards the relations of things simply as relations; considering thoughts, not in their integral unity, but as the algebraical representations which conduct to certain general results. Reason is the enumeration of quantities already known; imagination is the perception of the value of those quantities, both separately and as a whole. Reason respects the differences, and imagination the similitudes of things. Reason is to imagination as the instrument to the agent, as the body to the spirit, as the shadow to the substance.

Poetry, in a general sense, may be defined to be "the pression of the imagination:" and poetry is connate

II.   A

with the origin of man. Man is an instrument over
which a series of external and internal impressions are
driven, like the alternations of an ever-changing wind
over an Æolian lyre, which move it by their motion to
ever-changing melody. But there is a principle within
the human being, and perhaps within all sentient beings,
which acts otherwise than in a lyre, and produces not
melody alone, but harmony, by an internal adjustment
of the sounds and motions thus excited to the impressions
which excite them. It is as if the lyre could accommodate its chords to the motions of that which strikes
them, in a determined proportion of sound ; even as the
musician can accommodate his voice to the sound of the
lyre. A child at play by itself will express its delight by
its voice and motions ; and every inflexion of tone and
gesture will bear exact relation to a corresponding anti-
type in the pleasurable impressions which awakened
it ; it will be the reflected image of that impression ;
and as the lyre trembles and sounds after the wind has
died away, so the child seeks, by prolonging in its voice
and motions the duration of the effect, to prolong also a
consciousness of the cause. In relation to the objects
which delight a child, these expressions are what poetry
is to higher objects. The savage (for the savage is to
ages what the child is to years) expresses the emotions
produced in him by surrounding objects in a similar
manner ; and language and gesture, together with plastic
or pictorial imitation, become the image of the combined effect of those objects and his apprehension of
them. Man in society, with all his passions and his
pleasures, next becomes the object of the passions and
pleasures of man ; an additional class of emotions
produces an augmented treasure of expression ; and
language, gesture, and the imitative arts become at
once the representation and the medium, the pencil and
the picture, the chisel and the statue, the chord and
the harmony. The social sympathies, or those

from which as from its elements society results, begin
to develop themselves from the moment that two human
beings coexist ; the future is contained within the
present as the plant within the seed ; and equality,
diversity, unity, contrast, mutual dependence, become
the principles alone capable of affording the motives
according to which the will of a social being is determined
to action, inasmuch as he is social ; and constitute
pleasure in sensation, virtue in sentiment, beauty in art,
truth in reasoning, and love in the intercourse of kind.
Hence men, even in the infancy of society, observe a
certain order in their words and actions, distinct from
that of the objects and the impressions represented by
them, all expression being subject to the laws of that
from which it proceeds. But let us dismiss those more
general considerations which might involve an inquiry
into the principles of society itself, and restrict our view
to the manner in which the imagination is expressed
upon its forms.

In the youth of the world, men dance and sing and
imitate natural objects, observing in these actions, as in
all others, a certain rhythm or order. And, although
all men observe a similar, they observe not the same
order, in the motions of the dance, in the melody of the
song, in the combinations of language, in the series of
their imitations of natural objects. For there is a certain order or rhythm belonging to each of these classes
of mimetic representation, from which the hearer and
the spectator receive an intenser and purer pleasure
than from any other : the sense of an approximation to
this order has been called taste by modern writers.
Every man in the infancy of art, observes an order which
approximates more or less closely to that from which
this highest delight results : but the diversity is not
sufficiently marked, as that its gradations should be
sensible, except in those instances where the predominance of this faculty of approximation to the beautiful

(for so we may be permitted to name the relation
between this highest pleasure and its cause) is very
great. Those in whom it exists to excess are poets, in
the most universal sense of the word ; and the pleasure
resulting from the manner in which they express the
influence of society or nature upon their own minds,
communicates itself to others, and gathers a sort of
reduplication from the community. Their language is
vitally metaphorical ; that is, it marks the before unapprehended relations of things and perpetuates their
apprehension, until words, which represent them, become,
through time, signs for portions or classes of thought,
instead of pictures of integral thoughts ; and then, if
no new poets should arise to create afresh the associations which have been thus disorganised, language will
be dead to all the nobler purposes of human intercourse. These similitudes or relations are finely said by
Bacon to be "the same footsteps of nature impressed
upon the various subjects of the world ;" *—and he considers the faculty which perceives them as the storehouse of axioms common to all knowledge. In the
infancy of society every author is necessarily a poet,
, because language itself is poetry ; and to be a poet is to
apprehend the true and the beautiful, in a word, the good
which exists in the relation subsisting, first between
existence and perception, and secondly between perception and expression. Every original language near
/ to its source is in itself the chaos of a cyclic poem :
the copiousness of lexicography and the distinctions of
grammar are the works of a later age, and are merely
the catalogue and the form of the creations of poetry.
But poets, or those who imagine and express this
indestructible order, are not only the authors of language
and of music, of the dance, and architecture, and statuary, and painting ; they are the institutors of laws and

* *De Augment. Scient.*, cap. l., lib. iii.

the founders of civil society, and the inventors of the
arts of life, and the teachers, who draw into a certain
propinquity with the beautiful and the true, that partial
apprehension of the agencies of the invisible world which
is called religion. Hence all original religions are
allegorical or susceptible of allegory, and, like Janus,
have a double face of false and true. Poets, according
to the circumstances of the age and nation in which
they appeared, were called, in the earlier epochs of the
world, legislators or prophets : a poet essentially com-
prises and unites both these characters. For he not
only beholds intensely the present as it is, and discovers
those laws according to which present things ought to be
ordered, but he beholds the future in the present, and
his thoughts are the germs of the flower and the fruit of
latest time. Not that I assert poets to be prophets in
the gross sense of the word, or that they can foretell the
form as surely as they foreknow the spirit of events :
such is the pretence of superstition, which would make
poetry an attribute of prophecy, rather than prophecy an
attribute of poetry. A poet participates in the eternal,
the infinite, and the one ; as far as relates to his conceptions, time and place and number are not. The
grammatical forms which express the moods of time,
and the difference of persons, and the distinction of
place, are convertible with respect to the highest poetry
without injuring it as poetry; and the choruses of
Æschylus, and the book of Job, and Dante's *Paradiso*,
would afford, more than any other writings, examples of
this fact, if the limits of this essay did not forbid citation.
The creations of sculpture, painting, and music, are illustrations still more decisive.

Language, colour, form, and religious and civil habits
of action, are all the instruments and materials of poetry ;
they may be called poetry by that figure of speech
which considers the effect as a synonym of the cause.
But poetry in a more restricted sense expresses those

arrangements of language, and especially metrical language, which are created by that imperial faculty, whose throne is curtained within the invisible nature of man. And this springs from the nature itself of language, which is a more direct representation of the actions and passions of our internal being, and is susceptible of more various and delicate combinations, than colour, form, or motion, and is more plastic and obedient to the control of that faculty of which it is the creation. For language is arbitrarily produced by the imagination, and has relation to thoughts alone; but all other materials, instruments, and conditions of art, have relations among each other, which limit and interpose between conception and expression. The former is as a mirror which reflects, the latter as a cloud which enfeebles, the light of which both are mediums of communication. Hence the fame of sculptors, painters, and musicians, although the intrinsic powers of the great masters of these arts may yield in no degree to that of those who have employed language as the hieroglyphic of their thoughts, has never equalled that of poets in the ⸺restricted sense of the term; as two performers of equal skill will produce unequal effects from a guitar and a harp. The fame of legislators and founders of religion, so long as their institutions last, alone seems to exceed that of poets in the restricted sense; but it can scarcely be a question, whether, if we deduct the celebrity which their flattery of the gross opinions of the vulgar usually conciliates, together with that which belonged to them in their higher character of poets, any excess will remain.

We have thus circumscribed the word poetry within the limits of that art which is the most familiar and the most perfect expression of the faculty itself. It is necessary, however, to make the circle still narrower, and to determine the distinction between measured and unmeasured language; for the popular division

into prose and verse is inadmissible in accurate philosophy.

Sounds as well as thoughts have relation both between each other and towards that which they represent, and a perception of the order of those relations
has always been found connected with a perception of
the order of the relations of thought. Hence the
language of poets has ever affected a sort of uniform
and harmonious recurrence of sound, without which it
were not poetry, and which is scarcely less indispensable
to the communication of its influence, than the words
themselves, without reference to that peculiar order.
Hence the vanity of translation ; it were as wise to cast
a violet into a crucible that you might discover the
formal principle of its colour and odour, as seek to
transfuse from one language into another the creations
of a poet. The plant must spring again from its seed,
or it will bear no flower—and this is the burthen of the
curse of Babel.

An observation of the regular mode of the recurrence
of harmony in the language of poetical minds, together
with its relation to music, produced metre, or a certain
system of traditional forms of harmony and language.
Yet it is by no means essential that a poet should
accommodate his language to this traditional form, so
that the harmony, which is its spirit, be observed. The
practice is indeed convenient and popular, and to be
preferred, especially in such composition as includes
much action : but every great poet must inevitably
innovate upon the example of his predecessors in the
exact structure of his peculiar versification. The distinction between poets and prose-writers is a vulgar
error. The distinction between philosophers and poets
has been anticipated. Plato was essentially a poet—
the truth and splendour of his imagery, and the melody
of his language, are the most intense that it is possible
to conceive. He rejected the harmony of the epic,

dramatic, and lyrical forms, because he sought to kindle a harmony in thoughts divested of shape and action, and he forbore to invent any regular plan of rhythm which would include, under determinate forms, the varied pauses of his style. Cicero sought to imitate the cadence of his periods, but with little success. Bacon was a poet.* His language has a sweet and majestic rhythm, which satisfies the sense, no less than the almost superhuman wisdom of his philosophy satisfies the intellect; it is a strain which distends, and then bursts the circumference of the reader's mind, and pours itself forth together with it into the universal element with which it has perpetual sympathy. All the authors of revolutions in opinion are not only necessarily poets as they are inventors, nor even as their words unveil the permanent analogy of things by images which participate in the life of truth; but as their periods are harmonious and rhythmical, and contain in themselves the elements of verse; being the echo of the eternal music. Nor are those supreme poets, who have employed traditional forms of rhythm on account of the form and action of their subjects, less capable of perceiving and teaching the truth of things, than those who have omitted that form. Shakespeare, Dante, and Milton (to confine ourselves to modern writers) are philosophers of the very loftiest power.

A poem is the very image of life expressed in its eternal truth. There is this difference between a story and a poem, that a story is a catalogue of detached facts, which have no other connexion than time, place, circumstance, cause, and effect : the other is the creation of actions according to the unchangeable forms of human nature, as existing in the mind of the Creator, which is itself the image of all other minds. The one is partial, and applies only to a definite period of time, and a cer-

---

* See the *Filum Labyrinthi*, and the Essay on Death particularly.

tain combination of events which can never again recur; the other is universal, and contains within itself the germ of a relation to whatever motives or actions have place in the possible varieties of human nature. Time, which destroys the beauty and the use of the story of particular facts, stripped of the poetry which should invest them, augments that of poetry, and for ever develops new and wonderful applications of the eternal truth which it contains. Hence epitomes have been called the moths of just history; they eat out the poetry of it. A story of particular facts is as a mirror which obscures and distorts that which should be beautiful: poetry is a mirror which makes beautiful that which is distorted.

The parts of a composition may be poetical, without the composition as a whole being a poem. A single sentence may be considered as a whole, though it may be found in the midst of a series of unassimilated portions; a single word even may be a spark of inextinguishable thought. And thus all the great historians, Herodotus, Plutarch, Livy, were poets; and although the plan of these writers, especially that of Livy, restrained them from developing this faculty in its highest degree, they made copious and ample amends for their subjection, by filling all the interstices of their subjects with living images.

Having determined what is poetry, and who are poets, let us proceed to estimate its effects upon society.

Poetry is ever accompanied with pleasure: all spirits upon which it falls open themselves to receive the wisdom which is mingled with its delight. In the infancy of the world, neither poets themselves nor their auditors are fully aware of the excellence of poetry: for it acts in a divine and unapprehended manner, beyond and above consciousness; and it is reserved for future generations to contemplate and measure the mighty cause and effect in all the strength and splendour of

their union. Even in modern times, no living poet ever
arrived at the fulness of his fame; the jury which sits
in judgment upon a poet, belonging as he does to all
time, must be composed of his peers : it must be
empannelled by time from the selectest of the wise of
many generations. A poet is a nightingale, who sits
in darkness and sings to cheer its own solitude with
sweet sounds; his auditors are as men entranced by
the melody of an unseen musician, who feel that they
are moved and softened, yet know not whence or why.
The poems of Homer and his contemporaries were the
delight of infant Greece; they were the elements of
that social system which is the column upon which all
succeeding civilisation has reposed. Homer embodied
the ideal perfection of his age in human character ; nor
can we doubt that those who read his verses were
awakened to an ambition of becoming like to Achilles,
Hector, and Ulysses : the truth and beauty of friendship,
patriotism, and persevering devotion to an object, were
unveiled to their depths in these immortal creations :
the sentiments of the auditors must have been refined
and enlarged by a sympathy with such great and lovely
impersonations, until from admiring they imitated, and
from imitation they identified themselves with the objects
of their admiration. Nor let it be objected, that these
characters are remote from moral perfection, and that
they are by no means to be considered as edifying
patterns for general imitation. Every epoch, under
names more or less specious, has deified its peculiar
errors ; Revenge is the naked idol of the worship of a
semibarbarous age ; and Self-deceit is the veiled image
of unknown evil, before which luxury and satiety lie
prostrate. But a poet considers the vices of his contemporaries as the temporary dress in which his
creations must be arrayed, and which cover without
concealing the eternal proportions of their beauty. An
epic or dramatic personage is understood to wear

them around his soul, as he may the ancient armour or modern uniform around his body; whilst it is easy to conceive a dress more graceful than either. The beauty of the internal nature cannot be so far concealed by its accidental vesture, but that the spirit of its form shall communicate itself to the very disguise, and indicate the shape it hides from the manner in which it is worn. A majestic form and graceful motions will express themselves through the most barbarous and tasteless costume. Few poets of the highest class have chosen to exhibit the beauty of their conceptions in its naked truth and splendour; and it is doubtful whether the alloy of costume, habit, &c., be not necessary to temper this planetary music for mortal ears.

The whole objection, however, of the immorality of poetry rests upon a misconception of the manner in which poetry acts to produce the moral improvement of man. Ethical science arranges the elements which poetry has created, and propounds schemes and pro- poses examples of civil and domestic life: nor is it for want of admirable doctrines that men hate, and despise, and censure, and deceive, and subjugate one another. But poetry acts in another and diviner manner. It awakens and enlarges the mind itself by rendering it the receptacle of a thousand unapprehended combina- tions of thought. Poetry lifts the veil from the hidden beauty of the world, and makes familiar objects be as if they were not familiar; it reproduces all that it re- presents, and the impersonations clothed in its Elysian light stand thenceforward in the minds of those who have once contemplated them, as memorials of that gentle and exalted content which extends itself over all thoughts and actions with which it coexists. The great secret of morals is love; or a going out of our own nature, and an identification of ourselves with the beautiful which exists in thought, action, or person, not our own. A man, to be greatly good, must imagine

intensely and comprehensively; he must put himself in
the place of another and of many others; the pains and
pleasures of his species must become his own.   The
great instrument of moral good is the imagination;
and p etry administers to the effect by acting upon
the cause.   Poetry enlarges the circumference of the
imagination by replenishing it with thoughts of ever new
delight, which have the power of attracting and assimilating to their own nature all other thoughts, and which
form new intervals and interstices whose void for ever
craves fresh food.   Poetry strengthens the faculty which
is the organ of the moral nature of man, in the same
manner as exercise strengthens a limb.   A poet therefore
would do ill to embody his own conceptions of right and
wrong, which are usually those of his place and time, in
his poetical creations, which participate in neither.   By
this assumption of the inferior office of interpreting
the effect, in which perhaps after all he might acquit
himself but imperfectly, he would resign a glory in the
participation of the cause.   There was little danger
that Homer, or any of the eternal poets, should have
so far misunderstood themselves as to have abdicated
this throne of their widest dominion.   Those in whom
the poetical faculty, though great, is less intense, as
Euripides, Lucan, Tasso, Spenser, have frequently
affected a moral aim, and the effect of their poetry is
diminished in exact proportion to the degree in which
they compel us to advert to this purpose.

Homer and the cyclic poets were followed at a certain
interval by the dramatic and lyrical poets of Athens,
who flourished contemporaneously with all that is most
perfect in the kindred expressions of the poetical faculty;
architecture, painting, music, the dance, sculpture, philosophy, and we may add, the forms of civil life.   For
although the scheme of Athenian society was deformed
by many imperfections which the poetry existing in
chivalry and Christianity has erased from the habits

and institutions of modern Europe; yet never at any other period has so much energy, beauty and virtue, been developed; never was blind strength and stubborn form so disciplined and rendered subject to the will of man, or that will less repugnant to the dictates of the beautiful and the true, as during the century which preceded the death of Socrates. Of no other epoch in the history of our species have we records and fragments stamped so visibly with the image of the divinity in man. But it is poetry alone, in form, in action, and in language, which has rendered this epoch memorable above all others, and the storehouse of examples to everlasting time. For written poetry existed at that epoch simultaneously with the other arts, and it is an idle inquiry to demand which gave and which received the light, which all, as from a common focus, have scattered over the darkest periods of succeeding time. We know no more of cause and effect than a constant conjunction of events: poetry is ever found to co-exist with whatever other arts contribute to the happiness and perfection of man. I appeal to what has already been established to distinguish between the cause and the effect.

It was at the period here adverted to, that the drama had its birth; and however a succeeding writer may have equalled or surpassed those few great specimens of the Athenian drama which have been preserved to us, it is indisputable that the art itself never was understood, or practised according to the true philosophy of it, as at Athens. For the Athenians employed language, action, music, painting, the dance, and religious institutions, to produce a common effect in the representation of the highest idealisms of passion and of power; each division in the art was made perfect in its kind by artists of the most consummate skill, and was disciplined into a beautiful proportion and unity one towards the other. On the modern stage a few only of the elements capable

of expressing the image of the poet's conception are employed at once. We have tragedy without music and
dancing; and music and dancing without the highest
impersonations of which they are the fit accompaniment,
and both without religion and solemnity. Religious
institution has indeed been usually banished from the
stage. Our system of divesting the actor's face of a
mask, on which the many expressions appropriated to
his dramatic character might be moulded into one
permanent and unchanging expression, is favourable
only to a partial and inharmonious effect; it is fit for
nothing but a monologue, where all the attention may
be directed to some great master of ideal mimicry.
The modern practice of blending comedy with tragedy,
though liable to great abuse in point of practice, is
undoubtedly an extension of the dramatic circle; but
the comedy should be as in King Lear, universal, ideal,
and sublime. It is perhaps the intervention of this
principle which determines the balance in favour of
King Lear against the Œdipus Tyrannus or the
Agamemnon, or, if you will, the trilogies with which
they are connected; unless the intense power of the
choral poetry, especially that of the latter, should be
considered as restoring the equilibrium. King Lear, if
it can sustain this comparison, may be judged to be the
most perfect specimen of the dramatic art existing in
the world; in spite of the narrow conditions to which
the poet was subjected by the ignorance of the philosophy
of the drama which has prevailed in modern Europe.
Calderon, in his religious Autos, has attempted to fulfil
some of the high conditions of dramatic representation
neglected by Shakespeare; such as the establishing a
relation between the drama and religion, and the accom-
modating them to music and dancing; but he omits the
observation of conditions still more important, and more
is lost than gained by the substitution of the rigidly-
defined and ever-repeated idealisms of a distorted

superstition for the living impersonations of the truth of
human passions.

But I digress.—The connexion of scenic exhibitions
with the improvement or corruption of the manners
of men, has been universally recognised: in other
words, the presence or absence of poetry, in its most
perfect and universal form, has been found to be connected with good and evil in conduct or habit. The
corruption which has been imputed to the drama as
an effect, begins, when the poetry employed in its
constitution ends: I appeal to the history of manners
whether the periods of the growth of the one and the
decline of the other have not corresponded with an
exactness equal to any example of moral cause and
effect.

The drama at Athens, or wheresoever else it may
have approached to its perfection, ever co-existed with
the moral and intellectual greatness of the age. The
tragedies of the Athenian poets are as mirrors in which
the spectator beholds himself, under a thin disguise
of circumstance, stript of all but that ideal perfection
and energy which every one feels to be the internal
type of all that he loves, admires, and would become.
The imagination is enlarged by a sympathy with pains
and passions so mighty, that they distend in their conception the capacity of that by which they are conceived,
the good affections are strengthened by pity, indignation,
terror and sorrow; and an exalted calm is prolonged
from the satiety of this high exercise of them into the
tumult of familiar life: even crime is disarmed of half
its horror and all its contagion by being represented as
the fatal consequence of the unfathomable agencies of
nature; error is thus divested of its wilfulness; men
can no longer cherish it as the creation of their choice.
In the drama of the highest order there is little food for
censure or hatred; it teaches rather self-knowledge and
self-respect. Neither the eye nor the mind can see itself,

unless reflected upon that which it resembles. The
drama, so long as it continues to express poetry, is a
prismatic and many-sided mirror, which collects the
brightest rays of human nature and divides and reproduces them from the simplicity of these elementary
forms, and touches them with majesty and beauty, and
multiplies all that it reflects, and endows it with the
power of propagating its like wherever it may fall.

But in periods of the decay of social life, the drama
sympathises with that decay. Tragedy becomes a cold
imitation of the form of the great masterpieces of antiquity, divested of all harmonious accompaniment of the
kindred arts ; and often the very form misunderstood,
or a weak attempt to teach certain doctrines, which the
writer considers as moral truths ; and which are usually
no more than specious flatteries of some gross vice or
weakness, with which the author, in common with his
auditors, are infected. Hence what has been called
the classical and domestic drama. Addison's " Cato "
is a specimen of the one ; and would it were not superfluous to cite examples of the other ! To such purposes
poetry cannot be made subservient. Poetry is a sword
of lightning, ever unsheathed, which consumes the
scabbard that would contain it. And thus we observe
that all dramatic writings of this nature are unimagina-
tive in a singular degree ; they affect sentiment and
passion, which, divested of imagination, are other names
for caprice and appetite. The period in our own history
of the grossest degradation of the drama is the reign of
Charles II., when all forms in which poetry had been
accustomed to be expressed became hymns to the
triumph of kingly power over liberty and virtue. Milton
stood alone illuminating an age unworthy of him. At
such periods the calculating principle pervades all the
forms of dramatic exhibition, and poetry ceases to be
expressed upon them. Comedy loves its ideal univer-
sality : wit succeeds to humour ; we laugh from self-

complacency and triumph, instead of pleasure; malignity, sarcasm, and contempt succeed to sympathetic merriment; we hardly laugh, but we smile. Obscenity, which is ever blasphemy against the divine beauty in life, becomes, from the very veil which it assumes, more active if less disgusting: it is a monster for which the corruption of society for ever brings forth new food, which it devours in secret.

The drama being that form under which a greater number of modes of expression of poetry are susceptible of being combined than any other, the connexion of poetry and social good is more observable in the drama than in whatever other form. And it is indisputable that the highest perfection of human society has ever corresponded with the highest dramatic excellence; and that the corruption or the extinction of the drama in a nation where it has once flourished, is a mark of a corruption of manners, and an extinction of the energies which sustain the soul of social life. But, as Macchiavelli says of political institutions, that life may be preserved and renewed, if men should arise capable of bringing back the drama to its principles. And this is true with respect to poetry in its most extended sense: all language, institution and form require not only to be produced but to be sustained: the office and character of a poet participates in the divine nature as regards providence, no less than as regards creation.

Civil war, the spoils of Asia, and the fatal predominance first of the Macedonian, and then of the Roman arms, were so many symbols of the extinction or suspension of the creative faculty in Greece. The bucolic writers, who found patronage under the lettered tyrants of Sicily and Egypt, were the latest representatives of its most glorious reign. Their poetry is intensely melodious; like the odour of the tuberose, it overcomes and sickens the spirit with excess of sweetness; whilst the poetry of the preceding age was as a meadow-gale

of June, which mingles the fragrance of all the flowers
of the field, and adds a quickening and harmonising
spirit of its own which endows the sense with a power
of sustaining its extreme delight. The bucolic and
erotic delicacy in written poetry is correlative with that
softness in statuary, music, and the kindred arts, and
even in manners and institutions, which distinguished
the epoch to which I now refer. Nor is it the poetical
faculty itself, or any misapplication of it, to which this
want of harmony is to be imputed. An equal sensibility
to the influence of the senses and the affections is to be
found in the writings of Homer and Sophocles : the
former, especially, has clothed sensual and pathetic
images with irresistible attractions. The superiority in
these to succeeding writers consists in the presence of
those thoughts which belong to the inner faculties of our
nature, not in the absence of those which are connected
with the external : their incomparable perfection consists
in a harmony of the union of all. It is not what the
erotic poets have, but what they have not, in which
their imperfection consists. It is not inasmuch as they
were poets, but inasmuch as they were not poets, that
they can be considered with any plausibility as connected with the corruption of their age. Had that
corruption availed so as to extinguish in them the
sensibility to pleasure, passion, and natural scenery,
which is imputed to them as an imperfection, the last
triumph of evil would have been achieved. For the
end of social corruption is to destroy all sensibility to
pleasure ; and, therefore, it is corruption. It begins at
the imagination and the intellect as at the core, and
distributes itself thence as a paralysing venom, through
the affections into the very appetites, until all become
a torpid mass in which hardly sense survives. At the
approach of such a period, poetry ever addresses itself
to those faculties which are the last to be destroyed,
and its voice is heard, like the footsteps of Astræa,

departing from the world. Poetry ever communicates all the pleasure which men are capable of receiving : it is ever still the light of life ; the source of whatever of beautiful or generous or true can have place in an evil time. It will readily be confessed that those among the luxurious citizens of Syracuse and Alexandria, who were delighted with the poems of Theocritus, were less cold, cruel, and sensual than the remnant of their tribe. But corruption must utterly have destroyed the fabric of human society before poetry can ever cease. The sacred links of that chain have never been entirely disjoined, which descending through the minds of many men is attached to those great minds, whence as from a magnet the invisible effluence is sent forth, which at once connects, animates, and sustains the life of all. It is the faculty which contains within itself the seeds at once of its own and of social renovation. And let us not circumscribe the effects of the bucolic and erotic poetry within the limits of the sensibility of those to whom it was addressed. They may have perceived the beauty of those immortal compositions, simply as frag-ments and isolated portions : those who are more finely organised, or born in a happier age, may recognise them as episodes to that great poem, which all poets, like the co-operating thoughts of one great mind, have built up since the beginning of the world.

The same revolutions within a narrower sphere had place in ancient Rome ; but the actions and forms of its social life never seem to have been perfectly saturated with the poetical element. The Romans appear to have considered the Greeks as the selectest treasuries of the selectest forms of manners and of nature, and to have abstained from creating in measured language, sculp-ture, music, or architecture, any thing which might bear. a particular relation to their own condition, whilst it should bear a general one to the universal constitution of the world. But we judge from partial evidence, and we judge perhaps partially. Ennius, Varro, Pacuvius, and Accius, all great poets, have been lost. Lucretius is in the highest, and Virgil in a very high sense, a creator. The chosen delicacy of expressions of the latter are as a mist of light which conceal from us the intense and exceeding truth of his conceptions of nature. Livy is instinct with poetry. Yet Horace, Catullus, Ovid, and generally the other great writers of the Virgilian age, saw man and nature in the mirror of Greece. The institutions also, and the religion of Rome, were less poetical than those of Greece, as the shadow is less vivid than the substance. Hence poetry in Rome seemed to follow, rather than accompany, the perfection of political and domestic society. The true poetry of Rome lived in its institutions ; for whatever of beautiful, true, and majestic, they contained, could have sprung only from the faculty which creates the order in which they consist. The life of Camillus, the death of Regulus ; the expectation of the senators, in their godlike state, of the victorious Gauls ; the refusal of the republic to make peace with Hannibal, after the battle of Cannæ, were not the consequences of a refined calculation of the probable personal advantage to result from such a rhythm and order in the shows of life, to those who were at once the poets and the actors of these immortal dramas. The imagination beholding the beauty of this order, created it out of itself according to its own idea ; the consequence was empire, and the reward everlasting fame. These things are not the less poetry, *quia carent vate sacro.* They are the episodes of that cyclic poem written by Time upon the memories of men. The Past, like an inspired rhapsodist, fills the theatre of everlasting generations with their harmony.

At length the ancient system of religion and manners had fulfilled the circle of its evolutions. And the world would have fallen into utter anarchy and darkness, but

that there were found poets among the authors of the
Christian and chivalric systems of manners and religion,
who created forms of opinion and action never before
conceived ; which, copied into the imaginations of men,
became as generals to the bewildered armies of their
thoughts.   It is foreign to the present purpose to touch
upon the evil produced by these systems : except that
we protest, on the ground of the principles already
established, that no portion of it can be attributed to
the poetry they contain.

It is probable that the poetry of Moses, Job, David,
Solomon, and Isaiah, had produced a great effect upon
the mind of Jesus and his disciples.   The scattered
fragments preserved to us by the biographers of this
extraordinary person are all instinct with the most
vivid poetry.   But his doctrines seem to have been
quickly distorted.   At a certain period after the pre-
valence of a system of opinions founded upon those
promulgated by him, the three forms into which Plato
had distributed the faculties of mind underwent a sort
of apotheosis, and became the object of the worship of
the civilised world.   Here it is to be confessed that
" Light seems to thicken," and

"The crow makes wing to the rooky wood,
Good things of day begin to droop and drowse,
And night's black agents to their preys do rouse." *

But mark how beautiful an order has sprung from the
dust and blood of this fierce chaos ! how the world, as
from a resurrection, balancing itself on the golden wings
of knowledge and of hope, has reassumed its yet un-
wearied flight into the heaven of time.   Listen to the
music, unheard by outward ears, which is as a ceaseless
and invisible wind, nourishing its everlasting course
with strength and swiftness.

[' Macbeth, act iii. scene 2.]

The poetry in the doctrines of Jesus, and the mythology and institutions of the Celtic conquerors of the
Roman empire, outlived the darkness and the convul-
sions connected with their growth and victory, and
blended themselves in a new fabric of manners and
opinion.   It is an error to impute the ignorance of the
dark ages to the Christian doctrines or the predominance
of the Celtic nations.   Whatever of evil their agencies
may have contained sprang from the extinction of the
poetical principle, connected with the progress of despotism and superstition.   Men, from causes too intricate
to be here discussed, had become insensible and selfish :
their own will had become feeble, and yet they were its
slaves, and thence the slaves of the will of others : but
fear, avarice, cruelty, and fraud, characterised a race
amongst whom no one was to be found capable of
creating in form, language, or institution.   The moral
anomalies of such a state of society are not justly to be
charged upon any class of events immediately connected
with them, and those events are most entitled to our
approbation which could dissolve it most expeditiously.
It is unfortunate for those who cannot distinguish words
from thoughts, that many of these anomalies have been
incorporated into our popular religion.

It was not until the eleventh century that the effects
of the poetry of the Christian and chivalric systems
began to manifest themselves.   The principle of equality
had been discovered and applied by Plato in his Republic,
as the theoretical rule of the mode in which the materials
of pleasure and of power, produced by the common skill
and labour of human beings, ought to be distributed
among them.   The limitations of this rule were asserted
by him to be determined only by the sensibility of each,
or the utility to result to all.   Plato, following the
doctrines of Timæus and Pythagoras, taught also a
moral and intellectual system of doctrine, comprehending at once the past, the present, and the future con-

dition of man. Jesus divulged the sacred and eternal
truths contained in these views to mankind, and
Christianity, in its abstract purity, became the exoteric
expression of the esoteric doctrines of the poetry and
wisdom of antiquity. The incorporation of the Celtic
nations with the exhausted population of the south,
impressed upon it the figure of the poetry existing in
their mythology and institutions. The result was a sum
of the action and reaction of all the causes included in
it ; for it may be assumed as a maxim that no nation
or religion can supersede any other without incorporat-
ing into itself a portion of that which it supersedes.
The abolition of personal and domestic slavery, and the
emancipation of women from a great part of the degrading restraints of antiquity, were among the consequences of these events.

The abolition of personal slavery is the basis of the
highest political hope that it can enter into the mind of
man to conceive. The freedom of women produced the
poetry of sexual love. Love became a religion, the
idols of whose worship were ever present. It was as if
the statues of Apollo and the Muses had been endowed
with life and motion, and had walked forth among their
worshippers ; so that earth became peopled by the
inhabitants of a diviner world. The familiar appearance and proceedings of life became wonderful and
heavenly, and a paradise was created as out of the
wrecks of Eden. And as this creation itself is poetry,
so its creators were poets ; and language was the
instrument of their art : " Galeotto fù il libro, e chi lo
scrisse." The Provençal Trouveurs, or inventors, preceded Petrarch, whose verses are as spells, which
unseal the inmost enchanted fountains of the delight
which is in the grief of love. It is impossible to feel
them without becoming a portion of that beauty which
we contemplate : it were superfluous to explain how the
gentleness and elevation of mind connected with these

sacred emotions can render men more amiable, more
generous and wise, and lift them out of the dull vapours
of the little world of self. Dante understood the secret
things of love even more than Petrarch. His *Vita
Nuova* is an inexhaustible fountain of purity of sentiment and language : it is the idealised history of that
period, and those intervals of his life which were dedicated to love. His apotheosis to Beatrice in Paradise,
and the gradations of his own love and her loveliness,
by which as by steps he feigns himself to have ascended
to the throne of the Supreme Cause, is the most glorious
imagination of modern poetry. The acutest critics have
justly reversed the judgment of the vulgar, and the order
of the great acts of the " Divina Commedia," in the
measure of the admiration which they accord to the
Hell, Purgat ry. and Paradise. The latter is a perpetual hymn of everlasting love. Love, which found
a worthy poet in Plato alone of all the ancients, has
been celebrated by a chorus of the greatest writers of
the renovated world ; and the music has penetrated
the caverns of society, and its echoes still drown the
dissonance of arms and superstition. At successive
intervals, Ariosto, Tasso, Shakespeare, Spenser, Calderon, Rousseau, and the great writers of our own
age, have celebrated the dominion of love, planting as
it were trophies in the human mind of that sublimest
victory over sensuality and force. The true relation
borne to each other by the sexes into which human
kind is distributed, has become less misunderstood ;
and if the error which confounded diversity with
inequality of the powers of the two sexes has been
partially recognised in the opinions and institutions of
modern Europe, we owe this great benefit to the
worship of which chivalry was the law, and poets the
prophets.

The poetry of Dante may be considered as the bridge
thrown over the stream of time, which unites the modern

and ancient world. The distorted notions of invisible things which Dante and his rival Milton have idealised, are merely the mask and the mantle in which these great poets walk through eternity enveloped and disguised. It is a difficult question to determine how far they were conscious of the distinction which must have subsisted in their minds between their own creeds and that of the people. Dante at least appears to wish to mark the full extent of it by placing Riphæus, whom Virgil calls *justissimus unus*, in Paradise, and observing a most poetical caprice in his distribution of rewards and punishments. And Milton's poem contains within itself a philosophical refutation of that system of which, by a strange and natural antithesis, it has been a chief popular support. Nothing can exceed the energy and magnificence of the character of Satan as expressed in "Paradise Lost." It is a mistake to suppose that he could ever have been intended for the popular personification of evil. Implacable hate, patient cunning, and a sleepless refinement of device to inflict the extremest anguish on an enemy, these things are evil; and, although venial in a slave, are not to be forgiven in a tyrant; although redeemed by much that ennobles his defeat in one subdued, are marked by all that dishonours his conquest in the victor. Milton's Devil as a moral being is as far superior to his God, as one who perseveres in some purpose which he has conceived to be excellent in spite of adversity and torture, is to one who in the cold security of undoubted triumph inflicts the most horrible revenge upon his enemy, not from any mistaken notion of inducing him to repent of a perseverance in enmity, but with the alleged design of exasperating him to deserve new torments. Milton has so far violated the popular creed (if this shall be judged to be a violation) as to have alleged no superiority of moral virtue to his god over his devil. And this bold neglect of a direct moral purpose is the most decisive proof of the supremacy of Milton's genius. He mingled as it were the elements of human nature as colours upon a single palette, and arranged them in the composition of his great picture according to the laws of epic truth, that is, according to the laws of that principle by which a series of actions of the external universe and of intelligent and ethical beings is calculated to excite the sympathy of succeeding generations of mankind. The Divina Commedia and Paradise Lost have conferred upon modern mythology a systematic form ; and when change and time shall have added one more superstition to the mass of those which have arisen and decayed upon the earth, commentators will be learnedly employed in elucidating the religion of ancestral Europe, only not utterly forgotten because it will have been stamped with the eternity of genius.

Homer was the first and Dante the second epic poet : that is, the second poet, the series of whose creations bore a defined and intelligible relation to the knowledge and sentiment and religion of the age in which he lived, and of the ages which followed it : developing itself in correspondence with their development. For Lucretius had limed the wings of his swift spirit in the dregs of the sensible world ; and Virgil, with a modesty that ill became his genius, had affected the fame of an imitator, even whilst he created anew all that he copied ; and none among the flock of mock-birds, though their notes are sweet, Apollonius Rhodius, Quintus Calaber, Smyrnæus, Nonnus, Lucan, Statius, or Claudian, have sought even to fulfil a single condition of epic truth. Milton was the third epic poet. For if the title of epic in its highest sense be refused to the Æneid, still less can it be conceded to the Orlando Furioso, the Gerusalemme Liberata, the Lusiad, or the Fairy Queen.

Dante and Milton were both deeply penetrated with the ancient religion of the civilised world ; and its spirit

exists in their poetry probably in the same proportion as
its forms survived in the unreformed worship of modern
Europe. The one preceded and the other followed the
Reformation at almost equal intervals. Dante was the
first religious reformer, and Luther surpassed him
rather in the rudeness and acrimony, than in the bold-
ness of his censures, of papal usurpation. Dante was
the first awakener of entranced Europe ; he created a
language, in itself music and persuasion, out of a chaos
of inharmonious barbarisms. He was the congregator
of those great spirits who presided over the resurrection
of learning ; the Lucifer of that starry flock which in
the thirteenth century shone forth from republican Italy,
as from a heaven, into the darkness of the benighted
world. His very words are instinct with spirit ; each is
as a spark, a burning atom of inextinguishable thought ;
and many yet lie covered in the ashes of their birth, and
pregnant with a lightning which has yet found no con-
ductor. All high poetry is infinite ; it is as the first
acorn, which contained all oaks potentially. Veil after
veil may be undrawn, and the inmost naked beauty of
the meaning never exposed. A great poem is a fountain
for ever overflowing with the waters of wisdom and
delight ; and after one person and one age has exhausted
all of its divine effluence which their peculiar relations
enable them to share, another and yet another succeeds,
and new relations are ever developed, the source of an
unforeseen and an unconceived delight.

The age immediately succeeding to that of Dante,
Petrarch, and Boccaccio, was characterised by a revival
of painting, sculpture, and architecture. Chaucer caught
the sacred inspiration, and the superstructure of English
literature is based upon the materials of Italian invention.

But let us not be betrayed from a defence into a
critical history of poetry and its influence on society.
Be it enough to have pointed out the effects of poets, in

the large and true sense of the word, upon their own
and all succeeding times.

But poets have been challenged to resign the civic
crown to reasoners and mechanists, on another plea.
It is admitted that the exercise of the imagination is
most delightful, but it is alleged that that of reason is
more useful. Let us examine, as the grounds of this
distinction, what is here meant by utility. Pleasure or
good, in a general sense, is that which the consciousness
of a sensitive and intelligent being seeks, and in which,
when found, it acquiesces. There are two kinds of
pleasure, one durable, universal, and permanent ; the
other transitory and particular. Utility may either
express the means of producing the former or the latter.
In the former sense, whatever strengthens and purifies
the affections, enlarges the imagination, and adds spirit
to sense, is useful. But a narrower meaning may be
assigned to the word utility, confining it to express that
which banishes the importunity of the wants of our
animal nature, the surrounding men with security of
life, the dispersing the grosser delusions of superstition,
and the conciliating such a degree of mutual forbearance
among men as may consist with the motives of personal
advantage.

Undoubtedly the promoters of utility, in this limited
sense, have their appointed office in society. They
follow the footsteps of poets, and copy the sketches
of their creations into the book of common life. They
make space, and give time. Their exertions are of the
highest value, so long as they confine their administration of the concerns of the inferior powers of our nature
within the limits due to the superior ones. But while
the sceptic destroys gross superstitions, let him spare to
deface, as some of the French writers have defaced,
the eternal truths charactered upon the imaginations of
men. Whilst the mechanist abridges, and the political
economist combines, labour, let them beware that their

speculations, for want of correspondence with those first principles which belong to the imagination, do not tend, as they have in modern England, to exasperate at once the extremes of luxury and want. They have exemplified the saying, " To him that hath, more shall be given ; and from him that hath not, the little that he hath shall be taken away."* The rich have become richer, and the poor have become poorer ; and the vessel of the state is driven between the Scylla and Charybdis of anarchy and despotism. Such are the effects which must ever flow from an unmitigated exercise of the calculating faculty.

It is difficult to define pleasure in its highest sense ; the definition involving a number of apparent paradoxes. For, from an inexplicable defect of harmony in the constitution of human nature, the pain of the inferior is frequently connected with the pleasures of the superior portions of our being. Sorrow, terror, anguish, despair itself, are often the chosen expressions of an approximation to the highest good. Our sympathy in tragic fiction depends on this principle ; tragedy delights by affording a shadow of that pleasure which exists in pain. This is the source also of the melancholy which is inseparable from the sweetest melody. The pleasure that is in sorrow is sweeter than the pleasure of pleasure itself. And hence the saying, " It is better to go to the house of mourning than to the house of mirth." † Not that this highest species of pleasure is necessarily linked with pain. The delight of love and friendship, the ecstasy of the admiration of nature, the joy of the perception and still more of the creation of poetry, is often wholly unalloyed.

The production and assurance of pleasure in this highest sense is true utility. Those who produce and preserve this pleasure are poets or poetical philosophers.

* A misquotation of Mark iv. 25.—ED.
† A misquotation of Ecclesiastes vii. 2.—ED.

The exertions of Locke, Hume, Gibbon, Voltaire, Rousseau,* and their disciples, in favour of oppressed and deluded humanity, are entitled to the gratitude of mankind. Yet it is easy to calculate the degree of moral and intellectual improvement which the world would have exhibited, had they never lived. A little more nonsense would have been talked for a century or two ; and perhaps a few more men, women, and children, burnt as heretics. We might not at this moment have been congratulating each other on the abolition of the Inquisition in Spain. But it exceeds all imagination to conceive what would have been the moral condition of the world if neither Dante, Petrarch, Boccaccio, Chaucer, Shakespeare, Calderon, Bacon, nor Milton, had ever existed ; if Raphael and Michael Angelo had never been born ; if the Hebrew poetry had never been translated ; if a revival of the study of Greek literature had never taken place ; if no monuments of ancient sculpture had been handed down to us ; and if the poetry of the religion of the ancient world had been extinguished together with its belief. The human mind could never, except by the intervention of these excitements, have been awakened to the invention of the grosser sciences, and that application of analytical reasoning to the aberrations of society, which it is now attempted to exalt over the direct expression of the inventive and creative faculty itself.

We have more moral, political, and historical wisdom than we know how to reduce into practice ; we have more scientific and economical knowledge than can be accommodated to the just distribution of the produce which it multiplies. The poetry, in these systems of thought, is concealed by the accumulation of facts and

* Although Rousseau has been thus classed, he was essentially a poet. The others, even Voltaire, were mere reasoners. [*Author's note.*]

calculating processes. There is no want of knowledge respecting what is wisest and best in morals, government, and political economy, or at least what is wiser and better than what men now practise and endure. But we let "*I dare not* wait upon *I would*, like the poor cat in the adage." We want the creative faculty to imagine that which we know; we want the generous impulse to act that which we imagine; we want the poetry of life : our calculations have outrun conception ; we have eaten more than we can digest. The cultivation of those sciences which have enlarged the limits of the empire of man over the external world, has, for want of the poetical faculty, proportionally circumscribed those of the internal world ; and man, having enslaved the elements, remains himself a slave. To what but a cultivation of the mechanical arts in a degree disproportioned to the presence of the creative faculty, which is the basis of all knowledge, is to be attributed the abuse of all invention for abridging and combining labour, to the exasperation of the inequality of mankind ? From what other cause has it arisen that the discoveries which should have lightened, have added a weight to the curse imposed on Adam ? Poetry, and the principle of Self, of which money is the visible incarnation, are the God and Mammon of the world.

The functions of the poetical faculty are twofold ; by one it creates new materials of knowledge, and power, and pleasure ; by the other it engenders in the mind a desire to reproduce and arrange them according to a certain rhythm and order, which may be called the beautiful and the good. The cultivation of poetry is never more to be desired than at periods when, from an excess of the selfish and calculating principle, the accumulation of the materials of external life exceed the quantity of the power of assimilating them to the internal laws of human nature. The body has then become too unwieldy for that which animates it.

Poetry is indeed something divine. It is at once the
centre and circumference of knowledge ; it is that which
comprehends all science, and that to which all science
must be referred. It is at the same time the root and
blossom of all other systems of thought ; it is that from
which all spring, and that which adorns all ; and that
·which, if blighted, denies the fruit and the seed, and
withholds from the barren world the nourishment and
the succession of the scions of the tree of life. It is the
perfect and consummate surface and bloom of all things ;
it is as the odour and the colour of the rose to the
texture of the elements which compose it, as the form and
splendour of unfaded beauty to the secrets of anatomy
and corruption. What were virtue, love, patriotism,
friendship,—what were the scenery of this beautiful
universe which we inhabit ; what were our consolations
on this side of the grave—and what were our aspirations
beyond it, if poetry did not ascend to bring light and
fire from those eternal regions where the owl-winged
faculty of calculation dare not ever soar ? Poetry is
not like reasoning, a power to be exerted according to
the determination of the will. A man cannot say, " I
will compose poetry." The greatest poet even cannot
say it ; for the mind in creation is as a fading coal,
which some invisible influence, like an inconstant wind,
awakens to transitory brightness ; this power arises
from within, like the colour of a flower which fades and
changes as it is developed, and the conscious portions
of our nature are unprophetic either of its approach or
its departure. Could this influence be durable in its
original purity and force, it is impossible to predict the
greatness of the results ; but when composition begins,
inspiration is already on the decline, and the most
glorious poetry that has ever been communicated to the
world is probably a feeble shadow of the original conceptions of the poet. I appeal to the greatest poets of
the present day, whether it is not an error to assert that

the finest passages of poetry are produced by labour and study. The toil and the delay recommended by critics can be justly interpreted to mean no more than a careful observation of the inspired moments, and an artificial connexion of the spaces between their suggestions, by the intertexture of conventional expressions ; a necessity only imposed by the limitedness of the poetical faculty itself: for Milton conceived the Paradise Lost as a whole before he executed it in portions. We have his own authority also for the muse having "dictated" to him the "unpremeditated song." And let this be an answer to those who would allege the fifty-six various readings of the first line of the Orlando Furioso. Compositions so produced are to poetry what mosaic is to painting. The instinct and intuition of the poetical faculty is still more observable in the plastic and pictorial arts : a great statue or picture grows under the power of the artist as a child in the mother's womb ; and the very mind which directs the hands in formation, is incapable of accounting to itself for the origin, the gradations, or the media of the process.

Poetry is the record of the best and happiest moments of the happiest and best minds. We are aware of evanescent visitations of thought and feeling, sometimes associated with place or person, sometimes regarding our own mind alone, and always arising unforeseen and departing unbidden, but elevating and delightful beyond all expression : so that even in the desire and the regret they leave, there cannot but be pleasure, participating as it does in the nature of its object. It is as it were the interpenetration of a diviner nature through our own ; but its footsteps are like those of a wind over the sea, which the morning calm erases, and whose traces remain only, as on the wrinkled sand which paves it. These and corresponding conditions of being are experienced principally by those of the most delicate sensibility and the most enlarged imagination ; and the state of mind produced by them is at war with every base desire. The enthusiasm of virtue, love, patriotism, and friendship, is essentially linked with such emotions ; and whilst they last, self appears as what it is, an atom to a universe. Poets are not only subject to these experiences as spirits of the most refined organisation, but they can colour all that they combine with the evanescent hues of this ethereal world ; a word, a trait in the representation of a scene or a passion, will touch the enchanted chord, and reanimate, in those who have ever experienced those emotions, the sleeping, the cold, the buried image of the past. Poetry thus makes immortal all that is best and most beautiful in the world ; it arrests the vanishing apparitions which haunt the interlunations of life, and veiling them, or in language or in form, sends them forth among mankind, bearing sweet news of kindred joy to those with whom their sisters abide—abide, because there is no portal of expression from the caverns of the spirit which they inhabit into the universe of things. Poetry redeems from decay the visitations of the divinity in man.

Poetry turns all things to loveliness ; it exalts the beauty of that which is most beautiful, and it adds beauty to that which is most deformed ; it marries exultation and horror, grief and pleasure, eternity and change ; it subdues to union, under its light yoke, all irreconcilable things. It transmutes all that it touches, and every form moving within the radiance of its presence is changed by wondrous sympathy to an incarnation of the spirit which it breathes : its secret alchemy turns to potable gold the poisonous waters which flow from death through life ; it strips the veil of familiarity from the world, and lays bare the naked and sleeping beauty, which is the spirit of its forms.

All things exist as they are perceived ; at least in relation to the percipient.

" The mind is its own place, and in itself
Can make a heaven of hell, a hell of heaven." *

But poetry defeats the curse which binds us to be
subjected to the accident of surrounding impressions.
And whether it spreads its own figured curtain, or with-
draws life's dark veil from before the scene of things,
it equally creates for us a being within our being. It
makes us the inhabitant of a world to which the familiar
world is a chaos. It reproduces the common universe
of which we are portions and percipients, and it purges
from our inward sight the film of familiarity which
obscures from us the wonder of our being. It compels
us to feel that which we perceive, and to imagine that
which we know. It creates anew the universe, after it
has been annihilated in our minds by the recurrence of
impressions blunted by reiteration. It justifies the bold
and true word of Tasso : *Non merita nome di creatore,*
se non Iddio ed il Poeta.

A poet, as he is the author to others of the highest
wisdom, pleasure, virtue and glory, so he ought personally
to be the happiest, the best, the wisest, and the most
illustrious of men. As to his glory, let time be challenged
to declare whether the fame of any other institutor of
human life be comparable to that of a poet. That he
is the wisest, the happiest, and the best, inasmuch as
he is a poet, is equally incontrovertible : the greatest
poets have been men of the most spotless virtue, of the
most consummate prudence, and, if we would look into
the interior of their lives, the most fortunate of men :
and the exceptions, as they regard those who possessed
the poetic faculty in a high yet inferior degree, will be
found on consideration to confirm rather than destroy
the rule. Let us for a moment stoop to the arbitration
of popular breath, and usurping and uniting in our own
persons the incompatible characters of accuser, witness,

[* Paradise Lost, Book i. l. 254-5.]

judge and executioner, let us decide without trial, testimony, or form, that certain motives of those who are "there sitting where we dare not soar," are reprehensible. Let us assume that Homer was a drunkard, that Virgil was a flatterer, that Horace was a coward, that Tasso was a madman, that Bacon was a speculator, that Raphael was a libertine, that Spenser was a poet laureate. It is inconsistent with this division of our subject to cite living poets, but posterity has done ample justice to the great names now referred to. Their errors have been weighed and found to have been dust in the balance; if their sins "were as scarlet, they are now white as snow:" they have been washed in the blood of the mediator and redeemer, time. Observe in what a ludicrous chaos the imputations of real or fictitious crime have been confused in the contemporary calumnies against poetry and poets; consider how little is, as it appears—or appears, as it is, look to your own motives, and judge not, lest ye be judged.

Poetry, as has been said, differs in this respect from logic, that it is not subject to the control of the active powers of the mind, and that its birth and recurrence have no necessary connexion with the consciousness or will. It is presumptuous to determine that these are the necessary conditions of all mental causation, when mental effects are experienced insusceptible of being referred to them. The frequent recurrence of the poetical power, it is obvious to suppose, may produce in the mind a habit of order and harmony correlative with its own nature and with its effects upon other minds. But in the intervals of inspiration, and they may be frequent without being durable, a poet becomes a man, and is abandoned to the sudden reflux of the influences under which others habitually live. But as he is more delicately organised than other men, and sensible to pain and pleasure, both his own and that of others, in a degree unknown to them, he will avoid the one and pursue the other with an ardour proportioned to this difference. And he renders himself obnoxious to calumny, when he neglects to observe the circumstances under which these objects of universal pursuit and flight have disguised themselves in one another's garments.

But there is nothing necessarily evil in this error, and thus cruelty, envy, revenge, avarice, and the passions purely evil, have never formed any portion of the popular imputations on the lives of poets.

I have thought it most favourable to the cause of truth to set down these remarks according to the order in which they were suggested to my mind, by a consideration of the subject itself, instead of observing the formality of a polemical reply ; but if the view which they contain be just, they will be found to involve a refutation of the arguers against poetry, so far at least as regards the first division of the subject. I can readily conjecture what should have moved the gall of some learned and intelligent writers who quarrel with certain versifiers ; I, like them, confess myself unwilling to be stunned by the Theseids of the hoarse Codri of the day. Bavius and Mævius undoubtedly are, as they ever were, insufferable persons. But it belongs to a philosophical critic to distinguish rather than confound. The first part of these remarks has related to poetry in its elements and principles : and it has been shown, as well as the narrow limits assigned them would permit, that what is called poetry in a restricted sense, has a common source with all other forms of order and of beauty, according to which the materials of human life are susceptible of being arranged, and which is poetry in an universal sense.

The second part will have for its object an application of these principles to the present state of the cultivation of poetry, and a defence of the attempt to idealise the modern forms of manners and opinions, and compel them into a subordination to the imaginative and creative faculty. For the literature of England, an energetic development of which has ever preceded or accompanied a great and free development of the national will, has arisen as it were from a new birth. In spite of the low-thoughted envy which would undervalue contemporary merit, our own will be a memorable age in intellectual achievements, and we live among such philosophers and poets as surpass beyond comparison any who have appeared since the last national struggle for civil and religious liberty. The most unfailing herald, companion, and follower of the awakening of a great people to work a beneficial change in opinion or institution, is poetry. At such periods there is an accumulation of the power of communicating and receiving intense and impassioned conceptions respecting man and nature. The persons in whom this power resides may often, as far as regards many portions of their nature, have little apparent correspondence with that spirit of good of which they are the ministers. But even whilst they deny and abjure, they are yet compelled to serve, the power which is seated on the throne of their own soul. It is impossible to read the compositions of the most celebrated writers of the present day without being startled with the electric life which burns within their words. They measure the circumference and sound the depths of human nature with a comprehensive and all-penetrating spirit, and they are themselves perhaps the most sincerely astonished at its manifestations; for it is less their spirit than the spirit of the age. Poets are the hierophants of an unapprehended inspiration; the mirrors of the gigantic shadows which futurity casts upon the present; the words which express what they understand not; the trumpets which sing to battle and feel not what they inspire; the influence which is moved not, but moves. Poets are the unacknowledged legislators of the world.

ESSAY

ON THE LITERATURE, THE ARTS, AND
THE MANNERS OF THE ATHENIANS.

A Fragment.

THE period which intervened between the birth of Pericles and the death of Aristotle, is undoubtedly, whether considered in itself, or with reference to the effects which it has produced upon the subsequent destinies of civilised man, the most memorable in the history of the world. What was the combination of moral and political circumstances which produced so unparalleled a progress during that period in literature and the arts ;—why that progress, so rapid and so sustained, so soon received a check, and became retrograde,—are problems left to the wonder and conjecture of posterity. The wrecks and fragments of those subtle and profound minds, like the ruins of a fine statue, obscurely suggest to us the grandeur and perfection of the whole. Their very language—a type of the understandings of which it was the creation and the image— in variety, in simplicity, in flexibility, and in copiousness, excels every other language of the western world. Their sculptures are such as we, in our presumption, assume to be the models of ideal truth and beauty, and to which no artist of modern times can produce forms in any degree comparable. Their paintings, according to Pliny and Pausanias, were full of delicacy and harmony ; and some even were powerfully pathetic, so as to awaken, like tender music or tragic poetry, the most overwhelming emotions. We are accustomed to conceive the painters of the sixteenth century, as those who have brought their art to the highest perfection, probably because none of the ancient paintings have been preserved. For all the inventive arts maintain, as it were, a sympathetic connexion between each other, being no more than various expressions of one internal power, modified by different circumstances, either of an individual, or of society ; and the paintings of that period would probably bear the same relation as is confessedly borne by the sculptures to all succeeding ones. Of their music we know little ; but the effects which it is said to have produced, whether they be attributed to the skill of the composer, or the sensibility of his audience, are far more powerful than any which we experience from the music of our own times ; and if, indeed, the melody of their compositions were more tender and delicate, and inspiring, than the melodies of some modern European nations, their superiority in this art must have been something wonderful, and wholly beyond conception.

Their poetry seems to maintain a very high, though not so disproportionate a rank, in the comparison. Perhaps Shakespeare, from the variety and comprehension of his genius, is to be considered, on the whole, as the greatest individual mind, of which we have specimens remaining. Perhaps Dante created imaginations of greater loveliness and energy than any that are to be found in the ancient literature of Greece. Perhaps nothing has been discovered in the fragments of the Greek lyric poets equivalent to the sublime and chivalric sensibility of Petrarch.—But, as a poet, Homer must be acknowledged to excel Shake-speare in the truth, the harmony, the sustained grandeur, the satisfying completeness of his images, their exact fitness to the illustration, and to that to which they belong. Nor could Dante, deficient in conduct, plan, nature, variety, and temperance, have been brought into comparison with these men, but for those fortunate isles, laden with golden fruit, which alone could tempt any one to embark in the misty ocean of his dark and extravagant fiction.

But, omitting the comparison of individual minds, which can afford no general inference, how superior was the spirit and system of their poetry to that of any other period ! So that, had any other genius equal in other respects to the greatest that ever enlightened the world, arisen in that age, he would have been superior to all, from this circumstance alone—that his conceptions would have assumed a more harmonious and perfect form. For it is worthy of observation, that whatever the poets of that age produced is as harmonious and perfect as possible. If a drama, for instance, were the composition of a person of inferior talent, it was still homogeneous and free from inequalities ; it was a whole, consistent with itself. The compositions of great minds bore throughout the sustained stamp of their greatness. In the poetry of succeeding ages the expectations are often exalted on Icarian wings, and fall, too much dis-appointed to give a memory and a name to the oblivious pool in which they fell.

In physical knowledge Aristotle and Theophrastus had already—no doubt assisted by the labours of those of their predecessors whom they criticise—made advances worthy of the maturity of science. The astonishing invention of geometry, that series of discoveries which have enabled man to command the elements and foresee future events, before the subjects of his ignorant wonder, and which have opened as it were the doors of the mysteries of nature, had already been brought to great perfection. Metaphysics, the science of man's intimate nature, and logic, or the grammar and elementary principles of that science, received from the latter philosophers of the Periclean age a firm basis. All our more exact philosophy is built upon the labours of these great men, and many of the words which we employ in metaphysical distinctions were invented by them to give accuracy and system to their reasonings. The science of morals, or the voluntary conduct of men in relation to themselves or others, dates from this epoch. How inexpressibly bolder and more pure were the doctrines of those great men, in comparison with the timid maxims which prevail in the writings of the most esteemed modern moralists! They were such as Phocion, and Epaminondas, and Timoleon, who formed themselves on their influence, were to the wretched heroes of our own age.

Their political and religious institutions are more difficult to bring into comparison with those of other times. A summary idea may be formed of the worth of any political and religious system, by observing the comparative degree of happiness and of intellect produced under its influence. And whilst many institutions and opinions, which in ancient Greece were obstacles to the improvement of the human race, have been abolished among modern nations, how many pernicious superstitions and new contrivances of misrule, and unheard-of complications of public mischief, have not been invented among them by the ever-watchful spirit of avarice and tyranny!

The modern nations of the civilised world owe the progress which they have made—as well in those physical sciences in which they have already excelled their masters, as in the moral and intellectual inquiries, in which, with all the advantage of the experience of the latter, it can scarcely be said that they have yet equalled them,—to what is called the revival of learning ; that is, the study of the writers of the age which preceded and immediately followed the government of Pericles, or of subsequent writers, who were, so to speak, the rivers flowing from those immortal fountains. And though there seems to be a principle in the modern world, which, should circumstances analogous to those which modelled the intellectual resources of the age to which we refer, into so harmonious a proportion, again arise, would arrest and perpetuate them, and consign their results to a more equal, extensive, and lasting improvement of the condition of man—though justice and the true meaning of human society are, if not more accurately, more generally understood ; though perhaps men know more, and therefore are more, as a mass, yet this principle has never been called into action, and requires indeed a universal and an almost appalling change in the system of existing things. The study of modern history is the study of kings, financiers, statesmen, and priests. The history of ancient Greece is the study of legislators, philosophers, and poets ; it is the history of men, compared with the history of titles. What the Greeks were, was a reality, not a promise. And what we are and hope to be, is derived, as it were, from the influence and inspiration of these glorious generations.

Whatever tends to afford a further illustration of the manners and opinions of those to whom we owe so much, and who were perhaps, on the whole, the most perfect specimens of humanity of whom we have authentic record, were infinitely valuable. Let us see their errors, their weaknesses, their daily actions, their familiar conversation, and catch the tone of their society. When we discover how far the most admirable community ever framed was removed from that perfection to which human society is impelled by some active power within each bosom to aspire, how great ought to be our hopes, how resolute our struggles ! For the Greeks of the Periclean age were widely different from us. It is to be lamented that no modern writer has hitherto dared to show them precisely as they were. Barthélemi cannot be denied the praise of industry and system ; but he never forgets that he is a Christian and a Frenchman. Wieland, in his delightful novels, makes indeed a very tolerable Pagan, but cherishes too many political prejudices, and refrains from diminishing the interest of his romances by painting sentiments in which no European of modern times can possibly sympathise. There is no book which shows the Greeks precisely as they were ; they seem all written for children, with the caution that no practice or sentiment, highly inconsistent with our present manners, should be mentioned, lest those manners should receive outrage and violation. But there are many to whom the Greek language is inaccessible, who ought not to be excluded by this prudery from possessing an exact and comprehensive conception of the history of man ; for there is no knowledge concerning what man has been and may be, from partaking of which a person can depart, without becoming in some degree more philosophical, tolerant, and just.

One of the chief distinctions between the manners of ancient Greece and modern Europe, consisted in the regulations and the sentiments respecting sexual intercourse. Whether this difference arises from some imperfect influence of the doctrines of Jesus, who alleges the absolute and unconditional equality of all human beings, or from the institutions of chivalry, or from a certain fundamental difference of physical nature existing in the Celts, or from a combination of all or any of these causes acting on each other, is a question worthy of voluminous investigation. The fact is, that the modern Europeans have in this circumstance, and in the abolition of slavery, made an improvement the most decisive in the regulation of human society ; and all the virtue and the wisdom of the Periclean age arose under other institutions, in spite of the diminution which personal slavery and the inferiority of women, recognised by law and opinion, must have produced in the delicacy, the strength, the comprehensiveness, and the accuracy of their conceptions, in moral, political, and metaphysical science, and perhaps in every other art and science.

The women, thus degraded, became such as it was expected they would become. They possessed, except with extraordinary exceptions, the habits and the qualities of slaves. They were probably not extremely beautiful ; at least there was no such disproportion in the attractions of the external form between the female and male sex among the Greeks, as exists among the modern Europeans. They were certainly devoid · of that moral and intellectual loveliness with which the acquisition of knowledge and the cultivation of senti-ment animates, as with another life of overpowering grace, the lineaments and the gestures of every form which they inhabit. Their eyes could not have been deep and intricate from the workings of the mind, and could have entangled no heart in soul-enwoven labyrinths.

Let it not be imagined that because the Greeks were deprived of its legitimate object, they were incapable of sentimental love ; and that this passion is the mere child of chivalry and the literature of modern times. This object or its archetype forever exists in the mind, which selects among those who resemble it that which most resembles it ; and instinctively fills up the inter-stices of the imperfect image, in the same manner as the imagination moulds and completes the shapes in clouds, or in the fire, into the resemblances of whatever form, animal, building, &c., happens to be present to it. Man is in his wildest state a social being : a certain degree of civilisation and refinement ever produces the want of sympathies still more intimate and complete ; and the gratification of the senses is no longer all that is sought in sexual connexion. It soon becomes a very small part of that profound and complicated sentiment, which we call love, which is rather the universal thirst for a communion not only of the senses, but of our whole nature, intellectual, imaginative and sensitive, and which, when individualised, becomes an imperious necessity, only to be satisfied by the complete or partial, actual or supposed fulfilment of its claims. This want grows more powerful in proportion to the development which our nature receives from civilisation, for man never ceases to be a social being. The sexual impulse, which is only one, and often a small part of those claims, serves, from its obvious and external nature, as a kind of type or expression of the rest, a common basis, an acknow-- ledged and visible link. Still it is a claim which even derives a strength not its own from the accessory circumstances which surround it, and one which our nature thirsts to satisfy. To estimate this, observe the degree of intensity and durability of the love of the male towards the female in animals and savages ; and acknowledge all the duration and intensity observable in the love of civilised beings beyond that of savages to be produced from other causes. In the susceptibility of the external senses there is probably no important difference.

Among the ancient Greeks the male sex, one half of the human race, received the highest cultivation and refinement : whilst the other, so far as intellect is concerned, were educated as slaves, and were raised but few degrees in all that related to moral or intellectual excellence above the condition of savages. The gradations in the society of man present us with slow improve ment in this respect. The Roman women held a higher

consideration in society, and were esteemed almost as
the equal partners with their husbands in the regulation
of domestic economy and the education of their children.
The practices and customs of modern Europe are essentially different from and incomparably less pernicious
than either, however remote from what an enlightened
mind cannot fail to desire as the future destiny of
human beings.

ON THE SYMPOSIUM,

OR PREFACE TO THE BANQUET OF PLATO.

A Fragment.

THE dialogue entitled "The Banquet," was selected by the translator as the most beautiful and perfect among all the works of Plato.* He despairs of having communicated to the English language any portion of the surpassing graces of the composition, or having done more than present an imperfect shadow of the language and the sentiment of this astonishing production.

Plato is eminently the greatest among the Greek philosophers, and from, or, rather, perhaps through him, from his master Socrates, have proceeded those emanations of moral and metaphysical knowledge, on which a long series and an incalculable variety of popular superstitions have sheltered their absurdities

---

* The Republic, though replete with considerable errors of speculation, is, indeed, the greatest repository of important truths of all the works of Plato. This, perhaps, is because it is the longest. He first, and perhaps last, maintained that a state ought to be governed, not by the wealthiest, or the most ambitious, or the most cunning, but by the wisest; the method of selecting such rulers, and the laws by which such a selection is made, must correspond with and arise out of the moral freedom and refinement of the people.

from the slow contempt of mankind. Plato exhibits
the rare union of close and subtle logic with the
Pythian enthusiasm of poetry, melted by the splendour
and harmony of his periods into one irresistible stream
of musical impressions, which hurry the persuasions
onward, as in a breathless career. His language
is that of an immortal spirit, rather than a man.
Bacon is, perhaps, the only writer who, in these particulars, can be compared with him : his imitator,
Cicero, sinks in the comparison into an ape mocking
the gestures of a man. His views into the nature of
mind and existence are often obscure, only because
they are profound ; and though his theories respecting
the government of the world, and the elementary laws
of moral action, are not always correct, yet there is
scarcely any of his treatises which do not, however
stained by puerile sophisms, contain the most remarkable intuitions into all that can be the subject of the
human mind. His excellence consists especially in
intuition, and it is this faculty which raises him far
above Aristotle, whose genius, though vivid and various,
is obscure in comparison with that of Plato.

The dialogue entitled the "Banquet," is called
Ερωτικος, or a Discussion upon Love, and is supposed
to have taken place at the house of Agathon, at one of
a series of festivals given by that poet, on the occasion
of his gaining the prize of tragedy at the Dionysiaca.
The account of the debate on this occasion is supposed
to have been given by Apollodorus, a pupil of Socrates,
many years after it had taken place, to a companion
who was curious to hear it. This Apollodorus appears,
both from the style in which he is represented in this
piece, as well as from a passage in the Phædon, to have
been a person of an impassioned and enthusiastic disposition ; to borrow an image from the Italian painters,
he seems to have been the St. John of the Socratic
group. The drama (for so the lively distinction of .

IL.   D

character and the various and well-wrought circumstances of the story almost entitle it to be called)
begins by Socrates persuading Aristodemus to sup at
Agathon's, uninvited. The whole of this introduction
affords the most lively conception of refined Athenian
manners.

THE BANQUET.

TRANSLATED FROM PLATO.

THE PERSONS OF THE DIALOGUE

APOLLODORUS
A FRIEND OF APOLLODORUS
GLAUCO
ARISTODEMUS
SOCRATES
AGATHON
PHÆDRUS
PAUSANIAS
ERYXIMACHUS
ARISTOPHANES
DIOTIMA
ALCIBIADES

THE BANQUET.

Translated from Plato.

APOLLODORUS.

I THINK that the subject of your inquiries is still fresh in my memory ; for yesterday, as I chanced to be returning home from Phaleros, one of my acquaintance, seeing me before him, called out to me from a distance, jokingly, " Apollodorus, you Phalerian, will you not wait a minute ? "—I waited for him, and as soon as he overtook me, " I have just been looking for you, Apollodorus," he said, " for I wished to hear what those discussions were on Love, which took place at the party, when Agathon, Socrates, Alcibiadès, and some others, met at supper. Some one who heard it from Phœnix, the son of Philip, told me that you could give a full account, but he could relate nothing distinctly himself. Relate to me, then, I entreat you, all the circumstances. I know you are a faithful reporter of the discussions of your friends ; but, first tell me, were you present at the party or not ? "

" Your informant," I replied, " seems to have given you no very clear idea of what you wish to hear, if he thinks that these discussions took place so lately as that I could have been of the party."—" Indeed, I thought

so," replied he.—"For how," said I, "O Glauco! could
I have been present? Do you not know that Agathon
has been absent from the city many years? But, since
I began to converse with Socrates, and to observe each
day all his words and actions, three years are scarcely
past. Before this time I wandered about wherever it
might chance, thinking that I did something, but being
in truth, a most miserable wretch, not less than you are
now, who believe that you ought to do anything rather
than practise the love of wisdom."—"Do not cavil,"
interrupted Glauco, "but tell me, when did this party
take place?"

"Whilst we were yet children," I replied, "when
Agathon first gained the prize of tragedy, and the day
after that on which he and the chorus made sacrifices in
celebration of their success."—"A long time ago, it
seems. But who told you all the circumstances of the
discussion? Did you hear them from Socrates himself?"
"No, by Jupiter! But the same person from whom
Phœnix had his information, one Aristodemus, a Cyda-
thenean,—a little man who always went about without
sandals. He was present at this feast, being, I believe,
more than any of his contemporaries, a lover and
admirer of Socrates. I have questioned Socrates concerning some of the circumstances of his narration, who
confirms all that I have heard from Aristodemus."—
"Why, then," said Glauco, "why not relate them, as we
walk, to me? The road to the city is every way convenient, both for those who listen and those who speak."

Thus as we walked I gave him some account of those
discussions concerning Love; since, as I said before,
I remember them with sufficient accuracy. If I am
required to relate them also to you, that shall willingly
be done; for, whensoever either I myself talk of philosophy, or listen to others talking of it, in addition to
the improvement which I conceive there arises from
such conversation, I am delighted beyond measure;

but whenever I hear your discussions about moneyed men and great proprietors, I am weighed down with grief, and pity you, who, doing nothing, believe that you are doing something. Perhaps you think that I am a miserable wretch ; and, indeed, I believe that you think truly. I do not think, but well know, that you are miserable.

COMPANION.

You are always the' same, Apollodorus — always saying some ill of yourself and others. Indeed, you seem to me to think every one miserable except Socrates, beginning with yourself. I do not know what could have entitled you to the surname of the "Madman," for, I am sure, you are consistent enough, for ever inveighing with bitterness against yourself and all others, except Socrates.

APOLLODORUS.

My dear friend, it is manifest that I am out of my wits from this alone—that I have such opinion as you describe concerning myself and you.

COMPANION.

It is not worth while, Apollodorus, to dispute now about these things ; but do what I entreat you, and relate to us what were these discussions.

APOLLODORUS.

They were such as I will proceed to tell you. But let me attempt to relate them in the order which Aristodemus observed in relating them to me. He said that he met Socrates washed, and, contrary to his usual custom, sandalled, and having inquired whither he went so gaily dressed, Socrates replied, "I am going to sup

at Agathon's ; yesterday I avoided it, disliking the
crowd, which would attend at the prize sacrifices then
celebrated ; to-day I promised to be there, and I made
myself so gay, because one ought to be beautiful to
approach one who is beautiful. But you, Aristodemus,
what think you of coming uninvited to supper ? "—" I
will do," he replied, "as you command."—" Follow,
then, that we may, by changing its application, disarm
that proverb which says, *To the feasts of the good, the
good come uninvited.* Homer, indeed, seems not only
to destroy, but to outrage the proverb ; for, describing
Agamemnon as excellent in battle, and Menelaus but
a faint-hearted warrior, he represents Menelaus as
coming uninvited to the feast of one better and braver
than himself."—Aristodemus hearing this, said, " I also
am in some danger, Socrates, not as you say, but
according to Homer, of approaching like an unworthy
inferior, the banquet of one more wise and excellent
than myself. Will you not, then, make some excuse
for me ? for I shall not confess that I came uninvited,
but shall say that I was invited by you."—" As we walk
together," said Socrates, " we will consider together
what excuse to make—but let us go."

Thus discoursing, they proceeded. But, as they
walked, Socrates, engaged in some deep contemplation,
slackened his pace, and, observing Aristodemus waiting
for him, he desired him to go on before. When Aristodemus arrived at Agathon's house he found the
door open, and it occurred somewhat comically, that
a slave met him at the vestibule, and conducted him
where he found the guests already reclined. As soon
as Agathon saw him, " You arrive just in time to sup
with us, Aristodemus," he said ; " if you have any other
purpose in your visit, defer it to a better opportunity.
I was looking for you yesterday, to invite you to be of
our party ; I could not find you anywhere. But how is
it that you do not bring Socrates with you ? "

But he turning round, and not seeing Socrates behind him, said to Agathon, "I just came hither in his company, being invited by him to sup with you."— "You did well," replied Agathon, "to come; but where is Socrates?"—"He just now came hither behind me; I myself wonder where he can be."—"Go and look, boy," said Agathon, "and bring Socrates in; meanwhile, you, Aristodemus, recline there near Eryximachus." And he bade a slave wash his feet that he might recline. Another slave, meanwhile, brought word that Socrates had retired into a neighbouring vestibule, where he stood, and, in spite of his message, refused to come in.—"What absurdity you talk," cried Agathon, "call him, and do not leave him till he comes."—"Leave him alone, by all means," said Aristodemus, "it is customary with him sometimes to retire in this way and stand wherever it may chance. He will come presently, I do not doubt; do not disturb him."—"Well, be it as you will," said Agathon; "as it is, you boys, bring supper for the rest; put before us what you will, for I resolved that there should be no master of the feast. Consider me, and these, my friends, as guests, whom you have invited to supper, and serve them so that we may commend you."

After this they began supper, but Socrates did not come in. Agathon ordered him to be called, but Aristodemus perpetually forbade it. At last he came in, much about the middle of supper, not having delayed so long as was his custom. Agathon (who happened to be reclining at the end of the table, and alone,) said, as he entered, "Come hither, Socrates, and sit down by me; so that by the mere touch of one so wise as you are, I may enjoy the fruit of your meditations in the vestibule; for, I well know, you would not have departed till you had discovered and secured it."

Socrates having sat down as he was desired, replied, "It would be well, Agathon, if wisdom were of such a

nature, as that when we touched each other, it would
overflow of its own accord, from him who possesses
much to him who possesses little ; like the water in two
chalices, which will flow through a flock of wool from
the fuller into the emptier, until both are equal.   If
wisdom had this property, I should esteem myself most
fortunate in reclining near to you.   I should thus soon
be filled, I think, with the most beautiful and various
wisdom.   Mine, indeed, is something obscure, and
doubtful, and dreamlike.   But yours is radiant, and has
been crowned with amplest reward ; for, though you are
yet so young, it shone forth from you, and became so
manifest yesterday, that more than thirty thousand
Greeks can bear testimony to its excellence and loveliness."—" You are laughing at me, Socrates," said
Agathon, " but you and I will decide this controversy
about wisdom by and bye, taking Bacchus for our
judge.   At present turn to your supper."

After Socrates and the rest had finished supper, and
had reclined back on their couches, and the libations
had been poured forth, and they had sung hymns to the
god, and all other rites which are customary had been
performed, they turned to drinking.   Then Pausanias
made this kind of proposal.   " Come, my friends," said
he, " in what manner will it be pleasantest for us to
drink ?   I must confess to you that, in reality, I am not
very well from the wine we drank last night, and I have
need of some intermission.   I suspect that most of you
are in the same condition, for you were here yesterday.
Now, consider how we shall drink most easily and
comfortably."

" 'Tis a good proposal, Pausanias," said Aristophanes,
" to contrive, in some way or other, to place moderation
in our cups.   I was one of those who were drenched
last night."—Eryximachus, the son of Acumenius,
hearing this, said : " I am of your opinion ; I only wish
to know one thing—whether Agathon is in the humour

for hard drinking?"—"Not at all," replied Agathon,
"I confess that I am not able to drink much this
evening."—"It is an excellent thing for us," replied
Eryximachus, "I mean myself, Aristodemus, Phædrus,
and these others, if you who are such invincible drinkers,
now refuse to drink. I ought to except Socrates, for he
is capable of drinking everything, or nothing; and whatever we shall determine will equally suit him. Since,
then, no one present has any desire to drink much wine,
I shall perhaps give less offence if I declare the nature
of drunkenness. The science of medicine teaches us that
drunkenness is very pernicious : nor would I choose to
drink immoderately myself, or counsel another to do so,
especially if he had been drunk the night before."—
"Yes," said Phædrus, the Myrinusian, interrupting him,
"I have been accustomed to confide in you, especially
in your directions concerning medicine ; and I would
now willingly do so, if the rest will do the same." All
then agreed that they would drink at this present
banquet not for drunkenness, but for pleasure.

"Since, then," said Eryximachus, "it is decided that
no one shall be compelled to drink more than he pleases,
I think that we may as well send away the flute-player
to play to herself; or, if she likes, to the women within.
Let us devote the present occasion to conversation
between ourselves, and if you wish, I will propose to
you what shall be the subject of our discussion." All
present desired and entreated that he would explain.—
"The exordium of my speech," said Eryximachus, "will
be in the style of the Menalippe of Euripides, for the
story which I am about to tell belongs not to me, but to
Phædrus. Phædrus has often indignantly complained
to me, saying—'Is it not strange, Eryximachus, that
there are innumerable hymns and pæans composed for
the other gods, but that not one of the many poets who
spring up in the world have ever composed a verse in
honour of Love, who is such and so great a god ? Nor

any one of those accomplished sophists, who, like the famous Prodicus, have celebrated the praise of Hercules and others, have ever celebrated that of Love ; but what is more astonishing, I have lately met with the book of some philosopher, in which salt is extolled on account of its utility, and many other things of the same nature are in like manner celebrated with elaborate praise. That so much serious thought is expended on such trifles, and that no man has dared to this day to frame a hymn in honour of Love, who being so great a deity, is thus neglected, may well be sufficient to excite my indignation.'

" There seemed to me some justice in these complaints of Phædrus ; I propose, therefore, at the same time for the sake of giving pleasure to Phædrus, and that we may on the present occasion do something well and befitting us, that this God should receive from those who are now present the honour which is most due to him. If you agree to my proposal, an excellent discussion might arise on the subject. Every one ought, according to my plan, to praise Love with as much eloquence as he can. Let Phædrus begin first, both because he reclines the first in order, and because he is the father of the discussion."

" No one will vote against you, Eryximachus," said Socrates, " for how can I oppose your proposal, who am ready to confess that I know nothing on any subject but love ? Or how can Agathon, or Pausanias, or even Aristophanes, whose life is one perpetual ministration to Venus and Bacchus ? Or how can any other whom I see here ? Though we who sit last are scarcely on an equality with you ; for if those who speak before us shall have exhausted the subject with their eloquence and reasonings, our discourses will be superfluous. But in the name of Good Fortune, let Phædrus begin and praise Love." The whole party agreed to what Socrates said, and entreated Phædrus to begin.

What each then said on this subject, Aristodemus did not entirely recollect, nor do I recollect all that he related to me ; but only the speeches of those who said what was most worthy of remembrance. First, then, Phædrus began thus :—

"Love is a mighty deity, and the object of admiration, both to Gods and men, for many and for various claims ; but especially on account of his origin. For that he is to be honoured as one of the most ancient of the gods, this may serve as a testimony, that Love has no parents, nor is there any poet or other person who has ever affirmed that there are such. Hesiod says, that first 'Chaos was produced ; then the broad-bosomed Earth, to be a secure foundation for all things ; then Love.' He says that after Chaos these two were produced, the Earth and Love. Parmenides, speaking of generation, says :—'But he created Love before any of the gods.' Acusileus agrees with Hesiod. Love, therefore, is universally acknowledged to be among the oldest of things. And in addition to this, Love is the author of our greatest advantages ; for I cannot imagine a greater happiness and advantage to one who is in the flower of youth than an amiable lover, or to a lover, than an amiable object of his love. For neither birth, nor wealth, nor honours, can awaken in the minds of men the principles which should guide those who from their youth aspire to an honourable and excellent life, as Love awakens them. I speak of the fear of shame, 'which deters them from that which is disgraceful ; and the love of glory, which incites to honourable deeds. For it is not possible that a state or private person should accomplish, without these incitements, anything beautiful or great. I assert, then, that should one who loves be discovered in any dishonourable action, or tamely enduring insult through cowardice, he would feel more anguish and shame if observed by the object of his passion, than if he were observed by his father, or his companions, or any other person. In like manner, among warmly attached friends, a man is especially grieved to be discovered by his friend in any dishonourable act. If, then, by any contrivance, a state or army could be composed of friends bound by strong attachment, it is beyond calculation how excellently they would administer their affairs, refraining from anything base, contending with each other for the acquirement of fame, and exhibiting such valour in battle as that, though few in numbers, they might subdue all mankind. For should one friend desert the ranks or cast away his arms in the presence of the other, he would suffer far acuter shame from that one person's regard, than from the regard of all other men. A thousand times would he prefer to die, rather than desert the object of his attachment, and not succour him in danger.

"There is none so worthless whom Love cannot impel, as it were by a divine inspiration, towards virtue, even so that he may through this inspiration become equal to one who might naturally be more excellent ; and, in truth, as Homer says : The God breathes vigour into certain heroes—so Love breathes into those who love, the spirit which is produced from himself. Not only men, but even women who love, are those alone who willingly expose themselves to die for others. Alcestis, the daughter of Pelias, affords to the Greeks a remarkable example of this opinion ; she alone being willing to die for her husband, and so surpassing his parents in the affection with which love inspired her towards him, as to make them appear, in the comparison with her, strangers to their own child, and related to him merely in name ; and so lovely and admirable did this action appear, not only to men, but even to the Gods, that, although they conceded the prerogative of bringing back the spirit from death to few among the many who then performed excellent and honourable deeds, yet, delighted with this action, they redeemed her soul from the infernal regions : so highly do the Gods honour zeal and devotion in love. They sent back indeed Orpheus, the son of Œagrus, from Hell, with his purpose unfulfilled, and, showing him only the spectre of her for whom he came, refused to render up herself. For Orpheus seemed to them, not as Alcestis, to have dared die for the sake of her whom he loved, and thus to secure to himself a perpetual intercourse with her in the regions to which she had preceded him, but like a cowardly musician, to have contrived to descend alive into Hell ; and, indeed, they appointed as a punishment for his cowardice, that he should be put to death by women.

"Far otherwise did they reward Achilles, the son of Thetis, whom they sent to inhabit the islands of the blessed. For Achilles, though informed by his mother that his own death would ensue upon his killing Hector, but that if he refrained from it he might return home and die in old age, yet preferred revenging and honouring his beloved Patroclus ; not to die for him merely, but to disdain and reject that life which he had ceased to share. Therefore the Greeks honoured Achilles beyond all other men, because he thus preferred his friend to all things else.

"On this account have the Gods rewarded Achilles more amply than Alcestis ; permitting his spirit to inhabit the islands of the blessed. Hence do I assert that Love is the most ancient and venerable of deities, and most powerful to endow mortals with the possession of happiness and virtue, both whilst they live and after they die."

Thus Aristodemus reported the discourse of Phædrus ; and after Phædrus, he said that some others spoke, whose discourses he did not well remember. When they had ceased, Pausanias began thus :—

"Simply to praise Love, O Phædrus, seems to me too bounded a scope for our discourse. If Love were

one, it would be well.   But since Love is not one, I will
endeavour to distinguish which is the Love whom it
becomes us to praise, and having thus discriminated
one from the other, will attempt to render him who is
the subject of our discourse the honour due to his
divinity.   We all know that Venus is never without
Love ; and if Venus were one, Love would be one ; but
since there are two Venuses, of necessity also must
there be two Loves.   For assuredly are there two
Venuses ; one, the eldest, the daughter of Uranus,
born without a mother, whom we call the Uranian ;
the other younger, the daughter of Jupiter and Dione,
whom we call the Pandemian ;—of necessity must there
also be two Loves, the Uranian and Pandemian companions of these goddesses.   It is becoming to praise
all the Gods, but the attributes which fall to the lot of
each may be distinguished and selected.   For any particular action whatever in itself is neither good nor
evil ; what we are now doing—drinking, singing, talking, none of these things are good in themselves, but
the mode in which they are done stamps them with
its own nature ; and that which is done well, is good,
and that which is done ill, is evil.   Thus, not all love,
nor every mode of love is beautiful, or worthy of commendation, but that alone which excites us to love
worthily.   The Love, therefore, which attends upon
Venus Pandemos is, in truth, common to the vulgar,
and presides over transient and fortuitous connexions,
and is worshipped by the least excellent of mankind.
The votaries of this deity seek the body rather than the
soul, and the ignorant rather than the wise, disdaining
all that is honourable and lovely, and considering how
they shall best satisfy their sensual necessities.   This
Love is derived from the younger goddess, who partakes
in her nature both of male and female.   But the attendant on the other, the Uranian, whose nature is entirely
masculine, is the Love who inspires us with affection,

and exempts us from all wantonness and libertinism. Those who are inspired by this divinity seek the affections of those who are endowed by nature with greater excellence and vigour both of body and mind. And it is easy to distinguish those who especially exist under the influence of this power, by their choosing in early youth as the objects of their love those in whom the intellectual faculties have begun to develop. For those who begin to love in this manner seem to me to be preparing to pass their whole life together in a community of good and evil, and not ever lightly deceiving those who love them, to be faithless to their vows. There ought to be a law that none should love the very young ; so much serious affection as this deity enkindles should not be doubtfully bestowed ; for the body and mind of those so young are yet unformed, and it is difficult to foretell what will be their future tendencies and power. The good voluntarily impose this law upon themselves, and those vulgar lovers ought to be compelled to the same observance, as we deter them with all the power of the laws from the love of free matrons. For these are the persons whose shameful actions embolden those who observe their importunity and intemperance to assert, that it is dishonourable to serve and gratify the objects of our love. But no one who does this gracefully and according to law, can justly be liable to the imputation of blame.

" Not only friendship, but philosophy and the practice of the gymnastic exercises, are represented as dishonourable by the tyrannical governments under which the barbarians live. For I imagine it would little conduce to the benefit of the governors, that the governed should be disciplined to lofty thoughts and to the unity and communion of steadfast friendship, of which admirable effects the tyrants of our own country have also learned that Love is the author. For the love of Harmodius and Aristogiton, strengthened into a firm friendship,

II.   E dissolved the tyranny. Wherever, therefore, it is declared dishonourable in any case to serve and benefit friends, that law is a mark of the depravity of the legislator, the avarice and tyranny of the rulers, and the cowardice of those who are ruled. Wherever it is simply declared to be honourable without distinction of cases, such a declaration denotes dulness and want of subtlety of mind in the authors of the regulation. Here the degrees of praise or blame to be attributed by law are far better regulated ; but it is yet difficult to determine the cases to which they should refer.

"It is evident, however, for one in whom passion is enkindled, it is more honourable to love openly than secretly ; and most honourable to love the most excellent and virtuous, even if they should be less beautiful than others. It is honourable for the lover to exhort and sustain the object of his love in virtuous conduct. It is considered honourable to attain the love of those whom we seek, and the contrary shameful ; and to facilitate this attainment, opinion has given to the lover the permission of acquiring favour by the most extraordinary devices, which if a person should practise for any purpose besides this, he would incur the severest reproof of philosophy. For if any one desirous of accumulating money, or ambitious of procuring power, or seeking any other advantage, should, like a lover seeking to acquire the favour of his beloved, employ prayers and entreaties in his necessity, and swear such oaths as lovers swear, and sleep before the threshold, and offer to subject himself to such slavery as no slave even would endure ; he would be frustrated of the attainment of what he sought, both by his enemies and friends, these reviling him for his flattery, those sharply admonishing him, and taking to themselves the shame of his servility. But there is a certain grace in a lover who does all these things, so that he alone may do them without dishonour. It is commonly said that the Gods accord pardon to the lover alone if he should break his oath, and that there is no oath by Venus. Thus, as our law declares, both gods and men have given to lovers all possible indulgence.

" The affair, however, I imagine, stands thus: As I have before said, love cannot be considered in itself as either honourable or dishonourable : if it is honourably pursued, it is honourable ; if dishonourably, dishonourable : it is dishonourable basely to serve and gratify a worthless person ; it is honourable honourably to serve a person of virtue. That Pandemic lover who loves rather the body than the soul is worthless, nor can be constant and consistent, since he has placed his affections on that which has no stability. For as soon as the flower of the form, which was the sole object of his desire, has faded, then he departs and is seen no more ; bound by no faith nor shame of his many promises and persuasions. But he who is the lover of virtuous manners is constant during life, since he has placed himself in harmony and desire with that which is consistent with itself.

" These two classes of persons we ought to distinguish with careful examination, so that we may serve and converse with the one and avoid the other ; determining, by that inquiry, by what a man is attracted, and for what the object of his love is dear to him. On the same account it is considered as dishonourable to be inspired with love at once, lest time should be wanting to know and approve the character of the object. It is considered dishonourable to be captivated by the allurements of wealth and power, or terrified through injuries to yield up the affections, or not to despise in the comparison with an unconstrained choice all political influence and personal advantage. For no circumstance is there in wealth or power so invariable and consistent, as that no generous friendship can ever spring up from amongst them. We have an opinion with respect to

lovers which declares that it shall not be considered
servile or disgraceful, though the lover should submit
himself to any species of slavery for the sake of his
beloved. The same opinion holds with respect to those
who undergo any degradation for the sake of virtue.
And also it is esteemed among us, that if any one
chooses to serve and obey another for the purpose of
becoming more wise or more virtuous through the intercourse that might thence arise, such willing slavery
is not the slavery of a dishonest flatterer. Through
this we should consider in the same light a servitude
undertaken for the sake of love as one undertaken for
the acquirement of wisdom or any other excellence, if
indeed the devotion of a lover to his beloved is to be
considered a beautiful thing. For when the lover and
the beloved have once arrived at the same point, the
province of each being distinguished; the one able
to assist in the cultivation of the mind and in the
acquirement of every other excellence; the other yet
requiring education, and seeking the possession of
wisdom; then alone, by the union of these conditions,
and in no other case, is it honourable for the beloved
to yield up the affections to the lover. In this servitude
alone there is no disgrace in being deceived and defeated
of the object for which it was undertaken, whereas
every other is disgraceful, whether we are deceived
or no.

"On the same principle, if any one seeks the friendship of another, believing him to be virtuous, for the
sake of becoming better through such intercourse and
affection, and is deceived, his friend turning out to be
worthless, and far from the possession of virtue; yet
it is honourable to have been so deceived. For such
a one seems to have submitted to a kind of servitude,
because he would endure anything for the sake of becoming more virtuous and wise; a disposition of mind
eminently beautiful.

"This is that Love who attends on the Uranian deity, and is Uranian; the author of innumerable benefits both to the state and to individuals, and by the necessity of whose influence those who love are disciplined into the zeal of virtue. All other loves are the attendants on Venus Pandemos. So much, although unpremeditated, is what I have to deliver on the subject of love, O Phædrus."

Pausanias having ceased (for so the learned teach me to denote the changes of the discourse), Aristodemus said that it came to the turn of Aristophanes to speak; but it happened that, from repletion or some other cause, he had an hiccough which prevented him; so he turned to Eryximachus, the physician, who was reclining close beside him, and said—"Eryximachus, it is but fair that you should cure my hiccough, or speak instead of me until it is over."—"I will do both," said Eryximachus; "I will speak in your turn, and you, when your hiccough has ceased, shall speak in mine. Meanwhile, if you hold your breath some time, it will subside. If not, gargle your throat with water; and if it still continue, take something to stimulate your nostrils, and sneeze; do this once or twice, and even though it should be very violent it will cease."—"Whilst you speak," said Aristophanes, "I will follow your directions."—Eryximachus then began:—

"Since Pausanias, beginning his discourse excellently, placed no fit completion and development to it, I think it necessary to attempt to fill up what he has left unfinished. He has reasoned well in defining love as of a double nature. The science of medicine, to which I have addicted myself, seems to teach me that the love which impels towards those who are beautiful, does not subsist only in the souls of men, but in the bodies also of those of all other living beings which are produced upon earth, and, in a word, in all things which are. So wonderful and mighty is this divinity, and so widely is

his influence extended over all divine and human things !
For the honour of my profession, I will begin by ad-
ducing a proof from medicine.   The nature of the body
contains within itself this double love.   For that which
is healthy and that which is diseased in a body differ
and are unlike : that which is unlike loves and desires
that which is unlike.   Love, therefore, is different in a
sane and in a diseased body.   Pausanias has asserted
rightly that it is honourable to gratify those things in
the body which are good and healthy, and in this consists the skill of the physician ; whilst those which are
bad and diseased ought to be treated with no indulgence.
The science of medicine, in a word, is a knowledge of
the love affairs of the body, as they bear relation to
repletion and evacuation ; and he is the most skilful
physician who can trace those operations of the good
and evil love, can make the one change places with the
other, and attract love into those parts from which he is
absent, or expel him from those which he ought not to
occupy.   He ought to make those things which are
most inimical, friendly, and excite them to mutual love.
But those things are most inimical which are most
opposite to each other ; cold to heat, bitterness to sweetness, dryness to moisture.   Our progenitor, Æsculapius,
as the poets inform us, (and indeed I believe them,)
through the skill which he possessed to inspire love and
concord in these contending principles, established the
science of medicine.

" The gymnastic arts and agriculture, no less than
medicine, are exercised under the dominion of this God.
Music, as any one may perceive who yields a very
slight attention to the subject, originates from the same
source ; which Heraclitus probably meant, though he
could not express his meaning very clearly in words,
when he says, ' One though apparently differing, yet so
agrees with itself, as the harmony of a lyre and a bow.'
It is great absurdity to say that a harmony differs, and

can exist between things whilst they are dissimilar ; but probably he meant that from sounds which first differed, like the grave and the acute, and which afterwards agreed, harmony was produced according to musical art. For no harmony can arise from the grave and the acute whilst yet they differ. But harmony is symphony : symphony is, as it were, concord. But it is impossible that concord should subsist between things that differ, so long as they differ. Between things which are discordant and dissimilar there is then no harmony. A rhythm is produced from that which is quick, and that which is slow, first being distinguished and opposed to each other, and then made accordant ; so does medicine, no less than music, establish a concord between the objects of its art, producing love and agreement between adverse things.

" Music is then the knowledge of that which relates to love in harmony and system. In the very system of harmony and rhythm, it is easy to distinguish love. The double love is not distinguishable in music itself ; but it is required to apply it to the service of mankind by system and harmony, which is called poetry, or the composition of melody ; or by the correct use of songs and measures already composed, which is called discipline ; then one can be distinguished from the other, by the aid of an extremely skilful artist. And the better love ought to be honoured and preserved for the sake of those who are virtuous, and that the nature of the vicious may be changed through the inspiration of its spirit. This is that beautiful Uranian love, the attendant on the Uranian muse : the Pandemian is the attendant of Polyhymnia ; to whose influence we should only so far subject ourselves, as to derive pleasure from it without indulging to excess ; in the same manner as, according to our art, we are instructed to seek the pleasures of the table, only so far as we can enjoy them without the consequences of disease. In music, therefore, and in medicine, and in all other things, human and divine, this double love ought to be traced and discriminated; for it is in all things.

"Even the constitution of the seasons of the year is penetrated with these contending principles. For so often as heat and cold, dryness and moisture, of which I spoke before, are influenced by the more benignant love, and are harmoniously and temperately inter-mingled with the seasons, they bring maturity and health to men, and to all the other animals and plants. But when the evil and injurious love assumes the dominion of the seasons of the year, destruction is spread widely abroad. Then pestilence is accustomed to arise, and many other blights and diseases fall upon animals and plants: and hoar frosts, and hails, and mildew on the corn, are produced from that excessive and disorderly love, with which each season of the year is impelled towards the other; the motions of which and the knowledge of the stars, is called astronomy. All sacrifices, and all those things in which divination is concerned (for these things are the links by which is maintained an intercourse and communion between the Gods and men), are nothing else than the science of preservation and right government of Love. For impiety is accustomed to spring up, so soon as any one ceases to serve the more honourable Love, and worship him by the sacrifice of good actions; but submits him-self to the influences of the other, in relation to his duties towards his parents, and the Gods, and the living, and the dead. It is the object of divination to distinguish and remedy the effects of these opposite loves; and divination is therefore the author of the friendship of Gods and men, because it affords the knowledge of what in matters of love is lawful or unlawful to men.

"Thus every species of love possesses collectively a various and vast, or rather universal power. But love which incites to the acquirement of its objects according to virtue and wisdom, possesses the most exclusive dominion, and prepares for his worshippers the highest happiness through the mutual intercourse of social kindness which it promotes among them, and through the benevolence which he attracts to them from the Gods, our superiors.

"Probably in thus praising Love, I have unwillingly omitted many things; but it is your business, O Aristophanes, to fill up all that I have left incomplete; or, if you have imagined any other mode of honouring the divinity: for I observe your hiccough is over."

"Yes," said Aristophanes, "but not before I applied the sneezing. I wonder why the harmonious construction of our body should require such noisy operations as sneezing; for it ceased the moment I sneezed."— "Do you not observe what you do, my good Aristophanes?" said Eryximachus; "you are going to speak, and you predispose us to laughter, and compel me to watch for the first ridiculous idea which you may start in your discourse, when you might have spoken in peace." —"Let me unsay what I have said, then," replied Aristophanes, laughing. "Do not watch me, I entreat you; though I am not afraid of saying what is laughable (since that would be all gain, and quite in the accustomed spirit of my muse), but lest I should say what is ridiculous."—"Do you think to throw your dart, and escape with impunity, Aristophanes? Attend, and what you say be careful you maintain; then, perhaps, if it pleases me, I may dismiss you without question."

"Indeed, Eryximachus," proceeded Aristophanes, "I have designed that my discourse should be very different from yours and that of Pausanias. It seems to me that mankind are by no means penetrated with a conception of the power of Love, or they would have built sumptuous temples and altars, and have established magnificent rites of sacrifice in his honour; he deserves worship and homage more than all the other Gods, and he has yet received none. For Love is of all the Gods the most friendly to mortals; and the physician of those wounds, whose cure would be the greatest happiness which could be conferred upon the human race. I will endeavour to unfold to you his true power, and you can relate what I declare to others.

" You ought first to know the nature of man, and the adventures he has gone through; for his nature was anciently far different from that which it is at present. First, then, human beings were formerly not divided into two sexes, male and female; there was also a third, common to both the others, the name of which remains, though the sex itself has disappeared. The androgynous sex, both in appearance and in name, was common both to male and female; its name alone remains, which labours under a reproach.

" At the period to which I refer, the form of every human being was round, the back and the sides being circularly joined, and each had four arms and as many legs; two faces fixed upon a round neck, exactly like each other; one head between the two faces; four ears, and everything else as from such proportions it is easy to conjecture. Man walked upright as now, in whatever direction he pleased; but when he wished to go fast he made use of all his eight limbs, and proceeded in a rapid motion by rolling circularly round,—like tumblers, who, with their legs in the air, tumble round and round. We account for the production of three sexes by supposing that, at the beginning, the male was produced from the sun, the female from the earth; and that sex which participated in both sexes, from the moon, by reason of the androgynous nature of the moon. They were round, and their mode of proceeding was round, from the similarity which must needs subsist between them and their parent.

"They were strong also, and had aspiring thoughts. They it was who levied war against the Gods; and what Homer writes concerning Ephialtus and Otus, that they sought to ascend heaven and dethrone the Gods, in reality relates to this primitive people. Jupiter and the other Gods debated what was to be done in this emergency. For neither could they prevail on themselves to destroy them, as they had the giants, with thunder, so that the race should be abolished ; for in that case they would be deprived of the honours of the sacrifices which they were in the custom of receiving from them ; nor could they permit a continuance of their insolence and impiety. Jupiter, with some difficulty having desired silence, at length spoke. ' I think,' said he, ' I have contrived a method by which we may, by rendering the human race more feeble, quell the insolence which they exercise, without proceeding to their utter destruction. I will cut each of them in half ; and so they will at once be weaker and more useful on account of their numbers. They shall walk upright on two legs. If they show any more insolence, and will not keep quiet, I will cut them up in half again, so they shall go about hopping on one leg.'

"So saying, he cut human beings in half, as people cut eggs before they salt them, or as I have seen eggs cut with hairs. He ordered Apollo to take each one as he cut him, and turn his face and half his neck towards the operation, so that by contemplating it he might become more cautious and humble ; and then, to cure him, Apollo turned the face round, and drawing the skin upon what we now call the belly, like a contracted pouch, and leaving one opening, that which is called the navel, tied it in the middle. He then smoothed many other wrinkles, and moulded the breast with much such an instrument as the leather-cutters use to smooth the skins upon the block. He left only a few wrinkles in the belly, near the navel, to serve as a record of its former adventure. Immediately after this division, as each desired to possess the other half of himself, these divided people threw their arms around and embraced each other, seeking to grow together ; and from this resolution to do nothing without the other half, they died of hunger and weakness : when one half died and the other was left alive, that which was thus left sought the other and folded it to its bosom ; whether that half were an entire woman (for we now call it a woman) or a man ; and thus they perished. But Jupiter, pitying them, thought of another contrivance. In this manner is generation now produced, by the union of male and female ; so that from the embrace of a man and woman the race is propagated.

"From this period, mutual love has naturally existed between human beings ; that reconciler and bond of union of their original nature, which seeks to make two one, and to heal the divided nature of man. Every one of us is thus the half of what may be properly termed a man, and like a pselta cut in two, is the imperfect portion of an entire whole, perpetually necessitated to seek the half belonging to him.

"Such as I have described is ever an affectionate lover and a faithful friend, delighting in that which is in conformity with his own nature. Whenever, therefore, any such as I have described are impetuously struck, through the sentiment of their former union, with love and desire and the want of community, they are un- willing to be divided even for a moment. These are they who devote their whole lives to each other, with a vain and inexpressible longing to obtain from each other something they know not what ; for it is not merely the sensual delights of their intercourse for the sake of which they dedicate themselves to each other with such serious affection ; but the soul of each manifestly thirsts for, from the other, something which there are no words to describe, and divines that which it seeks, and traces

obscurely the footsteps of its obscure desire. If Vulcan
should say to persons thus affected, 'My good people,
what is it that you want with one another?' And if,
while they were hesitating what to answer, he should
proceed to ask, 'Do you not desire the closest union
and singleness to exist between you, so that you may
never be divided night or day? If so, I will melt you
together, and make you grow into one, so that both in
life and death ye may be undivided. Consider, is this
what you desire? Will it content you if you become
that which I propose?' We all know that no one would
refuse such an offer, but would at once feel that this was
what he had ever sought; and intimately to mix and
melt and to be melted together with his beloved, so that
one should be made out of two.

"The cause of this desire is, that according to our
original nature, we were once entire. The desire and
the pursuit of integrity and union is that which we all
love. First, as I said, we were entire, but now we
have been dwindled through our own weakness, as the
Arcadians by the Lacedemonians. There is reason to
fear, if we are guilty of any additional impiety towards
the Gods, that we may be cut in two again, and may go
about like those figures painted on the columns, divided
through the middle of our nostrils, as thin as lispæ.
On which account every man ought to be exhorted to
pay due reverence to the Gods, that we may escape so
severe a punishment, and obtain those things which
Love, our general and commander, incites us to desire;
against whom let none rebel by exciting the hatred of
the Gods. For if we continue on good terms with them,
we may discover and possess those lost and concealed
objects of our love; a good-fortune which now befalls to
few.

"I assert, then, that the happiness of all, both men
and women, consists singly in the fulfilment of their
love, and in that possession of its objects by which we

are in some degree restored to our ancient nature. If this be the completion of felicity, that must necessarily approach nearest to it, in which we obtain the possession and society of those whose natures most intimately accord with our own. And if we would celebrate any God as the author of this benefit, we should justly celebrate Love with hymns of joy ; who, in our present condition, brings good assistance in our necessity, and affords great hopes, if we persevere in piety towards the Gods, that he will restore us to our original state, and confer on us the complete happiness alone suited to our nature.

"Such, Eryximachus, is my discourse on the subject of Love ; different indeed from yours, which I nevertheless entreat you not to turn into ridicule, that we may not interrupt what each has separately to deliver on the subject.".

"I will refrain at present," said Eryximachus, "for your discourse delighted me. And if I did not know that Socrates and Agathon were profoundly versed in the science of love affairs, I should fear that they had nothing new to say, after so many and such various imaginations. As it is, I confide in the fertility of their geniuses."—"Your part of the contest, at least, was strenuously fought, Eryximachus," said Socrates, "but if you had been in the situation in which I am, or rather shall be, after the discourse of Agathon, like me, you would then have reason to fear, and be reduced to your wits' end."—"Socrates," said Agathon, "wishes to confuse me with the enchantments of his wit, sufficiently confused already with the expectation I see in the assembly in favour of my discourse."—"I must have lost my memory, Agathon," replied Socrates, "if I imagine that you could be disturbed by a few private persons, after having witnessed your firmness and courage in ascending the rostrum with the actors, and in calmly reciting your compositions in the presence of so great an assembly as that which decreed you the

prize of tragedy."—"What then, Socrates," retorted
Agathon, "do you think me so full of the theatre as to
be ignorant that the judgment of a few wise is more
awful than that of a multitude of others, to one who
rightly balances the value of their suffrages?"—"I
should judge ill indeed, Agathon," answered Socrates,
"in thinking you capable of any rude and unrefined
conception, for I well know that if you meet with any
whom you consider wise, you esteem such alone of more
value than all others. But we are far from being
entitled to this distinction, for we were also of that
assembly, and to be numbered among the rest. But
should you meet with any who are really wise, you
would be careful to say nothing in their presence which
you thought they would not approve—is it not so?"—
"Certainly," replied Agathon.—"You would not then
exercise the same caution in the presence of the multitude
in which they were included?"—"My dear Agathon,"
said Phædrus, interrupting him, "if you answer all the
questions of Socrates, they will never have an end; he
will urge them without conscience so long as he can get
any person, especially one who is so beautiful, to dispute with him. I own it delights me to hear Socrates
discuss; but at present, I must see that Love is not
defrauded of the praise, which it is my province to exact
from each of you. Pay the God his due, and then
reason between yourselves if you will."

"Your admonition is just, Phædrus," replied Agathon,
"nor need any reasoning I hold with Socrates impede
me: we shall find many future opportunities for discussion. I will begin my discourse then; first having
defined what ought to be the subject of it. All who
have already spoken seem to me not so much to have
praised Love, as to have felicitated mankind on the
many advantages of which that deity is the cause; what
he is, the author of these great benefits, none have yet
declared. There is one mode alone of celebration which

would comprehend the whole topic, namely, first to
declare what are those benefits, and then what he is
who is the author of those benefits, which are the subject
of our discourse. Love ought first to be praised, and
then his gifts declared. I assert, then, that although
all the Gods are immortally happy, Love, if I dare
trust my voice to express so awful a truth, is the happiest,
and most excellent, and the most beautiful. That he is
the most beautiful is evident ; first, O Phædrus, from
this circumstance, that he is the youngest of the Gods ;
and, secondly, from his fleetness, and from his repugnance to all that is old ; for he escapes with the swiftness
of wings from old age ; a thing in itself sufficiently swift,
since it overtakes us sooner than there is need ; and
which Love, who delights in the intercourse of the
young, hates, and in no manner can be induced to enter
into community with. The ancient proverb, which says
that like is attracted by like, applies to the attributes
of Love. I concede many things to you, O Phædrus,
but this I do not concede, that Love is more ancient
than Saturn and Jupiter. I assert that he is not only
the youngest of the Gods, but invested with everlasting
youth. Those ancient deeds among the Gods recorded
by Hesiod and Parmenides, if their relations are to be
considered as true, were produced not by Love, but by
Necessity. For if Love had been then in Heaven, those
violent and sanguinary crimes never would have taken
place ; but there would ever have subsisted that affection
and peace, in which the Gods now live, under the
influence of Love.

" He is young, therefore, and being young is tender
and soft. There were need of some poet like Homer
to celebrate the delicacy and tenderness of Love. For
Homer says, that the goddess Calamity is delicate, and
that her feet are tender. ' Her feet are soft,' he says,
' for she treads not upon the ground, but makes her path
upon the heads of men.' He gives as an evidence of

her tenderness, that she walks not upon that which is
hard, but that which is soft. The same evidence is
sufficient to make manifest the tenderness of Love. For
Love walks not upon the earth, nor over the heads of
men, which are not indeed very soft; but he dwells
within, and treads on the softest of existing things,
having established his habitation within the souls and
inmost nature of Gods and men; not indeed in all souls
—for wherever he chances to find a hard and rugged
disposition, there he will not inhabit, but only where it
is most soft and tender. Of needs must he be the
most delicate of all things, who touches lightly with his
feet only the softest parts of those things which are the
softest of all.

"He is then the youngest and the most delicate of
all divinities; and in addition to this, he is, as it were,
the most moist and liquid. For if he were otherwise,
he could not, as he does, fold himself around everything, and secretly flow out and into every soul. His
loveliness, that which Love possesses far beyond all
other things, is a manifestation of the liquid and flowing
symmetry of his form; for between deformity and Love
there is eternal contrast and repugnance. His life is spent
among flowers, and this accounts for the immortal fair-
ness of his skin; for the winged Love rests not in
his flight on any form, or within any soul the flower
of whose loveliness is faded, but there remains most
willingly where is the odour and radiance of blossoms,
yet unwithered. Concerning the beauty of the God, let
this be sufficient, though many things must remain un-
said. Let us next consider the virtue and power of
Love.

"What is most admirable in Love is, that he neither
inflicts nor endures injury in his relations either with
Gods or men. Nor if he suffers any thing does he suffer
it through violence, nor doing any thing does he act it
with violence, for Love is never even touched with

violence. Every one willingly administers every thing to
Love ; and that which every one voluntarily concedes
to another, the laws, which are the kings of the republic,
decree that is just for him to possess.   In addition to
justice, Love participates in the highest temperance ;
for if temperance is defined to be the being superior to
and holding under dominion pleasures and desires ;
then Love, than whom no pleasure is more powerful,
and who is thus more powerful than all persuasions and
delights, must be excellently temperate.   In power and
valour Mars cannot contend with Love : the love of
Venus possesses Mars ; the possessor is always superior
to the possessed, and he who subdues the most powerful
must of necessity be the most powerful of all.

    " The justice and temperance and valour of the God
have been thus declared ;—there remains to exhibit his
wisdom.   And first, that, like Eryximachus, I may
honour my own profession, the God is a wise poet ;
so wise that he can even make a poet one who was
not before : for every one, even if before he were ever
so undisciplined, becomes a poet as soon as he is
touched by Love ;—a sufficient proof that Love is a
great poet, and well skilled in that science according
to the discipline of music.   For what any one possesses
not, or knows not, that can he neither give nor teach
another.   And who will deny that the divine poetry,
by which all living things are produced upon the earth,
is not harmonised by the wisdom of Love ?   Is it not
evident that Love was the author of all the arts of life
with which we are acquainted, and that he whose teacher
has been Love, becomes eminent and illustrious, whilst
he who knows not Love, remains forever unregarded and
obscure ?   Apollo invented medicine, and divination,
and archery, under the guidance of desire and Love ;
so that Apollo was the disciple of Love.   Through him
the Muses discovered the arts of literature, and Vulcan
that of moulding brass, and Minerva the loom, and

Jupiter the mystery of the dominion which he now
exercises over gods and men. So were the Gods taught
and disciplined by the love of that which is beautiful;
for there is no love towards deformity.

"At the origin of things, as I have before said, many
fearful deeds are reported to have been done among the
Gods, on account of the dominion of Necessity. But
so soon as this deity sprang forth from the desire which
forever tends in the universe towards that which is lovely,
then all blessings descended upon all living things,
human and divine. Love seems to me, O Phædrus, a
divinity the most beautiful and the best of all, and the
author to all others of the excellencies with which his
own nature is endowed. Nor can I restrain the poetic
enthusiasm which takes possession of my discourse, and
bids me declare that Love is the divinity who creates
peace among men, and calm upon the sea, the windless
silence of storms, repose and sleep in sadness. Love
divests us of all alienation from each other, and fills our
vacant hearts with overflowing sympathy; he gathers us
together in such social meetings as we now delight to
celebrate, our guardian and our guide in dances, and
sacrifices, and feasts. Yes, Love, who showers benignity upon the world, and before whose presence all
harsh passions flee and perish; the author of all soft
affections; the destroyer of all ungentle thoughts; merciful, mild; the object of the admiration of the wise, and
the delight of gods; possessed by the fortunate, and
desired by the unhappy, therefore unhappy because they
possess him not; the father of grace, and delicacy, and
gentleness, and delight, and persuasion, and desire; the
cherisher of all that is good, the abolisher of all evil;
our most excellent pilot, defence, saviour and guardian
in labour and in fear, in desire and in reason; the
ornament and governor of all things human and divine;
the best, the loveliest; in whose footsteps every one
ought to follow, celebrating him excellently in song, and

bearing each his part in that divinest harmony which
Love sings to all things which live and are, soothing
the troubled minds of Gods and men. This, O Phædrus,
is what I have to offer in praise of the divinity ; partly
composed, indeed, of thoughtless and playful fancies,
and partly of such serious ones as I could well command."

No sooner had Agathon ceased, than a loud murmur
of applause arose from all present ; so becomingly had
the fair youth spoken, both in praise of the God, and
in extenuation of himself. Then Socrates, addressing
Eryximachus, said, " Was not my fear reasonable, son
of Acumenus ? Did I not divine what has, in fact,
happened,—that Agathon's discourse would be so wonderfully beautiful, as to preoccupy all interest in what
I should say ? "—" You, indeed, divined well so far,
O Socrates," said Eryximachus, " that Agathon would
speak eloquently, but not that, therefore, you would be
reduced to any difficulty."—" How, my good friend,
can I or any one else be otherwise than reduced to
difficulty, who speak after a discourse so various and
so eloquent, and which otherwise had been sufficiently
wonderful, if, at the conclusion, the splendour of the
sentences, and the choice selection of the expressions,
had not struck all the hearers with astonishment ; so
that I, who well know that I can never say anything
nearly so beautiful as this, would, if there had been any
escape, have run away for shame. The story of Gorgias came into my mind, and I was afraid lest in
reality I should suffer what Homer describes ; and lest
Agathon, scanning my discourse with the head of the
eloquent Gorgias, should turn me to stone for speech-
lessness. I immediately perceived how ridiculously I
had engaged myself with you to assume a part in
rendering praise to love, and had boasted that I was
well skilled in amatory matters, being so ignorant of
the manner in which it is becoming to render him

honour, as I now perceive myself to be. I, in my simplicity, imagined that the truth ought to be spoken concerning each of the topics of our praise, and that it would be sufficient, choosing those which are the most honourable to the God, to place them in as luminous an arrangement as we could. I had, therefore, great hopes that I should speak satisfactorily, being well aware that I was acquainted with the true foundations of the praise which we have engaged to render. But since, as it appears, our purpose has been, not to render Love his due honour, but to accumulate the most beautiful and the greatest attributes of his divinity, whether they in truth belong to it or not, and that the proposed question is not how Love ought to be praised, but how we should praise him most eloquently, my attempt must of necessity fail. It is on this account, I imagine, that in your discourses you have attributed everything to Love, and have described him to be the author of such and so great effects as, to those who are ignorant of his true nature, may exhibit him as the most beautiful and the best of all things. Not, indeed, to those who know the truth. Such praise has a splendid and imposing effect, but as I am unacquainted with the art of rendering it, my mind, which could not foresee what would be required of me, absolves me from that which my tongue promised. Farewell, then, for such praise I can never render.

"But if you desire, I will speak what I feel to be true ; and that I may not expose myself to ridicule, I entreat you to consider that I speak without entering into competition with those who have preceded me. Consider, then, Phædrus, whether you will exact from me such a discourse, containing the mere truth with respect to Love, and composed of such unpremeditated expressions as may chance to offer themselves to my mind."—Phædrus and the rest bade him speak in the manner which he judged most befitting.—"Permit me,

then, O Phædrus, to ask Agathon a few questions, so
that, confirmed by his agreement with me, I may proceed."—"Willingly," replied Phædrus, "ask."—Then
Socrates thus began :—

"I applaud, dear Agathon, the beginning of your
discourse, where you say we ought first to define and
declare what Love is, and then his works. This rule
I particularly approve. But, come, since you have
given us a discourse of such beauty and majesty concerning Love, you are able, I doubt not, to explain this
question, whether Love is the love of something or
nothing? I do not ask you of what parents Love is ;
for the inquiry, of whether Love is the love of any
father or mother, would be sufficiently ridiculous. But
if I were asking you to describe that which a father
is, I should ask, not whether a father was the love of
any one, but whether a father was the father of any one
or not ; you would undoubtedly reply, that a father was
the father of a son or daughter; would you not?"—
"Assuredly."—"You would define a mother in the
same manner?"—"Without doubt."—"Yet bear
with me, and answer a few more questions, for I would
learn from you that which I wish to know. If I should
inquire, in addition, is not a brother, through the very
nature of his relation, the brother of some one?"—
"Certainly."—"Of a brother or sister, is he not?"—
"Without question."—"Try to explain to me then the
nature of Love ; Love is the love of something or
nothing?"—"Of something, certainly."

"Observe and remember this concession. Tell me
yet farther, whether Love desires that of which it is the
Love or not?"—"It desires it, assuredly."—"Whether
possessing that which it desires and loves, or not
possessing it, does it desire and love?"—"Not possessing it, I should imagine."—"Observe now, whether it
does not appear, that, of necessity, desire desires that
which it wants and does not possess, and no longer

desires that which it no longer wants: this appears to me, Agathon, of necessity to be ; how does it appear to you ? "—" It appears so to me also."—" Would any one who was already illustrious, desire to be illustrious ; would any one already strong, desire to be strong ? From what has already been conceded, it follows that he would not. If any one already strong, should desire to be strong ; or any one already swift, should desire to be swift ; or any one already healthy, should desire to be healthy, it must be concluded that they still desired the advantages of which they already seemed possessed. To destroy the foundation of this error, observe, Agathon, that each of these persons must possess the several advantages in question, at the moment present to our thoughts, whether he will or no. And, now, is it possible that those advantages should be at that time the objects of his desire ? For, if any one should say, being in health, ' I desire to be in health ; ' being rich, ' I desire to be rich, and thus still desire those things which I already possess ; ' we might say to him, ' You, my friend, possess health, and strength, and riches ; you do not desire to possess now, but to continue to possess them in future ; for, whether you will or no, they now belong to you. Consider then, whether, when you say that you desire things present to you, and in your own possession, you say anything else than that you desire the advantages to be for the future also in your possession.' What else could he reply ? "— " Nothing, indeed."—" Is not Love, then, the love of that which is not within its reach, and which cannot hold in security, for the future, those things of which it obtains a present and transitory possession ? "— " Evidently."—" Love, therefore, and everything else that desires anything, desires that which is absent and beyond his reach, that which it has not, that which is not itself, that which it wants ; such are the things of which there are desire and love ? "—" Assuredly."

"Come," said Socrates, "let us review your concessions. Is Love anything else than the love first of something ; and, secondly, of those things of which it has need ? "—" Nothing."—" Now, remember of those things you said in your discourse, that Love was the love—if you wish I will remind you. I think you said something of this kind, that all the affairs of the gods were admirably disposed through the love of the things which are beautiful ; for, there was no love of things deformed ; did you not say so ? "—" I confess that I did."—" You said what was most likely to be true, my friend ; and if the matter be so, the love of beauty must be one thing, and the love of deformity another."— " Certainly."—" It is conceded, then, that Love loves that which he wants but possesses not ? "—" Yes, certainly." — " But Love wants and does not possess beauty ? " — " Indeed it must necessarily follow."— " What, then ! call you that beautiful which has need of beauty and possesses not ? "—" Assuredly no."—" Do you still assert, then, that Love is beautiful, if all that we have said be true ? "—" Indeed, Socrates," said Agathon, " I am in danger of being convicted of ignorance, with respect to all that I then spoke."— " You spoke most eloquently, my dear Agathon ; but bear with my questions yet a moment. You admit that things which are good are also beautiful ? "—" No doubt."—" If Love, then, be in want of beautiful things, and things which are good are beautiful, he must be in want of things which are good ? "—" I cannot refute your arguments, Socrates."—" You cannot refute truth, my dear Agathon : to refute Socrates is nothing difficult.

"But I will dismiss these questionings. At present let me endeavour, to the best of my power, to repeat to you, on the basis of the points which have been agreed upon between me and Agathon, a discourse concerning Love, which I formerly heard from the prophetess Diotima, who was profoundly skilled in this and many other doctrines, and who, ten years before the pestilence, procured to the Athenians, through their sacrifices, a delay of the disease ; for it was she who taught me the science of things relating to Love.

"As you well remarked, Agathon, we ought to declare who and what is Love, and then his works. It is easiest to relate them in the same order as the foreign prophetess observed when, questioning me, she related them. For I said to her much the same things that Agathon has just said to me—that Love was a great deity, and that he was beautiful ; and she refuted me with the same reasons as I have employed to refute Agathon, compelling me to infer that he was neither beautiful nor good, as I said.—'What then,' I objected, ' O Diotima, is Love ugly and evil ? '—' Good words, I entreat you,' said Diotima ; 'do you think that every thing which is not beautiful, must of necessity be ugly ? ' — ' Certainly.' — 'And everything that is not wise, ignorant ? Do you not perceive that there is something between ignorance and wisdom ? '—' What is that ? '— ' To have a right opinion or conjecture. Observe, that this kind of opinion, for which no reason can be rendered, cannot be called knowledge ; for how can that be called knowledge, which is without evidence or reason ? Nor ignorance, on the other hand ; for how can that be called ignorance which arrives at the persuasion of that which it really is? A right opinion is something between understanding and ignorance.'—I confessed that what she alleged was true.—' Do not then say,' she continued, ' that what is not beautiful is of necessity deformed, nor what is not good is of necessity evil ; nor, since you have confessed that Love is neither beautiful nor good, infer, therefore, that he is deformed or evil, but rather something intermediate.'

" ' But,' I said, ' love is confessed by all to be a great God.'—' Do you mean, when you say all, all those who know, or those who know not, what they say ? '—' All

collectively.'—'And how can that be, Socrates?' said
she laughing; 'how can he be acknowledged to be a
great God, by those who assert that he is not even a
God at all?'—'And who are they?' I said—'You for
one, and I for another.'—'How can you say that,
Diotima?'—'Easily,' she replied, 'and with truth; for
tell me, do you not own that all the Gods are beautiful
and happy? or will you presume to maintain that any
God is otherwise?'—'By Jupiter, not I!'—'Do you not
call those alone happy who possess all things that are
beautiful and good?'—'Certainly.'—'You have confessed that Love, through his desire for things beautiful
and good, possesses not those materials of happiness.'
—'Indeed such was my concession.'—But how can we
conceive a God to be without the possession of what is
beautiful and good?'—'In no manner, I confess.'—
'Observe, then, that you do not consider Love to be a
God.'—'What, then,' I said, 'is Love a mortal?'—
'By no means.' — 'But what, then?'—'Like those
things which I have before instanced, he is neither
mortal nor immortal, but something intermediate.'—
'What is that, O Diotima?' — 'A great dæmon,
Socrates; and everything dæmoniacal holds an intermediate place between what is divine and what is
mortal.'

   "'What is his power and nature?' I inquired.—'He
interprets and makes a communication between divine
and human things, conveying the prayers and sacrifices
of men to the Gods, and communicating the commands
and directions concerning the mode of worship most
pleasing to them, from Gods to men.   He fills up that
intermediate space between these two classes of beings,
so as to bind together, by his own power, the whole
universe of things.   Through him subsist all divination,
and the science of sacred things as it relates to sacrifices,
and expiations, and disenchantments, and prophecy,
and magic.   The divine nature cannot immediately

communicate with what is human, but all that intercourse and converse which is conceded by the Gods to men, both whilst they sleep and when they wake, subsists through the intervention of Love; and he who is wise in the science of this intercourse is supremely happy, and participates in the dæmoniacal nature; whilst he who is wise in any other science or art, remains a mere ordinary slave. These dæmons are, indeed, many and various, and one of them is Love.'

" 'Who are the parents of Love?' I inquired.—'The history of what you ask,' replied Diotima, 'is somewhat long; nevertheless I will explain it to you. On the birth of Venus the Gods celebrated a great feast, and among them came Plenty, the son of Metis. After supper, Poverty, observing the profusion, came to beg, and stood beside the door. Plenty being drunk with nectar, for wine was not yet invented, went out into Jupiter's garden, and fell into a deep sleep. Poverty wishing to have a child by Plenty, on account of her low estate, lay down by him, and from his embraces conceived Love. Love is, therefore, the follower and servant of Venus, because he was conceived at her birth, and because by nature he is a lover of all that is beautiful, and Venus was beautiful. And since Love is the child of Poverty and Plenty, his nature and fortune participate in that of his parents. He is for ever poor, and so far from being delicate and beautiful, as mankind imagine, he is squalid and withered; he flies low along the ground, and is homeless and unsandalled; he sleeps without covering before the doors, and in the unsheltered streets; possessing thus far his mother's nature, that he is ever the companion of want. But, inasmuch as he participates in that of his father, he is for ever scheming to obtain things which are good and beautiful; he is fearless, vehement, and strong; a dreadful hunter, for ever weaving some new contrivance; exceedingly cautious and prudent, and full of resources; he is also, during his whole existence, a philosopher, a powerful enchanter, a wizard, and a subtle sophist. And, as his nature is neither mortal nor immortal, on the same day when he is fortunate and successful, he will at one time flourish, and then die away, and then, according to his father's nature, again revive. All that he acquires perpetually flows away from him, so that Love is never either rich or poor, and holding for ever an intermediate state between ignorance and wisdom. The case stands thus ;—no God philosophises or desires to become wise, for he is wise ; nor, if there exist any other being who is wise, does he philosophise. Nor do the ignorant philosophise, for they desire not to become wise ; for this is the evil of ignorance, that he who has neither intelligence, nor virtue, nor delicacy of sentiment, imagines that he possesses all those things sufficiently. He seeks not, therefore, that possession, of whose want he is not aware.'—' Who, then, O Diotima,' I inquired, ' are philosophers, if they are neither the ignorant nor the wise ? '—' It is evident, even to a child, that they are those intermediate persons, among whom is Love. For Wisdom is one of the most beautiful of all things ; Love is that which thirsts for the beautiful, so that Love is of necessity a philosopher, philosophy being an intermediate state between ignorance and wisdom. His parentage accounts for his condition, being the child of a wise and well provided father, and of a mother both ignorant and poor.

" ' Such is the dæmoniacal nature, my dear Socrates ; nor do I wonder at your error concerning Love, for you thought, as I conjecture from what you say, that Love was not the lover but the beloved, and thence, well concluded that he must be supremely beautiful ; for that which is the object of Love must indeed be fair, and delicate, and perfect, and most happy ; but Love inherits, as I have declared, a totally opposite nature.' —' Your words have persuasion in them, O stranger,

I said; 'be it as you say. But this Love, what advantages does he afford to men?'—'I will proceed to explain it to you, Socrates. Love being such and so produced as I have described, is, indeed, as you say, the love of things which are beautiful. But if any one should ask us, saying : O Socrates and Diotima, why is Love the love of beautiful things? Or, in plainer words, what does the lover of that which is beautiful, love in the object of his love, and seek from it?'—'He seeks,' I said, interrupting her, 'the property and possession of it.'—'But that,' she replied, 'might still be met with another question, What has he, who possesses that which is beautiful?'—'Indeed, I cannot immediately reply.'—'But, if changing the beautiful for good, any one should inquire,—I ask, O Socrates, what is that which he who loves that which is good, loves in the object of his love?'—'To be in his possession,' I replied.—'And what has he, who has the possession of good?'—'This question is of easier solution, he is happy.'—'Those who are happy, then, are happy through the possession; and it is useless to inquire what he desires, who desires to be happy; the question seems to have a complete reply. But do you think that this wish and this love are common to all men, and that all desire that that which is good should be for ever present to them?'—'Certainly, common to all.'—'Why do we not say then, Socrates, that every one loves? if, indeed, all love perpetually the same thing? But we say that some love, and some do not.'—'Indeed I wonder why it is so.'—'Wonder not,' said Diotima, 'for we select a particular species of love, and apply to it distinctively, the appellation of that which is universal.'——

"'Give me an example of such a select application.' —'Poetry; which is a general name signifying every cause whereby anything proceeds from that which is not, into that which is; so that the exercise of every inventive art is poetry, and all such artists poets. Yet they are not called poets, but distinguished by other names ; and one portion or species of poetry, that which has relation to music and rhythm, is divided from all others, and known by the name belonging to all. For this is alone properly called poetry, and those who exercise the art of this species of poetry, poets. So with respect to Love. Love is indeed universally all that earnest desire for the possession of happiness and that which is good ; the greatest and the subtlest love, and which inhabits the heart of every living being ; but those who seek this object through the acquirement of wealth, or the exercise of the gymnastic arts, or philosophy, are not said to love, nor are called lovers ; one species alone is called love, and those alone are said to be lovers, and to love, who seek the attainment of the universal desire through one species of love, which is peculiarly distinguished by the name belonging to the whole. It is asserted by some, that they love, who are seeking the lost half of their divided being. But I assert, that Love is neither the love of half nor of the whole, unless, my friend, it meets with that which is good ; since men willingly cut off their own hands and feet, if they think that they are the cause of evil to them. Nor do they cherish and embrace that which may belong to themselves, merely because it is their own ; unless, indeed, any one should choose to say, that that which is good is attached to his own nature and is his own, whilst that which is evil is foreign and accidental ; but love nothing but that which is good. Does it not appear so to you ?'—' Assuredly.'—' Can we then simply affirm that men love that which is good ?'—' Without doubt.' —' What, then, must we not add, that, in addition to loving that which is good, they love that it should be present to themselves ?'—' Indeed that must be added.' —' And not merely that it should be present, but that it should ever be present ?'—' This also must be added.'

"'Love, then, is collectively the desire in men that
good should be for ever present to them.'—'Most true.'
—'Since this is the general definition of Love, can you
explain in what mode of attaining its object, and in what
species of actions, does Love peculiarly consist?'—
'If I knew what you ask, O Diotima, I should not have
so much wondered at your wisdom, nor have sought you
out for the purpose of deriving improvement from your
instructions.'—'I will tell you,' she replied: 'Love is
the desire of generation in the beautiful, both with relation to the body and the soul.'—'I must be a diviner
to comprehend what you say, for, being such as I am,
I confess that I do not understand it.'—'But I will
explain it more clearly. The bodies and the souls of all
human beings are alike pregnant with their future progeny, and when we arrive at a certain age, our nature
impels us to bring forth and propagate. This nature is
unable to produce in that which is deformed, but it can
produce in that which is beautiful. The intercourse of
the male and female in generation, a divine work,
through pregnancy and production, is, as it were, something immortal in mortality. These things cannot take
place in that which is incongruous; for that which is
deformed is incongruous, but that which is beautiful is
congruous with what is mortal and divine. Beauty is,
therefore, the fate, and the Juno Lucina to generation.
Wherefore, whenever that which is pregnant with the
generative principle, approaches that which is beautiful,
it becomes transported with delight, and is poured forth
in overflowing pleasure, and propagates. But when it
approaches that which is deformed it is contracted by
sadness, and being repelled and checked, it does not
produce, but retains unwillingly that with which it is
pregnant. Wherefore, to one pregnant, and, as it were,
already bursting with the load of his desire, the impulse
towards that which is beautiful is intense, on account of
the great pain of retaining that which he has conceived.

Love, then, O Socrates, is not as you imagine the love
of the beautiful.'—' What, then ?'—' Of generation and
production in the beautiful.'—' Why then of generation ? '—' Generation is something eternal and immortal
in mortality. It necessarily, from what has been confessed, follows, that we must desire immortality together
with what is good, since Love is the desire that good be
for ever present to us. Of necessity Love must also be
the desire of immortality.'

" Diotima taught me all this doctrine in the discourse
we had together concerning Love ; and, in addition,
she inquired, ' What do you think, Socrates, is the
cause of this love and desire ? Do you not perceive how
all animals, both those of the earth and of the air, are
affected when they desire the propagation of their species,
affected even to weakness and disease by the impulse of
their love ; first, longing to be mixed with each other,
and then seeking nourishment for their offspring, so
that the feeblest are ready to contend with the strongest
in obedience to this law, and to die for the sake of their
young, or to waste away with hunger, and do or suffer
anything so that they may not want nourishment. It
might be said that human beings do these things
through reason, but can you explain why other animals
are thus affected through love ? '—I confessed that I did
not know.—' Do you imagine yourself,' said she, ' to be
skilful in the science of Love, if you are ignorant of
these things ? '—' As I said before, O Diotima, I come
to you, well knowing how much I am in need of a
teacher. But explain to me, I entreat you, the cause of
these things, and of the other things relating to Love.'
—' If,' said Diotima, ' you believe that Love is of the
same nature as we have mutually agreed upon, wonder
not that such are its effects. For the mortal nature
seeks, so far as it is able, to become deathless and
eternal. But it can only accomplish this desire by
generation, which for ever leaves another new in place

of the old. For, although each human being is severally said to live, and be the same from youth to old age, yet, that which is called the same, never contains within itself the same things, but always is becoming new by the loss and change of that which it possessed before ; both the hair and the flesh, and the bones, and the entire body.

"'And not only does this change take place in the body, but also with respect to the soul. Manners, morals, opinions, desires, pleasures, sorrows, fears ; none of these ever remain unchanged in the same persons ; but some die away, and others are produced. And, what is yet more strange is, that not only does some knowledge spring up, and another decay, and that we are never the same with respect to our knowledge, but that each several object of our thoughts suffers the same revolution. That which is called meditation, or the exercise of memory, is the science of the escape or departure of memory ; for, forgetfulness is the going out of knowledge ; and meditation, calling up a new memory in the place of that which has departed, pre-serves knowledge ; so that, though for ever displaced and restored, it seems to be the same. In this manner every thing mortal is preserved : not that it is constant and eternal, like that which is divine ; but that in the place of what has grown old and is departed, it leaves another new like that which it was itself. By this con-trivance, O Socrates, does what is mortal, the body and all other things, partake of immortality ; that which is immortal, is immortal in another manner. Wonder not, then, if every thing by nature cherishes that which was produced from itself, for this earnest Love is a tendency towards eternity.'

" Having heard this discourse, I was astonished, and asked, ' Can these things be true, O wisest Diotima ? ' And she, like an accomplished sophist, said, ' Know well, O Socrates, that if you only regard that love of

II. G

which inspires men, you will wonder at your own
Lc_skilfulness in not having discovered all that I now
declare. Observe with how vehement a desire they
are affected to become illustrious and to prolong their
glory into immortal time, to attain which object, far
more ardently than for the sake of their children, all
men are ready to engage in many dangers, and expend
their fortunes, and submit to any labours and incur
any death. Do you believe that Alcestis would have
died in the place of Admetus, or Achilles for the revenge
of Patroclus, or Codrus for the kingdom of his posterity,
if they had not believed that the immortal memory
of their actions, which we now cherish, would have
remained after their death? Far otherwise; all such
deeds are done for the sake of ever-living virtue, and
this immortal glory which they have obtained; and
inasmuch as any one is of an excellent nature, so much
the more is he impelled to attain this reward. For
they love what is immortal.

" ' Those whose bodies alone are pregnant with this
principle of immortality are attracted by women, seeking
through the production of children what they imagine to
be happiness and immortality and an enduring remembrance; but they whose souls are far more pregnant
than their bodies, conceive and produce that which
is more suitable to the soul. What is suitable to the
soul? Intelligence, and every other power and excellence of the mind; of which all poets, and all other
artists who are creative and inventive, are the authors.
The greatest and most admirable wisdom is that which
regulates the government of families and states, and
which is called moderation and justice. Whosoever,
therefore, from his youth feels his soul pregnant with
the conception of these excellences, is divine; and when
due time arrives, desires to bring forth; and wandering
about, he seeks the beautiful in which he may propagate
what he has conceived: for there is no generation in

that which is deformed ; he embraces those bodies
which are beautiful rather than those which are deformed,
in obedience to the principle which is within him, which
is ever seeking to perpetuate itself. And if he meets,
in conjunction with loveliness of form, a beautiful,
generous, and gentle soul, he embraces both at once,
and immediately undertakes to educate this object of
his love, and is inspired with an overflowing persuasion
to declare what is virtue, and what he ought to be who
would attain to its possession, and what are the duties
which it exacts. For, by the intercourse with, and as
it were, the very touch of that which is beautiful, he
brings forth and produces what he had formerly conceived ; and nourishes and educates that which is thus
produced together with the object of his love, whose
image, whether absent or present, is never divided from
his mind. So that those who are thus united are linked
by a nobler community and a firmer love, as being the
common parents of a lovelier and more endearing progeny than the parents of other children. And every one
who considers what posterity Homer and Hesiod, and
the other great poets, have left behind them, the sources
of their own immortal memory and renown, or what
children of his soul Lycurgus has appointed to be the
guardians, not only of Lacedæmon, but of all Greece ;
or what an illustrious progeny of laws Solon has produced, and how many admirable achievements, both
among the Greeks and Barbarians, men have left as
the pledges of that love which subsisted between them
and the beautiful, would choose rather to be the parent
of such children than those in a human shape. For
divine honours have often been rendered to them on
account of such children, but on account of those in
human shape, never.

" ' Your own meditation, O Socrates, might perhaps
have initiated you in all these things which I have
already taught you on the subject of Love. But those

ɟerfect and sublime ends to which these are only the
means, I know not that you would have been competent
to discover. I will declare them, therefore, and will
render them as intelligible as possible : do you meanwhile strain all your attention to trace the obscure depth
of the subject. He who aspires to love rightly, ought
from his earliest youth to seek an intercourse with
beautiful forms, and first to make a single form the
object of his love, and therein to generate intellectual
excellences. He ought, then, to consider that beauty
in whatever form it resides is the brother of that beauty
which subsists in another form ; and if he ought to
pursue that which is beautiful in form, it would be
absurd to imagine that beauty is not one and the same
thing in all forms, and would therefore remit much of
his ardent preference towards one, through his perception of the multitude of claims upon his love. In
addition, he would consider the beauty which is in
souls more excellent than that which is in form. So
that one endowed with an admirable soul, even though
the flower of the form were withered, would suffice him
as the object of his love and care, and the companion
with whom he might seek and produce such conclusions
as tend to the improvement of youth ; so that it might
be led to observe the beauty and the conformity which
there is in the observation of its duties and the laws,
and to esteem little the mere beauty of the outward
form. He would then conduct his pupil to (science)
so that he might look upon the loveliness of wisdom ;
and that contemplating thus the universal beauty, no
longer would he unworthily and meanly enslave himself
to the attractions of one form in love, nor one subject
of discipline or science, but would turn towards the
wide ocean of intellectual beauty, and from the sight
of the lovely and majestic forms which it contains,
would abundantly bring forth his conceptions in philosophy ; until, strengthened and confirmed, he should at

length steadily contemplate one science, which is the
science of this universal beauty.

" 'Attempt, I entreat you, to mark what I say with
as keen an observation as you can. He who has been
disciplined to this point in Love, by contemplating
beautiful objects gradually, and in their order, now
arriving at the end of all that concerns Love, on a
sudden beholds a beauty wonderful in its nature. This
is it, O Socrates, for the sake of which all the former
labours were endured. It is eternal, unproduced, indestructible; neither subject to increase nor decay : not,
like other things, partly beautiful and partly deformed;
not at one time beautiful and at another time not ; not
beautiful in relation to one thing and deformed in relation to another ; not here beautiful and there deformed ;
not beautiful in the estimation of one person and
deformed in that of another; nor can this supreme
beauty be figured to the imagination like a beautiful
face, or beautiful hands, or any portion of the body,
nor like any discourse, nor any science. Nor does
it subsist in any other that lives or is, either in earth,
or in heaven, or in any other place ; but it is eternally
uniform and consistent, and monoeidic with itself. All
other things are beautiful through a participation of it,
with this condition, that although they are subject to
production and decay, it never becomes more or less,
or endures any change. When any one, ascending
from a correct system of Love, begins to contemplate
this supreme beauty, he already touches the consumma-
tion of his labour. For such as discipline themselves
upon this system, or are conducted by another beginning
to ascend through these transitory objects which are
beautiful, towards that which is beauty itself, proceeding
as on steps from the love of one form to that of two,
and from that of two, to that of all forms which are
beautiful; and from beautiful forms to beautiful habits
and institutions, and from institutions to beautiful doc-

trines; until, from the meditation of many doctrines, they arrive at that which is nothing else than the doctrine of the supreme beauty itself, in the knowledge and contemplation of which at length they repose.

"'Such a life as this, my dear Socrates,' exclaimed the stranger Prophetess, 'spent in the contemplation of the beautiful, is the life for men to live; which if you chance ever to experience, you will esteem far beyond gold and rich garments, and even those lovely persons whom you and many others now gaze on with astonishment, and are prepared neither to eat nor drink so that you may behold and live for ever with these objects of your love! What then shall we imagine to be the aspect of the supreme beauty itself, simple, pure, uncontaminated with the intermixture of human flesh and colours, and all other idle and unreal shapes attendant on mortality; the divine, the original, the supreme, the monoeidic beautiful itself? What must be the life of him who dwells with and gazes on that which it becomes us all to seek? Think you not that to him alone is accorded the prerogative of bringing forth, not images and shadows of virtue, for he is in contact not with a shadow but with reality; with virtue itself, in the production and nourishment of which he becomes dear to the Gods, and if such a privilege is conceded to any human being, himself immortal.'

"Such, O Phædrus, and my other friends, was what Diotima said. And being persuaded by her words, I have since occupied myself in attempting to persuade others, that it is not easy to find a better assistant than Love in seeking to communicate immortality to our human natures. Wherefore I exhort every one to honour Love; I hold him in honour, and chiefly exercise myself in amatory matters, and exhort others to do so; and now and ever do I praise the power and excellence of Love, in the best manner that I can. Let this discourse, if it pleases you, Phædrus, be considered as an

encomium of Love; or call it by what other name you
will."

The whole assembly praised his discourse, and
Aristophanes was on the point of making some remarks
on the allusion made by Socrates to him in a part of
his discourse, when suddenly they heard a loud knocking
at the door of the vestibule, and a clamour as of revellers,
attended by a flute-player.—"Go, boys," said Agathon,
"and see who is there: if they are any of our friends,
call them in; if not, say that we have already done
drinking."—A minute afterwards, they heard the voice
of Alcibiades in the vestibule excessively drunk and
roaring out:—"Where is Agathon? Lead me to
Agathon!"—The flute-player, and some of his companions then led him in, and placed him against the
door-post, crowned with a thick crown of ivy and violets,
and having a quantity of fillets on his head.—"My
friends," he cried out, "hail! I am excessively drunk
already, but I'll drink with you, if you will. If not, we
will go away after having crowned Agathon, for which
purpose I came. I assure you that I could not come
yesterday, but I am now here with these fillets round my
temples, that from my own head I may crown his who,
with your leave, is the most beautiful and wisest of men.
Are you laughing at me because I am drunk? Ay, I
know what I say is true, whether you laugh or not.
But tell me at once whether I shall come in, or no.
Will you drink with me?"

Agathon and the whole party desired him to come in,
and recline among them; so he came in, led by his
companions. He then unbound his fillets that he might
crown Agathon, and though Socrates was just before his
eyes, he did not see him, but sat down by Agathon,
between Socrates and him, for Socrates moved out of
the way to make room for him. When he sat down, he
embraced Agathon and crowned him; and Agathon
desired the slaves to untie his sandals, that he might

make a third, and recline on the same couch. " By all
means," said Alcibiades, " but what third companion
have we here ? " And at the same time turning round
and seeing Socrates, he leaped up and cried out :—" O
Hercules ! what have we here ? You, Socrates, lying in
ambush for me wherever I go ! and meeting me just as
you always do, when I least expected to see you ! And,
now, what are you come here for ? Why have you
chosen to recline exactly in this place, and not near
Aristophanes, or any one else who is, or wishes to be
ridiculous, but have contrived to take your place beside
the most delightful person of the whole party ? "—
" Agathon," said Socrates, " see if you cannot defend
me. I declare my friendship for this man is a bad
business : from the moment that I first began to know
him I have never been permitted to converse with, or
so much as look upon any one else. If I do, he is so
jealous and suspicious that he does the most extravagant
things, and hardly refrains from beating me. I entreat
you to prevent him from doing anything of that kind at
present. Procure a reconciliation : or, if he perseveres
in attempting any violence, I entreat you to defend me."
—" Indeed," said Alcibiades, " I will not be reconciled
to you ; I shall find another opportunity to punish you
for this. But now," said he, addressing Agathon, " lend
me some of those fillets, that I may crown the wonderful
head of this fellow, lest I incur the blame, that having
crowned you, I neglected to crown him who conquers
all men with his discourses, not yesterday alone as you
did, but ever."

Saying this he took the fillets, and having bound the
head of Socrates, and again having reclined, said :
" Come, my friends, you seem to be sober enough.
You must not flinch, but drink, for that was your agreement with me before I came in. I choose as president,
until you have drunk enough—myself. Come, Agathon,
if you have got a great goblet, fetch it out. But no

matter, that wine-cooler will do ; bring it, boy !" And observing that it held more than eight cups, he first drank it off, and then ordered it to be filled for Socrates, and said :—"Observe, my friends, I cannot invent any scheme against Socrates, for he will drink as much as any one desires him, and not be in the least drunk." Socrates, after the boy had filled up, drank it off; and Eryximachus said :—"Shall we then have no conversation or singing over our cups, but drink down stupidly, just as if we were thirsty ?" And Alcibiades said : "Ah, Eryximachus, I did not see you before ; hail, you excellent son of a wise and excellent father !"—"Hail to you also," replied Eryximachus, "but what shall we do ?"—"Whatever you command, for we ought to submit to your directions ; a physician is worth a hundred common men. Command us as you please."—"Listen then," said Eryximachus, " before you came in, each of us had agreed to deliver as eloquent a discourse as he could in praise of Love, beginning at the right hand ; all the rest of us have fulfilled our engagement ; you have not spoken, and yet have drunk with us : you ought to bear your part in the discussion ; and having done so, command what you please to Socrates, who shall have the privilege of doing so to his right-hand neighbour, and so on to the others."—" Indeed, there appears some justice in your proposal, Eryximachus, though it is rather unfair to induce a drunken man to set his discourse in competition with that of those who are sober. And, besides, did Socrates really persuade you that what he just said about me was true, or do you not know that matters are in fact exactly the reverse of his representation ? For I seriously believe that, should I praise in his presence, be he god or man, any other beside himself, he would not keep his hands off me. But I assure you, Socrates, I will praise no one beside yourself in your presence."

"Do so, then," said Eryximachus, "praise Socrates

if you please."—"What," said Alcibiades, "shall I
attack him, and punish him before you all?"—"What
have you got into your head now," said Socrates, "are
you going to expose me to ridicule, and to misrepresent
me? Or what are you going to do?"—"I will only
speak the truth; will you permit me on this condition?"
—"I not only permit, but exhort you to say all the truth
you know," replied Socrates. "I obey you willingly,"
said Alcibiades, "and if I advance anything untrue, do
you, if you please, interrupt me, and convict me of mis-
representation, for I would never willingly speak falsely.
And bear with me if I do not relate things in their order,
but just as I remember them, for it is not easy for a
man in my present condition to enumerate systemati-
cally all your singularities.

"I will begin the praise of Socrates by comparing
him to a certain statue. Perhaps he will think that
this statue is introduced for the sake of ridicule, but I
assure you that it is necessary for the illustration of
truth. I assert, then, that Socrates is exactly like those
Silenuses that sit in the sculptors' shops, and which are
carved holding flutes or pipes, but which, when divided
in two, are found to contain withinside the images of
the gods. I assert that Socrates is like the satyr
Marsyas. That your form and appearance are like
these satyrs', I think that even you will not venture to
deny; and how like you are to them in all other things,
now hear. Are you not scornful and petulant? If you
deny this, I will bring witnesses. Are you not a piper,
and far more wonderful a one than he? For Marsyas,
and whoever now pipes the music that he taught, for
that music which is of heaven, and described as being
taught by Marsyas, enchants men through the power of
the mouth. For if any musician, be he skilful or not,
awakens this music, it alone enables him to retain the
minds of men, and from the divinity of its nature makes
evident those who are in want of the gods and initiation.

You differ only from Marsyas in this circumstance, that you effect without instruments, by mere words, all that he can do. For when we hear Pericles, or any other accomplished orator, deliver a discourse, no one, as it were, cares any thing about it. But when any one hears you, or even your words related by another, though ever so rude and unskilful a speaker, be that person a woman, man or child, we are struck and retained, as it were, by the discourse clinging to our mind.

" If I was not afraid that I am a great deal too drunk, I would confirm to you by an oath the strange effects which I assure you I have suffered from his words, and suffer still ; for when I hear him speak, my heart leaps up far more than the hearts of those who celebrate the Corybantic mysteries ; my tears are poured out as he talks, a thing I have seen happen to many others beside myself. I have heard Pericles and other excellent orators, and have been pleased with their discourses, but I suffered nothing of this kind ; nor was my soul ever on those occasions disturbed and filled with self-reproach, as if it were slavishly laid prostrate. But this Marsyas here has often affected me in the way I describe, until the life which I lead seemed hardly worth living. Do not deny it, Socrates, for I well know that if even now I chose to listen to you, I could not resist, but should again suffer the same effects. For, my friends, he forces me to confess that while I myself am still in want of many things, I neglect my own necessities, and attend to those of the Athenians. I stop my ears, therefore, as from the Syrens, and flee away as fast as possible, that I may not sit down beside him and grow old in listening to his talk. For this man has reduced me to feel the sentiment of shame, which I imagine no one would readily believe was in me ; he alone inspires me with remorse and awe. For I feel in his presence my incapacity of refuting what he says, or of refusing to do that which he directs ; but when I depart from him, the glory which the multitude confers overwhelms me. I escape, therefore, and hide myself from him, and when I see him I am overwhelmed with humiliation, because I have neglected to do what I have confessed to him ought to be done ; and often and often have I wished that he were no longer to be seen among men. But if that were to happen, I well know that I should suffer far greater pain ; so that where I can turn, or what I can do with this man, I know not. All this have I and many others suffered from the pipings of this satyr.

" And observe, how like he is to what I said, and what a wonderful power he possesses. Know that there is not one of you who is aware of the real nature of Socrates ; but since I have begun, I will make him plain to you. You observe how passionately Socrates affects the intimacy of those who are beautiful, and how ignorant he professes himself to be ; appearances in themselves excessively Silenic. This, my friends, is the external form with which, like one of the sculptured Sileni, he has clothed himself ; for if you open him, you will find within admirable temperance and wisdom. For he cares not for mere beauty, but despises more than any one can imagine all external possessions, whether it be beauty or wealth, or glory, or any other thing for which the multitude felicitates the possessor. He esteems these things and us who honour them, as nothing, and lives among men, making all the objects of their admiration the playthings of his irony. But I know not if any one of you have ever seen the divine images which are within, when he has been opened and is serious. I have seen them, and they are so supremely beautiful, so golden, so divine, and wonderful, that everything which Socrates commands surely ought to be obeyed, even like the voice of a God.

" At one time we were fellow-soldiers, and had our mess together in the camp before Potidæa. Socrates

there overcame not only me, but every one beside, in
endurance of toils : when, as often happens in a cam-
paign, we were reduced to few provisions, there were
none who could sustain hunger like Socrates ; and when
we had plenty, he alone seemed to enjoy our military
fare. He never drank much willingly, but when he was
compelled he conquered all even in that to which he
was least accustomed ; and what is most astonishing,
no person ever saw Socrates drunk either then or at
any other time. In the depth of winter (and the
winters there are excessively rigid,) he sustained calmly
incredible hardships ; and amongst other things, whilst
the frost was intolerably severe, and no one went out of
their tents, or if they went out, wrapt themselves up
carefully, and put fleeces under their feet, and bound
their legs with hairy skins, Socrates went out only with
the same cloak on that he usually wore, and walked
barefoot upon the ice ; more easily, indeed, than those
who had sandalled themselves so delicately : so that the
soldiers thought that he did it to mock their want of
fortitude. It would indeed be worth while to commemorate all that this brave man did and endured in
that expedition. In one instance he was seen early in
the morning, standing in one place wrapt in meditation;
and as he seemed not to be able to unravel the subject
of his thoughts, he still continued to stand as inquiring
and discussing within himself, and when noon came, the
soldiers observed him, and said to one another—'Socrates
has been standing there thinking, ever since the morning.'
At last some Ionians came to the spot, and having
supped, as it was summer, bringing their blankets, they
lay down to sleep in the cool ; they observed that
Socrates continued to stand there the whole night until
morning, and that, when the sun rose, he saluted it with
a prayer and departed.

" I ought not to omit what Socrates is in battle. For
in that battle after which the generals decreed to me

the prize of courage, Socrates alone of all men was the saviour of my life, standing by me when I had fallen and was wounded, and preserving both myself and my arms from the hands of the enemy. On that occasion I entreated the generals to decree the prize, as it was most due, to him. And this, O Socrates, you cannot deny, that the generals wishing to conciliate a person of my rank, desired to give me the prize, you were far more earnestly desirous than the generals that this glory should be attributed not to yourself, but me.

"But to see Socrates when our army was defeated and scattered in flight at Delius, was a spectacle worthy to behold. On that occasion I was among the cavalry, and he on foot, heavily armed. After the total rout of our troops, he and Laches retreated together; I came up by chance, and seeing them, bade them be of good cheer, for that I would not leave them. As I was on horseback, and therefore less occupied by a regard of my own situation, I could better observe than at Potidæa the beautiful spectacle exhibited by Socrates on this emergency. How superior was he to Laches in presence of mind and courage! Your representation of him on the stage, O Aristophanes, was not wholly unlike his real self on this occasion, for he walked and darted his regards around with a majestic composure, looking tranquilly both on his friends and enemies; so that it was evident to every one, even from afar, that whoever should venture to attack him would encounter a desperate resistance. He and his companion thus departed in safety; for those who are scattered in flight are pursued and killed, whilst men hesitate to touch those who exhibit such a countenance as that of Socrates even in defeat.

"Many other and most wonderful qualities might well be praised in Socrates; but such as these might singly be attributed to others. But that which is unparalleled in Socrates, is, that he is unlike, and above comparison,

with all other men, whether those who have lived in
ancient times, or those who exist now. For it may be
conjectured, that Brasidas and many others are such as
was Achilles. Pericles deserves comparison with Nestor
and Antenor; and other excellent persons of various
times may, with probability, be drawn into comparison
with each other. But to such a singular man as this,
both himself and his discourses are so uncommon, no
one, should he seek, would find a parallel among the
present or the past generations of mankind ; unless they
should say that he resembled those with whom I lately
compared him, for, assuredly, he and his discourses are
like nothing but the Silen and the Satyrs. At first I
forgot to make you observe how like his discourses are
to those Satyrs when they are opened, for, if any one
will listen to the talk of Socrates, it will appear to him
at first extremely ridiculous ; the phrases and expressions
which he employs, fold around his exterior the skin, as
it were, of a rude and wanton Satyr. He is always
talking about great market-asses, and brass-founders,
and leather-cutters, and skin-dressers ; and this is his
perpetual custom, so that any dull and unobservant
person might easily laugh at his discourse. But if any
one should see it opened, as it were, and get within the
sense of his words, he would then find that they alone
of all that enters into the mind of man to utter, had a
profound and persuasive meaning, and that they were
most divine ; and that they presented to the mind
innumerable images of every excellence, and that they
tended towards objects of the highest moment, or rather
towards all that he who seeks the possession of what is
supremely beautiful and good need regard as essential
to the accomplishment of his ambition.

"These are the things, my friends, for which I praise
Socrates."

Alcibiades having said this, the whole party burst
into a laugh at his frankness, and Socrates said, "You

seem to be sober enough, Alcibiades, else you would not have made such a circuit of words, only to hide the main design for which you made this long speech, and which, as it were carelessly, you just throw in at the last; now, as if you had not said all this for the mere purpose of dividing me and Agathon? You think that I ought to be your friend, and to care for no one else. I have found you out; it is evident enough for what design you invented all this Satyrical and Silenic drama. But, my dear Agathon, do not let his device succeed. I entreat you to permit no one to throw discord between us."—" No doubt," said Agathon, " he sat down between us only that he might divide us; but this shall not assist his scheme, for I will come and sit near you." —" Do so," said Socrates, " come, there is room for you by me."—" Oh, Jupiter!" exclaimed Alcibiades, " what I endure from that man! He thinks to subdue every way; but, at least, I pray you, let Agathon remain between us."—" Impossible," said Socrates, " you have just praised me; I ought to praise him sitting at my right hand. If Agathon is placed beside you, will he not praise me before I praise him? Now, my dear friend, allow the young man to receive what praise I can give him. I have a great desire to pronounce his encomium."—" Quick, quick, Alcibiades," said Agathon, " I cannot stay here, I must change my place, or Socrates will not praise me."—Agathon then arose to take his place near Socrates.

He had no sooner reclined than there came in a number of revellers—for some one who had gone out had left the door open—and took their places on the vacant couches, and everything became full of confusion; and no order being observed, every one was obliged to drink a great quantity of wine. Eryximachus, and Phædrus, and some others, said Aristodemus, went home to bed; that, for his part, he went to sleep on his couch, and slept long and soundly—the nights were then long—until the cock crew in the morning. When he awoke he found that some were still fast asleep, and others had gone home, and that Aristophanes, Agathon, and Socrates had alone stood it out, and were still drinking out of a great goblet which they passed round and round. Socrates was disputing between them. The beginning of their discussion Aristodemus said that he did not recollect, because he was asleep; but it was terminated by Socrates forcing them to confess, that the same person is able to compose both tragedy and comedy, and that the foundations of the tragic and comic arts were essentially the same. They, rather convicted than convinced, went to sleep. Aristophanes first awoke, and then, it being broad daylight, Agathon. Socrates, having put them to sleep, went away, Aristodemus following him, and coming to the Lyceum he washed himself, as he would have done anywhere else, and after having spent the day there in his accustomed manner, went home in the evening.

ION;

OR, OF THE ILIAD.

Translated from Plato.

SOCRATES *and* ION.

Socrates. HAIL to thee, O Ion! from whence returnest thou amongst us now?— from thine own native Ephesus?

Ion. No, Socrates; I come from Epidaurus and the feasts in honour of Æsculapius.

Socrates. Had the Epidaurians instituted a contest of rhapsody in honour of the God?

Ion. And not in rhapsodies alone; there were contests in every species of music.

Socrates. And in which did you contend? And what was the success of your efforts?

Ion. I bore away the first prize at the games, O Socrates.

Socrates. Well done! You have now only to consider how you shall win the Panathenæa.

Ion. That may also happen, God willing.

Socrates. Your profession, O Ion, has often appeared to me an enviable one. For, together with the nicest care of your person, and the most studied elegance of dress, it imposes upon you the necessity of a familiar acquaintance with many and excellent poets, and especially with Homer, the most admirable of them all. Nor is it merely because you can repeat the verses of this great poet, that I envy you, but because you fathom his inmost thoughts. For he is no rhapsodist who does not understand the whole scope and intention of the poet, and is not capable of interpreting it to his audience. This he cannot do without a full comprehension of the meaning of the author he undertakes to illustrate; and worthy, indeed, of envy are those who can fulfil these conditions.

Ion. Thou speakest truth, O Socrates. And, indeed, I have expended my study particularly on this part of my profession. I flatter myself that no man living excels me in the interpretation of Homer; neither Metrodorus of Lampsacus, nor Stesimbrotus the Thasian, nor Glauco, nor any other rhapsodist of the present times can express so many various and beautiful thoughts upon Homer as I can.

Socrates. I am persuaded of your eminent skill, O Ion. You will not, I hope, refuse me a specimen of it?

Ion. And, indeed, it would be worth your while to hear me declaim upon Homer. I deserve a golden crown from his admirers.

Socrates. And I will find leisure some day or other to request you to favour me so far. At present, I will only trouble you with one question. Do you excel in explaining Homer alone, or are you conscious of a similar power with regard to Hesiod and Archilochus?

Ion. I possess this high degree of skill with regard to Homer alone, and I consider that sufficient.

Socrates. Are there any subjects upon which Homer and Hesiod say the same things?

Ion. Many, as it seems to me.

Socrates. Whether do you demonstrate these things better in Homer or Hesiod?

Ion. In the same manner, doubtless; inasmuch as they say the same words with regard to the same things.

Socrates. But with regard to those things in which they differ;—Homer and Hesiod both treat of divination, do they not?

Ion. Certainly.

Socrates. Do you think that you or a diviner would make the best exposition, respecting all that these poets say of divination, both as they agree and as they differ?

Ion. A diviner probably.

Socrates. Suppose you were a diviner, do you not think that you could explain the discrepancies of those poets on the subject of your profession, if you understand their agreement?

Ion. Clearly so.

Socrates. How does it happen then that you are possessed of skill to illustrate Homer, and not Hesiod, or any other poet in an equal degree? Is the subject-matter of the poetry of Homer different from all other poets'? Does he not principally treat of war and social intercourse, and of the distinct functions and characters of the brave man and the coward, the professional and private person, the mutual relations which subsist between the Gods and men; together with the modes of their intercourse, the phænomena of Heaven, the secrets of Hades, and the origin of Gods and heroes? Are not these the materials from which Homer wrought his poem?

Ion. Assuredly, O Socrates.

Socrates. And the other poets, do they not treat of the same matter?

Ion. Certainly: but not like Homer.

Socrates. How! Worse?

Ion. Oh! far worse.

Socrates. Then Homer treats of them better than they?

Ion. Oh ! Jupiter !—how much better !

Socrates. Amongst a number of persons employed in solving a problem of arithmetic, might not a person know, my dear Ion, which had given the right answer?

Ion. Certainly.

Socrates. The same person who had been aware of the false one, or some other ?

Ion. The same, clearly.

Socrates. That is, some one who understood arith metic ?

Ion. Certainly.

Socrates. Among a number of persons giving their opinions on the wholesomeness of different foods, whether would one person be capable to pronounce upon the rectitude of the opinions of those who judged rightly, and another on the erroneousness of those which were incorrect, or would the same person be competent to decide respecting them both ?

Ion. The same, evidently.

Socrates. What would you call that person ?

Ion. A physician.

Socrates. We may assert then, universally, that the same person who is competent to determine the truth, is competent also to determine the falsehood of whatever assertion is advanced on the same subject ; and, it is manifest, that he who cannot judge respecting the false-hood, or unfitness of what is said upon a given subject, is equally incompetent to determine upon its truth or beauty ?

Ion. Assuredly.

Socrates. The same person would then be competent or incompetent for both ?

Ion. Yes.

Socrates. Do you not say that Homer and the other poets, and among them Hesiod and Archilochus, speak of the same things, but unequally ; one better and the other worse?

Ion. And I speak truth.

Socrates. But if you can judge of what is well said by the one, you must also be able to judge of what is ill said by another, inasmuch as it expresses less correctly.

Ion. It should seem so.

Socrates. Then, my dear friend, we should not err if we asserted that Ion possessed a like power of illustration respecting Homer and all other poets ; especially since he confesses that the same person must be esteemed a competent judge of all those who speak on the same subjects ; inasmuch as those subjects are understood by him when spoken of by one, and the subject-matter of almost all the poets is the same.

Ion. What can be the reason then, O Socrates, that when any other poet is the subject of conversation I cannot compel my attention, and I feel utterly unable to declaim anything worth talking of, and positively go to sleep ?   But when any one makes mention of Homer, my mind applies itself without effort to the subject ; I awaken as if it were from a trance, and a profusion of eloquent expressions suggest themselves involuntarily ?

Socrates. It is not difficult to suggest the cause of this, my dear friend.   You are evidently unable to declaim on Homer according to art and knowledge ; for did your art endow you with this faculty, you would be equally capable of exerting it with regard to any other of the poets.   Is not poetry, as an art or a faculty, a thing entire and one ?

Ion. Assuredly.

Socrates. The same mode of consideration must be admitted with respect to all arts which are severally one and entire.   Do you desire to hear what I understand by this, O Ion ?

Ion. Yes, by Jupiter, Socrates, I am delighted with listening to you wise men.

Socrates. It is you who are wise, my dear Ion ; you rhapsodists, actors, and the authors of the poems you recite. I, like an unprofessional and private man, can only speak the truth. Observe how common, vulgar, and level to the comprehension of any one, is the question which I now ask relative to the same consideration belonging to one entire art. Is not painting an art whole and entire?

Ion. Certainly.

Socrates. Did you ever know a person competent to judge of the paintings of Polygnotus, the son of Aglaophon, and incompetent to judge of the production of any other painter; who, on the supposition of the works of other painters being exhibited to him, was wholly at a loss, and very much inclined to go to sleep, and lost all faculty of reasoning on the subject; but when his opinion was required of Polygnotus, or any one single painter you please, awoke, paid attention to the subject, and discoursed on it with great eloquence and sagacity?

Ion. Never, by Jupiter!

Socrates. Did you ever know any one very skilful in determining the merits of Dædalus, the son of Metion, Epius, the son of Panopus, Theodorus the Samian, or any other great sculptor, who was immediately at a loss, and felt sleepy the moment any other sculptor was mentioned?

Ion. I never met with such a person certainly.

Socrates. Nor, do I think, that you ever met with a man professing himself a judge of poetry and rhapsody, and competent to criticise either Olympus, Thamyris, Orpheus, or Phemius of Ithaca, the rhapsodist, who, the moment he came to Ion the Ephesian, felt himself quite at a loss, and utterly incompetent to judge whether he rhapsodised well or ill.

Ion. I cannot refute you, Socrates, but of this I am conscious to myself: that I excel all men in the copiousness and beauty of my illustrations of Homer, as all who have heard me will confess, and with respect to other poets, I am deserted of this power. It is for you to consider what may be the cause of this distinction.

Socrates. I will tell you, O Ion, what appears to me to be the cause of this inequality of power. It is that you are not master of any art for the illustration of Homer, but it is a divine influence which moves you, like that which resides in the stone called magnet by Euripides, and Heraclea by the people. For not only does this stone possess the power of attracting iron rings, but it can communicate to them the power of attracting other rings; so that you may see sometimes a long chain of rings, and other iron substances, attached and suspended one to the other by this influence. And as the power of the stone circulates through all the links of this series, and attaches each to each, so the Muse, communicating through those whom she has first inspired, to all others capable of sharing in the inspiration, the influence of that first enthusiasm, creates a chain and a succession. For the authors of those great poems which we admire, do not attain to excellence through the rules of any art, but they utter their beautiful melodies of verse in a state of inspiration, and, as it were, *possessed* by a spirit not their own. Thus the composers of lyrical poetry create those admired songs of theirs in a state of divine insanity, like the Corybantes, who lose all control over their reason in the enthusiasm of the sacred dance; and, during this supernatural possession, are excited to the rhythm and harmony which they communicate to men. Like the Bacchantes, who, when possessed by the God, draw honey and milk from the rivers, in which, when they come to their senses, they find nothing but simple water. For the souls of the poets, as poets tell us, have this peculiar ministration in the world. They tell us that these souls, flying like bees from flower to flower, and wandering over the gardens and the meadows, and the honey-flowing fountains of the Muses, return to us laden with the sweetness of melody ; and arrayed as they are in the plumes of rapid imagination, they speak truth. For a Poet is indeed a thing ethereally light, winged, and sacred, nor can he compose anything worth calling poetry until he becomes inspired, and, as it were, mad, or whilst any reason remains in him. For whilst a man retains any portion of the thing called reason, he is utterly incompetent to produce poetry or to vaticinate. Thus, those who declaim various and beautiful poetry upon any subject, as for instance upon Homer, are not enabled to do so by art or study ; but every rhapsodist or poet, whether dithyrambic, encomiastic, choral, epic, or iambic, is excellent in proportion to the extent of his participation in the divine influence, and the degree in which the Muse itself has descended on him. In other respects, poets may be sufficiently ignorant and incapable. For they do not compose according to any art which they have acquired, but from the impulse of the divinity within them ; for did they know any rules of criticism according to which they could compose beautiful verses upon one subject, they would be able to exert the same faculty with respect to all or any other. The God seems purposely to have deprived all poets, prophets, and soothsayers of every particle of reason and understanding, the better to adapt them to their employment as his ministers and interpreters ; and that we, their auditors, may acknowledge that those who write so beautifully, are possessed, and address us, inspired by the God. Tynnicus the Chalcidean, is a manifest proof of this, for he never before composed any poem worthy to be remembered ; and yet, was the author of that Pæan which everybody sings, and which excels almost every other hymn, and which he himself acknowledges to have been inspired by the Muse. And, thus, it appears to me that the God proves beyond a doubt, that these transcendent poems are not human as the work of men, but divine as coming from the God. Poets then are the interpreters of the divinities—each being possessed by some one deity ; and to make this apparent, the God designedly inspires the worst poets with the sublimest verse.   Does it seem to you that I am in the right, O Ion ?

Ion. Yes, by Jupiter !   My mind is enlightened by your words, O Socrates, and it appears to me that great poets interpret to us through some divine election of the God.

Socrates. And do not you rhapsodists interpret poets ?
Ion. We do.
Socrates. Thus you interpret the interpreters ?
Ion. Evidently.
Socrates. Remember this, and tell me ; and do not conceal that which I ask.   When you declaim well, and strike your audience with admiration ; whether you sing of Ulysses rushing upon the threshold of his palace, discovering himself to the suitors, and pouring his shafts out at his feet ; or of Achilles assailing Hector ; or those affecting passages concerning Andromache, or Hecuba, or Priam, are you then self-possessed ? or, rather, are you not rapt and filled with such enthusiasm by the deeds you recite, that you fancy yourself in Ithaca or Troy, or wherever else the poem transports you ?

Ion. You speak most truly, Socrates, nor will I deny it ; for, when I recite of sorrow my eyes fill with tears ; and, when of fearful or terrible deeds, my hair stands on end, and my heart beats fast.

Socrates. Tell me, Ion, can we call him in his senses, who weeps while dressed in splendid garments, and crowned with a golden coronal, not losing any of these things ? and is filled with fear when surrounded by ten thousand friendly persons, not one among whom desires to despoil or injure him ?

Ion. To say the truth, we could not.
Socrates. Do you often perceive your audience moved also ?

Ion. Many among them, and frequently. I, standing on the rostrum, see them weeping; with eyes fixed earnestly on me, and overcome by my declamation. I have need so to agitate them; for if they weep, I laugh, taking their money; if they should laugh, I must weep, going without it.

Socrates. Do you not perceive that your auditor is the last link of that chain which I have described as held together through the power of the magnet? You rhapsodists and actors are the middle links, of which the poet is the first—and through all these the God influences whichever mind he selects, as they conduct this power one to the other; and thus, as rings from the stone, so hangs a long series of chorus-dancers, teachers, and disciples from the Muse. Some poets are influenced by one Muse, some by another; we call them possessed, and this word really expresses the truth, for they are held. Others, who are interpreters, are inspired by the first links, the poets, and are filled with enthusiasm, some by one, some by another; some by Orpheus, some by Musæus, but the greater number are possessed and inspired by Homer. You, O Ion, are influenced by Homer. If you recite the works of any other poet, you get drowsy, and are at a loss what to say; but when you hear any of the compositions of that poet you are roused, your thoughts are excited, and you grow eloquent;—for what you say of Homer is not derived from any art or knowledge, but from divine inspiration and possession. As the Corybantes feel acutely the melodies of him by whom they are inspired, and abound with verse and gesture for his songs alone, and care for no other; thus, you, O Ion, are eloquent when you expound Homer, and are barren of words with regard to every other poet. And this explains the question you asked, wherefore Homer, and no other poet, inspires you with eloquence. It is that you are thus excellent in your praise, not through science but from divine inspiration.

Ion. You say the truth, Socrates. Yet, I am surprised that you should be able to persuade me that I am possessed and insane when I praise Homer. I think I shall not appear such to you when you hear me.

Socrates. I desire to hear you, but not before you have answered me this one question. What subject does Homer treat best? for, surely, he does not treat all equally.

Ion. You are aware that he treats of every thing.

Socrates. Does Homer mention subjects on which you are ignorant?

Ion. What can those be?

Socrates. Does not Homer frequently dilate on various arts—on chariot-driving, for instance? if I remember the verses I will repeat them.

Ion. I will repeat them, for I remember them.

Socrates. Repeat what Nestor says to his son Antilochus, counselling him to be cautious in turning, during the chariot-race at the funeral games of Patroclus.

Ion (repeats). Αὐτὸς δὲ κλινθῆναι εὐπλέκτῳ ἐνὶ δίφρῳ
Ἦκ' ἐπ' ἀριστερὰ τοῖιν ἀτὰρ τὸν δεξιὸν ἵππον
Κένσαι ὁμοκλήσας, εἶξαί τέ οἱ ἡνία χερσίν.
Ἐν νύσσῃ δέ τοι ἵππος ἀριστερὸς ἐγχριμφθήτω,
Ὡς ἄν τοι πλήμνη γε δοάσσεται ἄκρον ἱκέσθαι
Κύκλου ποιητοῖο· λίθου δ' ἀλέασθαι ἐπαυρεῖν.

Il. ψ. 335.

Socrates. Enough. Now, O Ion, would a physician or a charioteer be the better judge as to Homer's sagacity on this subject?

Ion. Of course, a charioteer.

Socrates. Because he understands the art—or from what other reason?

Ion. From his knowledge of the art.

Socrates. For one science is not gifted with the power of judging of another—a steersman, for instance, does not understand medicine?

Ion. Without doubt.

Socrates. Nor a physician, architecture?

Ion. Of course not.

Socrates. Is it not thus with every art? If we are adepts in one, we are ignorant of another. But first, tell me, do not all arts differ one from the other?

Ion. They do.

Socrates. For you, as well as I, can testify that when we say an art is the knowledge of one thing, we do not mean that it is the knowledge of another.

Ion. Certainly.

Socrates. For, if each art contained the knowledge of all things, why should we call them by different names? we do so that we may distinguish them one from the other. Thus, you as well as I, know that these are five fingers ; and if I asked you whether we both meant the same thing or another, when we speak of arithmetic—would you not say the same?

Ion. Yes.

Socrates. And tell me, when we learn one art we must both learn the same things with regard to it ; and other things if we learn another?

Ion. Certainly.

Socrates. And he who is not versed in an art, is not a good judge of what is said or done with respect to it?

Ion. Certainly not.

Socrates. To return to the verses which you just recited, do you think that you or a charioteer would be better capable of deciding whether Homer had spoken rightly or not?

Ion. Doubtless a charioteer.

Socrates. For you are a rhapsodist, and not a charioteer?

Ion. Yes.

Socrates. And the art of reciting verses is different from that of driving chariots?

Ion. Certainly.

Socrates. And if it is different, it supposes a knowledge of different things ?

Ion. Certainly.

Socrates. And when Homer introduces Hecamede, the concubine of Nestor, giving Machaon a posset to drink, and he speaks thus :—

Οἴνῳ πραμνείῳ, φησίν· ἐπὶ δ' αἴγειον κνῆ τυρὸν
Κνήστι χαλκείῃ· παρὰ δὲ κρόμιον ποτῷ ὄψον.

Il. λ'. 639.

does it belong to the medical or rhapsodical art, to determine whether Homer speaks rightly on this sub-ject ?

Ion. The medical.

Socrates. And when he says—

Ἡ δὲ μολυβδαίνη ἰκέλη ἐς βυσσὸν ἵκανεν,
Ἡ τε κατ' ἀγραύλοιο βοὸς κέρας ἐμμεμαυῖα
Ἔρχεται ὠμηστῇσι μετ' ἰχθύσι πῆμα φέρουσα.

Il. ω. 80.

does it belong to the rhapsodical or the piscatorial art, to determine whether he speaks rightly or not ?

Ion. Manifestly to the piscatorial art.

Socrates. Consider whether you are not inspired to make some such demand as this to me :—Come, Socrates, since you have found in Homer an accurate description of these arts, assist me also in the inquiry as to his competence on the subject of soothsayers and divination ; and how far he speaks well or ill on such subjects ; for he often treats of them in the Odyssey, and especially when he introduces Theoclymenus the Soothsayer of the Melampians, prophesying to the Suitors :—

Δαίμονι, τί κακὸν τόδε πάσχετε ; νυκτὶ μὲν ὑμέων
Εἰλύαται κεφαλαί τε προσωπά τε νέρθε τε γυῖα,

Οἰμωγὴ δὲ δέδηε, δεδάκρυνται δὲ παρειαί.
Εἰδώλων τε πλέον πρόθυρον, πλείη δὲ καὶ αὐλὴ
'Ισμένων ἐρεβόςδε ὑπὸ ζόφον· ἠέλιος δὲ
Οὐρανοῦ ἐξαπόλωλε, κακὴ δ' ἐπιδέδρομεν ἀχλύς.
                              Odyss. υ. 351.

Often too in the Iliad, as at the battle at the walls ; for
he there says—

Ορνις γάρ σφιν ἐπῆλθε περησέμεναι μεμαῶσιν,
Αἰετὸς ὑψιπέτης, ἐπ' ἀριστερὰ λαὸν ἐέργων,
Φοινήεντα δράκοντα φέρων ὀνύχεσσι πέλωρον,
Ζωὸν, ἔτ' ἀσπαίροντα· καὶ οὔπω λήθετο χάρμης.
Κόψε γὰρ αὐτὸν ἔχοντα κατὰ στῆθος παρὰ δειρὴν,
'Ιδνωθεὶς ὀπίσω. ὁ δ' ἀπὸ ἕθεν ἧκε χαμάζε
'Αλγήσας ὀδύνῃσι, μέσῳ δ' ἐγκάββαλ' ὁμίλῳ·
Αὐτὸς δὲ κλάγξας ἕπετο πνοιῇς ἀνέμοιο.
                              Il. μ'.

I assert, it belongs to a soothsayer both to observe and
to judge respecting such appearances as these.

Ion. And you assert the truth, O Socrates.

Socrates. And you also, my dear Ion. For we have
in our turn recited from the Odyssey and the Iliad,
passages relating to vaticination, to medicine and the
piscatorial art ; and as you are more skilled in Homer
than I can be, do you now make mention of whatever
relates to the rhapsodist and his art ; for a rhapsodist
is competent above all other men to consider and pronounce on whatever has relation to his art.

Ion. Or with respect to everything else mentioned
by Homer.

Socrates. Do not be so forgetful as to say everything. A good memory is particularly necessary for a
rhapsodist.

Ion. And what do I forget ?

Socrates. Do you not remember that you admitted

the art of reciting verses was different from that of
driving chariots?

Ion. I remember.

Socrates. And did you not admit that being different,
the subjects of its knowledge must also be different?

Ion. Certainly.

Socrates. You will not assert that the art of rhapsody is that of universal knowledge; a rhapsodist may
be ignorant of some things.

Ion. Except, perhaps, such things as we now discuss,
O Socrates.

Socrates. What do you mean by *such* subjects, besides those which relate to other arts?   And with which
among them do you profess a competent acquaintance,
since not with all?

Ion. I imagine that the rhapsodist has a perfect
knowledge of what it is becoming for a man to
speak—what for a woman; what for a slave, what
for a free man; what for the ruler, what for him who is
governed.

Socrates. How! do you think that a rhapsodist
knows better than a pilot what the captain of a ship in
a tempest ought to say?

Ion. In such a circumstance I allow that the pilot
would know best.

Socrates. Has the rhapsodist or the physician the
clearest knowledge of what ought to be said to a sick
man?

Ion. In that case the physician.

Socrates. But you assert that he knows what a slave
ought to say?

Ion. Certainly.

Socrates. To take for example, in the driving of
cattle; a rhapsodist would know much better than the
herdsman what ought to be said to a slave engaged in
bringing back a herd of oxen run wild?

Ion. No, indeed.

Socrates. But what a woman should say concerning spinning wool ?

Ion. Of course not.

Socrates. He would know, however, what a man, who is a general, should say when exhorting his troops ?

Ion. Yes ; a rhapsodist would know that.

Socrates. How I is rhapsody and strategy the same art ?

Ion. I know what it is fitting for a general to say.

Socrates. Probably because you are learned in war, O Ion. For if you are equally expert in horsemanship and playing on the harp, you would know whether a man rode well or ill. But if I should ask you which understands riding best, a horseman or a harper, what would you answer ?

Ion. A horseman, of course.

Socrates. And if you knew a good player on the harp, you would in the same way say that he understood harp-playing and not riding ?

Ion. Certainly.

Socrates. Since you understand strategy, you can tell me which is the most excellent, the art of war or rhapsody ?

Ion. One does not appear to me to excel the other.

Socrates. One is not better than the other, say you ? Do you say that tactics and rhapsody are two arts or one ?

Ion. They appear to me to be the same.

Socrates. Then a good rhapsodist is also a good general.

Ion. Of course.

Socrates. And a good general is a good rhapsodist ?

Ion. I do not say that.

Socrates. You said that a good rhapsodist was also a good general.

Ion. I did.

Socrates. Are you not the best rhapsodist in Greece ?

II.   I

Ion. By far, O Socrates.

Socrates. And you are also the most excellent general among the Greeks ?

Ion. I am.   I learned the art from Homer.

Socrates. How is it then, by Jupiter, that being both the best general and the best rhapsodist among us, you continually go about Greece rhapsodising, and never lead our armies ?   Does it seem to you that the Greeks greatly need golden-crowned rhapsodists, and have no want of generals ?

Ion. My native town, O Socrates, is ruled by yours, and requires no general for her wars ;—and neither will your city nor the Lacedemonians elect me to lead their armies—you think your own generals sufficient.

Socrates. My good Ion, are you acquainted with Apollodorus the Cyzicenian ?

Ion. Who do you mean ?

Socrates. He whom, though a stranger, the Athenians often elected general ; and Phanosthenes the Andrian, and Heraclides the Clazomenian, all foreigners, but whom this city has chosen, as being great men, to lead its armies, and to fill other high offices.   Would not, there-fore, Ion the Ephesian be elected and honoured if he were esteemed capable ?   Were not the Ephesians originally from Athens, and is Ephesus the least of cities ?   But if you spoke true, Ion, and praise Homer according to art and knowledge, you have deceived me, —since you declared that you were learned on the subject of Homer, and would communicate your knowledge to me—but you have disappointed me, and are far from keeping your word.   For you will not explain in what you are so excessively clever, though I greatly desire to learn ; but, as various as Proteus, you change from one thing to another, and to escape at last, you disappear in the form of a general, without disclosing your Homeric wisdom.   If, therefore, you possess the learning which you promised to expound on the subject of Homer, you deceive me and are false. But if you are eloquent on the subject of this Poet, not through knowledge, but by inspiration, being possessed by him, ignorant the while ' of the wisdom and beauty you display, then I allow that you are no deceiver. Choose then whether you will be considered false or inspired ?

Ion. It is far better, O Socrates, to be thought inspired.

Socrates. It is better both for you and for us, O Ion, to say that you are the inspired, and not the learned, eulogist of Homer.

MENEXENUS,

OR

THE FUNERAL ORATION.

A Fragment.

SOCRATES *and* MENEXENUS.

Socrates. HENCE comest thou, O Menexenus? from the forum?
Menexenus. Even so ; and from the senate-house.
Socrates. What was thy business with the senate? Art thou persuaded that thou hast attained to that perfection of discipline and philosophy, from which thou mayest aspire to undertake greater matters? Wouldst thou, at thine age, my wonderful friend, assume to thyself the government of us who are thine elders, lest thy family should at any time fail in affording us a protector?
Menexenus. Thou, O Socrates, shouldst permit and counsel me to enter into public life. I would earnestly endeavour to fit myself for the attempt. If otherwise, I would abstain. On the present occasion, I went to the senate-house, merely from having heard that the senate was about to elect one to speak concerning those who

are dead. Thou knowest that the celebration of their funeral approaches?

Socrates. Assuredly. But whom have they chosen?

Menexenus. The election is deferred until to-morrow; I imagine that either Dion or Archinus will be chosen.

Socrates. In truth, Menexenus, the condition of him who dies in battle is, in every respect, fortunate and glorious. If he is poor, he is conducted to his tomb with a magnificent and honourable funeral, amidst the praises of all; if even he were a coward, his name is included in a panegyric pronounced by the most learned men; from which all the vulgar expressions, which unpremeditated composition might admit, have been excluded by the careful labour of leisure; who praise so admirably, enlarging upon every topic remotely or immediately connected with the subject, and blending so eloquent a variety of expressions, that, praising in every manner the state of which we are citizens, and those who have perished in battle, and the ancestors who preceded our generation, and ourselves who yet live, they steal away our spirits as with enchantment. Whilst I listen to their praises, O Menexenus, I am penetrated with a very lofty conception of myself, and overcome by their flatteries. I appear to myself immeasurably more honourable and generous than before, and many of the strangers who are accustomed to accompany me, regard me with additional veneration, after having heard these relations; they seem to consider the whole state, including me, much more worthy of admiration, after they have been soothed into persuasion by the orator. The opinion thus inspired of my own majesty will last me more than three days sometimes, and the penetrating melody of the words descends through the ears into the mind, and clings to it; so that it is often three or four days before I come to my senses sufficiently to perceive in what part of the world I am, or succeed in persuading myself

that I do not inhabit one of the islands of the blessed.
So skilful are these orators of ours.

Menexenus. Thou always laughest at the orators, O
Socrates.   On the present occasion, however, the unforeseen election will preclude the person chosen from the
advantages of a preconcerted speech : the speaker will
probably be reduced to the necessity of extemporising.

Socrates. How so, my good friend ?   Every one of
the candidates has, without doubt, his oration prepared ;
and if not, there were little difficulty, on this occasion, of
inventing an unpremeditated speech.   If, indeed, the
question were of Athenians, who should speak in the
Peloponnesus ; or of Peloponnesians, who should speak
at Athens, an orator who would persuade and be
applauded, must employ all the resources of his skill.
But to the orator who contends for the approbation of
those whom he praises, success will be little difficult.

Menexenus. Is that thy opinion, O Socrates ?

Socrates. In truth it is.

Menexenus. Shouldst thou consider thyself competent
to pronounce this oration, if thou shouldst be chosen by
the senate ?

· *Socrates.* There would be nothing astonishing if I
should consider myself equal to such an undertaking.
My mistress in oratory was perfect in the science which
she taught, and had formed many other excellent orators,
and one of the most eminent among the Greeks, Pericles,
the son of Xantippus.

Menexenus. Who is she ?   Assuredly thou meanest
Aspasia.

Socrates. Aspasia, and Connus the son of Metrobius,
the two instructors.   From the former of these I learned
rhetoric, and from the latter music.   There would be
nothing wonderful if a man so educated should be capable
of great energy of speech.   A person who should have
been instructed in a manner totally different from me ;
who should have learned rhetoric from Antiphon the

son of Rhamnusius, and music from Lampses, would be competent to succeed in such an attempt as praising the Athenians to the Athenians.

Menexenus. And what shouldst thou have to say, if thou wert chosen to pronounce the oration ?

Socrates. Of my own, probably nothing. But yesterday I heard Aspasia declaim a funeral oration over these same persons. She had heard, as thou sayest, that the Athenians were about to choose an orator, and she took the occasion of suggesting a series of topics proper for such an orator to select ; in part extemporaneously, and in part such as she had already prepared. I think it probable that she composed the oration by interweaving such fragments of oratory as Pericles might have left.

Menexenus. Rememberest thou what Aspasia said ?

Socrates. Unless I am greatly mistaken. I learned it from her ; and she is so good a school-mistress, that I should have been beaten if I had not been perfect in my lesson.

Menexenus. Why not repeat it to me ?

Socrates. I fear lest my mistress be angry, should I publish her discourse.

Menexenus. O, fear not. At least deliver a discourse ; you will do what is exceedingly delightful to me, whether it be of Aspasia or any other. I entreat you to do me this pleasure.

Socrates. But you will laugh at me, who, being old, attempt to repeat a pleasant discourse.

Menexenus. O no, Socrates ; I entreat you to speak, however it may be.

Socrates. I see that I must do what you require. In a little while, if you should ask me to strip naked and dance, I shall be unable to refuse you, at least, if we are alone. Now, listen. She spoke thus, if I recollect, beginning with the dead, in whose honour the oration is supposed to have been delivered.

FRAGMENTS

FROM THE REPUBLIC OF PLATO.

I. **B**UT it would be almost impossible to build your city in such a situation that it would need no imposts?—Impossible.—Other persons would then be required, who might undertake to conduct from another city those things of which they stood in need?—Certainly.—But the merchant who should return to his own city, without any of those articles which it needed, would return empty-handed. It will be necessary, therefore, not only to produce a sufficient supply, but such articles, both in quantity and in kind, as may be required to remunerate those who conduct the imports. There will be needed then more husbandmen, and other artificers, in our city. There will be needed also other persons who will undertake the conveyance of the imports and the exports, and these persons are called merchants. If the commerce which these necessities produce is carried on by sea, other persons will be required who are accustomed to nautical affairs. And, in the city itself, how shall the products of each man's labour be transported from one to another; those products, for the sake of the enjoyment and the ready distribution of which, they were first induced to institute a civil society?—By selling and buying, surely.—A market and money, as a symbol of exchange, arises out of this necessity ?—Evidently.—When the husbandman, or any other artificer, brings the produce of his labours to the public place, and those who desire to barter their produce for it do not happen to arrive exactly at the same time, would he not lose his time, and the profit of it, if he were to sit in the market waiting for them ?— Assuredly.—But, there are persons, who, perceiving this, will take upon themselves the arrangement between the buyer and the seller. In constituted civil societies, those who are employed on this service, ought to be the infirm, and unable to perform any other ; but, exchanging on one hand for money, what any person comes to sell, and giving the articles thus bought for a similar equivalent to those who might wish to buy.

II. Description of a frugal enjoyment of the goods of the world.

III. But with this system of life some are not contented. They must have beds and tables, and other furniture. They must have scarce ointments and perfumes, women, and a thousand superfluities of the same character. The things which we mentioned as sufficient, houses, and clothes, and food, are not enough. Painting and mosaic-work must be cultivated, and works in gold and ivory. The society must be enlarged in consequence. This city, which is of a healthy proportion, will not suffice, but it must be replenished with a multitude of persons, whose occupations are by no means indispensable. Huntsmen and mimics, persons whose occupation it is to arrange forms and colours, persons whose trade is the cultivation of the more delicate arts, poets and their ministers, rhapsodists, actors, dancers, manufacturers of all kinds of instruments and schemes of female dress, and an immense crowd of other ministers to pleasure and necessity. Do you not think we should want schoolmasters, tutors, nurses, hair-dressers, barbers, manufacturers and cooks? Should we not want pig-drivers, which were not wanted in our more modest city, in this one, and a multitude of others to administer to other animals, which would then become necessary articles of food,—or should we not?— Certainly we should.—Should we not want physicians much more, living in this manner than before? The same tract of country would no longer provide sustenance for the state. Must we then not usurp from the territory of our neighbours, and then we should make aggressions, and so we have discovered the origin of war; which is the principal cause of the greatest public and private calamities.—C. xi.

IV. And first, we must improve upon the composers of fabulous histories in verse, to compose them according to the rules of moral beauty; and those not composed according to the rules must be rejected; and we must persuade mothers and nurses to teach those which we approve to their children, and to form their minds by moral fables, far more than their bodies by their hands.—Lib. ii.

V. ON THE DANGER OF THE STUDY OF ALLEGORICAL COMPOŠITION (IN A LARGE SENSE) FOR YOUNG PEOPLE.

For a young person is not competent to judge what portions of a fabulous composition are allegorical and what literal; but the opinions produced by a literal acceptation of that which has no meaning, or a bad one, except in an allegorical sense, are often irradicable. —Lib ii.

VI.—God then, since he is good, cannot be, as is vulgarly supposed, the cause of all things; he is the

cause, indeed, of very few things. Among the great
variety of events which happen in the course of human
affairs, evil prodigiously overbalances good in everything which regards men. Of all that is good there can
be no other cause than God; but some other cause
ought to be discovered for evil, which should never be
imputed as an effect to God.—L. ii.

VII.—Plato's doctrine of punishment, as laid down
[here], is refuted by his previous reasonings.

VIII.—THE UNCHANGEABLE NATURE OF GOD.

Do you think that God is like a vulgar conjuror, and
that he is capable for the sake of effect, of assuming,
at one time, one form, and at another time, another?
Now, in his own character, converting his proper form
into a multitude of shapes, now deceiving us, and
offering vain images of himself to our imagination?
Or do you think that God is single and one, and least
of all things capable of departing from his permanent
nature and appearance?

IX.—THE PERMANENCY OF WHAT IS EXCELLENT.

But everything, in proportion as it is excellent, either
in art or nature, or in both, is least susceptible of
receiving change from any external influence.

X.—AGAINST SUPERSTITIOUS TALES.

Nor should mothers terrify their children by these
fables, that Gods go about in the night-time, resembling
strangers, in all sorts of forms: at once blaspheming
the Gods and rendering their children cowardly.

XI.—THE TRUE ESSENCE OF FALSEHOOD AND ITS ORIGIN.

Know you not that, that which is truly false, if it may be permitted me so to speak, all, both gods and men detest ?—How do you mean ?—Thus : No person is willing to falsify in matters of the highest concern to himself concerning those matters, but fears, above all things, lest he should accept falsehood.—Yet, I understand you not.—You think that I mean something profound. I say that no person is willing in his own mind to receive or to assert a falsehood, to be ignorant, to be in error, to possess that which is not true. This is truly to be called falsehood, this ignorance and error in the mind itself. What is usually called falsehood, or deceit in words, is but a voluntary imitation of what the mind itself suffers in the involuntary possession of that falsehood, an image of later birth, and scarcely, in a strict and complete sense, deserving the name of falsehood.—Lib. ii.

XII.—AGAINST A BELIEF IN HELL.

If they are to possess courage, are not those doctrines alone to be taught, which render death least terrible ? Or do you conceive that any man can be brave who is subjected to a fear of death ? that he who believes the things that are related of hell, and thinks that they are truth, will prefer in battle, death to slavery, or defeat ? —Lib. iii.—*Then follows a criticism on the poetical accounts of hell.*

XIII.—ON GRIEF.

We must then abolish the custom of lamenting and commiserating the deaths of illustrious men. Do we assert that an excellent man will consider it anything

dreadful that his intimate friend, who is also an excellent man, should die?—By no means (*an excessive
refinement*). He will abstain then from lamenting over
his loss, as if he had suffered some great evil?—Surely.
—May we not assert in addition, that such a person as
we have described suffices to himself for all purposes
of living well and happily, and in no manner needs the
assistance or society of another? that he would endure
with resignation the destitution of a son, or a brother,
or possessions, · or whatever external adjuncts of life
might have been attached to him? and that, on the
occurrence of such contingencies, he would support
them with moderation and mildness, by no means
bursting into lamentations, or resigning himself to
despondence?—Lib. iii.

*Then he proceeds to allege passages of the poets in
which opposite examples were held up to approbation
and imitation.*

XIV.—THE INFLUENCE OF EARLY CONSTANT IMITATION.

Do you not apprehend that imitations, if they shall
have been practised and persevered in from early youth,
become established in the habits and nature, in the
gestures of the body, and the tones of the voice, and
lastly, in the intellect itself?—C. iii.

XV.—ON THE EFFECT OF BAD TASTE IN ART.

Nor must we restrict the poets alone to an exhibition
of the example of virtuous manners in their compositions, but all other artists must be forbidden, either in
sculpture, or painting, or architecture, to employ their
skill upon forms of an immoral, unchastened, monstrous,
or illiberal type, either in the forms of living beings, or

in architectural arrangements. And the artist capable
of this employment of his art, must not be suffered in
our community, lest those destined to be guardians of
the society, nourished upon images of deformity and
vice, like cattle upon bad grass, gradually gathering and
depasturing every day a little, may ignorantly establish
one great evil composed of these many evil things, in
their minds.—C. iii.

*The monstrous figures called Arabesques, however in
some of them is to be found a mixture of a truer and
simpler taste, which are found in the ruined palaces of
the Roman Emperors, bear, nevertheless, the same relation to the brutal profligacy and killing luxury which
required them, as the majestic figures of Castor and
Pollux, and the simple beauty of the sculpture of the
frieze of the Parthenon, bear to the more beautiful and
simple manners of the Greeks of that period. With a
liberal interpretation, a similar analogy might be extended into literary composition.*

XVI.—AGAINST THE LEARNED PROFESSIONS.

What better evidence can you require of a corrupt
and pernicious system of discipline in a state, than that
not merely persons of base habits and plebeian employ-
ments, but men who pretend to have received a liberal
education, require the assistance of lawyers and physicians, and those too who have attained to a singular
degree (so desperate are these diseases of body and
mind) of skill. Do you not consider it an abject necessity, a proof of the deepest degradation, to need to be
instructed in what is just or what is needful, as by a
master and a judge, with regard to your personal knowledge and suffering ?

*What would Plato have said to a priest, such as his
office is in modern times ?*—C. iii.

XVII.—ON MEDICINE.

Do you not think it an abject thing to require the assistance of the medicinal art, not for the cure of wounds, or such external diseases as result from the accidents of the seasons (επητιην), but on account of sloth and the superfluous indulgences which we have already condemned; this being filled with wind and water, like holes in earth, and compelling the elegant successors of Æsculapius to invent new names, flatulences, and catarrhs, &c., for the new diseases which are the progeny of your luxury and sloth?—L. iii.

XVIII.—THE EFFECT OF THE DIETETIC SYSTEM.

Herodicus being pædotribe (παιδοτρίβης, *Magister palæstræ*), and his health becoming weak, united the gymnastic with the medical art, and having condemned himself to a life of weariness, afterwards extended the same pernicious system to others. He made his life a long death. For humouring the disease, mortal in its own nature, to which he was subject, without being able to cure it, he postponed all other purposes to the care of medicating himself, and through his whole life was subject to an access of his malady, if he departed in any degree from his accustomed diet, and by the employment of this skill, dying by degrees, he arrived at an old age.—L. iii.

Æsculapius never pursued these systems, nor Machaon or Podalirius. They never undertook the treatment of those whose frames were inwardly and thoroughly diseased, so to prolong a worthless existence, and bestow on a man a long and wretched being, during which they might generate children in every respect the inheritors of their infirmity.—L. iii.

XIX.—AGAINST WHAT IS FALSELY CALLED " KNOW-
LEDGE OF THE WORLD."

A man ought not to be a good judge until he be old ;
because he ought not have acquired a knowledge of
what injustice is, until his understanding has arrived
at maturity : not apprehending its nature from a consideration of *its* existence in himself ; but having contemplated it distinct from his own nature in that of
others, for a long time, until he shall perceive what an
evil it is, not from his own experience and its effects
within himself, but from his observations of them as
resulting in others.   Such a one were indeed an honourable judge, and a good ; for he who has a good mind,
is good.   But that judge who is considered so wise,
who having himself committed great injustice, is supposed to be qualified for the detection of it in others,
and who is quick to suspect, appears keen, indeed, as
long as he associates with those who resemble him ;
because, deriving experience from the example afforded
by a consideration of his own conduct and character,
he acts with caution ; but when he associates with men
of universal experience and real virtue, he exposes the
defects resulting from such experience as he possesses,
by distrusting men unreasonably and mistaking true
virtue, having no example of it within himself with which
to compare the appearances manifested in others : yet,
such a one finding more associates who are virtuous
than such as are wise, necessarily appears, both to himself and others, rather to be wise than foolish.—But we
ought rather to search for a wise and good judge ; one
who has examples within himself of that upon which he
is to pronounce.—C. iii.

XX.—Those who use gymnastics unmingled with
music become too savage, whilst those who use music
unmingled with gymnastics, become more delicate than
is befitting.

ON A PASSAGE IN CRITO.

[Prefatory note by Mrs. Shelley.]

It is well known that when Socrates was condemned to death, his friends made arrangements for his escape from prison and his after security ; of which he refused to avail himself, from the reason, that a good citizen ought to obey the laws of his country. On this Shelley makes the following remarks—

HE reply is simple, Indeed, your city cannot subsist, because the laws are no longer of avail. For how can the laws be said to exist, when those who deserve to be nourished in the **Prytanea** at the public expense, are condemned to suffer the penalties only due to the most atrocious criminals ; whilst those against, and to protect from whose injustice, the laws were framed, live in honour and security ? I neither overthrow your state, nor infringe your laws. Although you have inflicted an injustice on me, which is sufficient, according to the opinions of the multitude, to authorise me to consider you and me as in a state of warfare ; yet, had I the power, so far from inflicting any revenge, I would endeavour to overcome you by benefits. All that I do at present is, that which the peaceful traveller would do, who, caught by robbers in a forest, escapes from them whilst they are engaged in the division of the spoil. And this I do, when it would not only be indifferent, but delightful to me to die, surrounded by my friends, secure of the inheritance of glory, and escaping, after such a life as mine, from the decay of mind and body which must soon begin to be my portion should I live. But I prefer the good, which I have it in my power yet to perform.

Such are the arguments which overturn the sophism placed in the mouth of Socrates by Plato. But there are others which prove that he did well to die.

THE ASSASSINS.

🎕 Fragment of a Romance.

CHAPTER I.

JERUSALEM, goaded on to resistance by the
incessant usurpations and insolence of Rome,
leagued together its discordant factions to rebel
against the common enemy and tyrant. Inferior to
their foe in all but the unconquerable hope of liberty,
they surrounded their city with fortifications of uncommon strength, and placed in array before the temple a
band rendered desperate by patriotism and religion.
Even the women preferred to die, rather than survive
the ruin of their country. When the Roman army
approached the walls of the sacred city, its preparations,
its discipline, and its numbers, evinced the conviction of
its leader, that he had no common barbarians to subdue.
At the approach of the Roman army, the strangers
withdrew from the city.

Among the multitudes which from every nation of the
East had assembled at Jerusalem, was a little congrega-
tion of Christians. They were remarkable neither for
their numbers nor their importance. They contained
among them neither philosophers nor poets. Acknow-
ledging no laws but those of God, they modelled their

conduct towards their fellow-men by the conclusions of
their individual judgment on the practical application of
these laws. And it was apparent from the simplicity and
severity of their manners, that this contempt for human
institutions had produced among them a character
superior in singleness and sincere self-apprehension to
the slavery of pagan customs and the gross delusions of
antiquated superstition. Many of their opinions considerably resembled those of the sect afterwards known
by the name of Gnostics. They esteemed the human
understanding to be the paramount rule of human
conduct ; they maintained that the obscurest religious
truth required for its complete elucidation no more than
the strenuous application of the energies of mind. It
appeared impossible to them that any doctrine could be
subversive of social happiness which is not capable of
being confuted by arguments derived from the nature of
existing things. With the devoutest submission to the
law of Christ, they united an intrepid spirit of inquiry as
to the correctest mode of acting in particular instances
of conduct that occur among men. Assuming the
doctrines of the Messiah concerning benevolence and
justice for the regulation of their actions, they could not
be persuaded to acknowledge that there was apparent
in the divine code any prescribed rule whereby, for
its own sake, one action rather than another, as ful-
filling the will of their great Master, should be preferred.

The contempt with which the magistracy and priest-
hood regarded this obscure community of speculators,
had hitherto protected them from persecution. But
they had arrived at that precise degree of eminence and
prosperity which is peculiarly obnoxious to the hostility
of the rich and powerful. The moment of their departure
from Jerusalem was the crisis of their future destiny.
Had they continued to seek a precarious refuge in a city
of the Roman empire, this persecution would not have

delayed to impress a new character on their opinions and their conduct; narrow views, and the illiberality of sectarian patriotism, would not have failed speedily to obliterate the magnificence and beauty of their wild and wonderful condition.

Attached from principle to peace, despising and hating the pleasures and the customs of the degenerate mass of mankind, this unostentatious community of good and happy men fled to the solitudes of Lebanon. To Arabians and enthusiasts the solemnity and grandeur of these desolate recesses possessed peculiar attractions. It well accorded with the justice of their conceptions on the relative duties of man towards his fellow in society, that they should labour in unconstrained equality to dispossess the wolf and the tiger of their empire, and establish on its ruins the dominion of intelligence and virtue. No longer would the worshippers of the God of Nature be indebted to a hundred hands for the accommodation of their simple wants. No longer would the poison of a diseased civilization embrue their very nutriment with pestilence. They would no longer owe their very existence to the vices, the fears, and the follies of mankind. Love, friendship, and philanthropy, would now be the characteristic disposers of their industry. It is for his mistress or his friend that the labourer consecrates his toil; others are mindful, but he is forgetful, of himself. "God feeds the hungry ravens, and clothes the lilies of the fields, and yet Solomon in all his glory is not like to one of these."

Rome was now the shadow of her former self. The light of her grandeur and loveliness had passed away. The latest and the noblest of her poets and historians had foretold in agony her approaching slavery and degradation. The ruins of the human mind, more awful and portentous than the desolation of the most solemn temples, threw a shade of gloom upon her golden palaces which the brutal vulgar could not see, but which

the mighty felt with inward trepidation and despair.
The ruins of Jerusalem lay defenceless and uninhabited
upon the burning sands; none visited, but in the depth
of solemn awe, this accursed and solitary spot. Tradition says that there was seen to linger among the
scorched and shattered fragments of the temple, one
being, whom he that saw dared not to call man, with
clasped hands, immoveable eyes, and a visage horribly
serene. Not on the will of the capricious multitude,
nor the constant fluctuations of the many and the weak,
depends the change of empires and religions. These
are the mere insensible elements from which a subtler
intelligence moulds its enduring statuary. They that
direct the changes of this mortal scene breathe the decrees of their dominion from a throne of darkness and
of tempest. The power of man is great.

After many days of wandering, the Assassins pitched
their tents in the valley of Bethzatanai. For ages had
this fertile valley lain concealed from the adventurous
search of man, among mountains of everlasting snow.
The men of elder days had inhabited this spot. Piles
of monumental marble and fragments of columns that in
their integrity almost seemed the work of some intelligence more sportive and fantastic than the gross conceptions of mortality, lay in heaps beside the lake, and
were visible beneath its transparent waves. The flowering orange-tree, the balsam, and innumerable odoriferous
shrubs, grew wild in the desolated portals. The
fountain tanks had overflowed, and amid the luxuriant
vegetation of their margin, the yellow snake held its
unmolested dwelling. Hither came the tiger and the
bear to contend for those once domestic animals who
had forgotten the secure servitude of their ancestors.
No sound, when the famished beast of prey had retreated
in despair from the awful desolation of this place, at
whose completion he had assisted, but the shrill cry of
the stork, and the flapping of his heavy wings from the

capital of the solitary column, and the scream of the hungry vulture baffled of its only victim. The lore of ancient wisdom was sculptured in mystic characters on the rocks. The human spirit and the human hand had been busy here to accomplish its profoundest miracles. It was a temple dedicated to the god of knowledge and of truth. The palaces of the Caliphs and the Cæsars might easily surpass these ruins in magnitude and sumptuousness : but they were the design of tyrants and the work of slaves. Piercing genius and consummate prudence had planned and executed Bethzatanai. There was deep and important meaning in every lineament of its fantastic sculpture. The unintelligible legend, once so beautiful and perfect, so full of poetry and history, spoke, even in destruction, volumes of mysterious import, and obscure significance.

But in the season of its utmost prosperity and magnificence, art might not aspire to vie with nature in the valley of Bethzatanai. All that was wonderful and lovely was collected in this deep seclusion. The fluctuating elements seemed to have been rendered everlastingly permanent in forms of wonder and delight. The mountains of Lebanon had been divided to their base to form this happy valley ; on every side their icy summits darted their white pinnacles into the clear blue sky, imaging, in their grotesque outline, minarets, and ruined domes, and columns worn with time. Far below, the silver clouds rolled their bright volumes in many beautiful shapes, and fed the eternal springs, that, spanning the dark chasms like a thousand radiant rainbows, leaped into the quiet vale, then, lingering in many a dark glade among the groves of cypress and of palm, lost themselves in the lake. The immensity of these precipitous mountains with their starry pyramids of snow, excluded the sun, which overtopped not, even in its meridian, their overhanging rocks. But a more heavenly and serener light was reflected from their icy mirrors, which, piercing through the many-tinted clouds, produced lights and colours of inexhaustible variety. The herb-age was perpetually verdant, and clothed the darkest recesses of the caverns and the woods.

Nature, undisturbed, had become an enchantress in these solitudes; she had collected here all that was wonderful and divine from the armoury of her omnipotence. The very winds breathed health and renovation, and the joyousness of youthful courage. Fountains of crystalline water played perpetually among the aromatic flowers, and mingled a freshness with their odour. The pine boughs became instruments of exquisite contrivance, among which every varying breeze waked music of new and more delightful melody. Meteoric shapes, more effulgent than the moonlight, hung on the wandering clouds, and mixed in discordant dance around the spiral fountains. Blue vapours assumed strange lineaments under the rocks and among the ruins, lingering like ghosts with slow and solemn step. Through a dark chasm to the east, in the long perspective of a portal glittering with the unnumbered riches of the subterranean world, shone the broad moon, pouring in one yellow and unbroken stream her horizontal beams. Nearer the icy region, autumn and spring held an alternate reign. The sere leaves fell and choked the sluggish brooks; the chilling fogs hung diamonds on every spray; and in the dark cold evening the howling winds made melancholy music in the trees. Far above, shone the bright throne of winter, clear, cold, and dazzling. Sometimes there was seen the snow-flakes to fall before the sinking orb of the beamless sun, like a shower of fiery sulphur. The cataracts, arrested in their course, seemed, with their transparent columns, to support the dark-browed rocks. Sometimes the icy whirlwind scooped the powdery snow aloft, to mingle with the hissing meteors, and scatter spangles through the rare and rayless atmosphere.

Such strange scenes of chaotic confusion and harrowing sublimity, surrounding and shutting in the vale, added to the delights of its secure and voluptuous tranquillity. No spectator could have refused to believe that some spirit of great intelligence and power had hallowed these wild and beautiful solitudes to a deep and solemn mystery.

The immediate effect of such a scene, suddenly presented to the contemplation of mortal eyes, is seldom the subject of authentic record. The coldest slave of custom cannot fail to recollect some few moments in which the breath of spring or the crowding clouds of sunset, with the pale moon shining through their fleecy skirts, or the song of some lonely bird perched on the only tree of an unfrequented heath, has awakened the touch of nature. And they were Arabians who entered the valley of Bethzatanai ; men who idolized nature and the God of nature ; to whom love and lofty thoughts, and the apprehensions of an uncorrupted spirit, were sustenance and life. Thus securely excluded from an abhorred world, all thought of its judgment was cancelled by the rapidity of their fervid imaginations. They ceased to acknowledge, or deigned not to advert to, the distinctions with which the majority of base and vulgar minds control the longings and struggles of the soul towards its place of rest. A new and sacred fire was kindled in their hearts and sparkled in their eyes. Every gesture, every feature, the minutest action, was modelled to beneficence and beauty by the holy inspiration that had descended on their searching spirits. The epidemic transport communicated itself through every heart with the rapidity of a blast from heaven. They were already disembodied spirits ; they were already the inhabitants of paradise. To live, to breathe, to move, was itself a sensation of immeasurable transport. Every new contemplation of the condition of his nature brought to the happy enthusiast an added measure of delight, and impelled to every organ, where mind is united with external things, a keener and more exquisite perception of all that they contain of lovely and divine. To love, to be beloved, suddenly became an insatiable famine of his nature, which the wide circle of the universe, comprehending beings of such inexhaustible variety and stupendous magnitude of excellence appeared too narrow and confined to satiate.

Alas, that these visitings of the spirit of life should fluctuate and pass away ! That the moments when the human mind is commensurate with all that it can conceive of excellent and powerful, should not endure with its existence and survive its most momentous change ! But the beauty of a vernal sunset, with its overhanging curtains of empurpled cloud, is rapidly dissolved, to return at some unexpected period, and spread an alleviating melancholy over the dark vigils of despair.

It is true the enthusiasm of overwhelming transport which had inspired every breast among the Assassins is no more. The necessity of daily occupation and the ordinariness of that human life, the burthen of which it is the destiny of every human being to bear, had smothered, not extinguished, that divine and eternal fire. Not the less indelible and permanent were the impressions communicated to all ; not the more unalterably were the features of their social character modelled and determined by its influence.

CHAPTER II.

ROME had fallen. Her senate-house had become a polluted den of thieves and liars : her solemn temples, the arena of theological disputants, who made fire and sword the missionaries of their inconceivable beliefs. The city of the monster Constantine, symbolising, in the consequences of its foundation, the wickedness and weakness of his successors, feebly imaged with declining power the substantial eminence of the Roman name. Pilgrims of a new and mightier faith crowded to visit the lonely ruins of Jerusalem, and weep and pray before the sepulchre of the Eternal God. The earth was filled with discord, tumult, and ruin. The spirit of disinterested virtue had armed one-half of the civilised world against the other. Monstrous and detestable creeds poisoned and blighted the domestic charities. There was no appeal to natural love, or ancient faith, from pride, superstition, and revenge.

Four centuries had passed thus terribly characterised by the most calamitous revolutions. The Assassins, meanwhile, undisturbed by the surrounding tumult, possessed and cultivated their fertile valley. The gradual operation of their peculiar condition had matured and perfected the singularity and excellence of their character. That cause, which had ceased to act as an immediate and overpowering excitement, became the unperceived law of their lives, and sustenance of their natures. Their religious tenets had also undergone a change, corresponding with the exalted condition of their moral being. The gratitude which they owed to the benignant Spirit by which their limited intelligences had not only been created but redeemed, was less frequently adverted to, became less the topic of comment or contemplation ; not, therefore, did it cease to be their presiding guardian, the guide of their inmost thoughts, the tribunal of appeal for the minutest particulars of their conduct. They learned to identify this mysterious benefactor with the delight that is bred among the solitary rocks, and has its dwelling alike in the changing colours of the clouds and the inmost recesses of the caverns. Their future also no longer existed, but in the blissful tranquillity of the present. Time was measured and created by the vices and the miseries of men, between whom and the happy nation of the Assassins there was no analogy nor comparison. Already had their eternal peace commenced. The darkness had passed away from the open gates of death.

The practical results produced by their faith and condition upon their external conduct were singular and memorable. Excluded from the great and various community of mankind, these solitudes became to them a sacred hermitage, in which all formed, as it were, one being, divided against itself by no contending will or factious passions. Every impulse conspired to one end, and tended to a single object. Each devoted his powers to the happiness of the other. Their republic was the scene of the perpetual contentions of benevolence ; not the heartless and assumed kindness of commercial man, but the genuine virtue that has a legible superscription in every feature of the countenance, and every motion of the frame. The perverseness and calamities of those who dwelt beyond the mountains that encircled their undisturbed possessions, were unknown and unimagined. Little embarrassed by the complexities of civilised society, they knew not to conceive any happiness that can be satiated without participation, or that thirsts not to reproduce and perpetually generate itself. The path of virtue and felicity was plain and unimpeded. They clearly acknowledged, in every case, that conduct to be entitled to preference which would obviously produce the greatest pleasure. They could not conceive an instance in which it would be their duty to hesitate, in causing, at whatever expense, the greatest and most unmixed delight.

Hence arose a peculiarity which only failed to germinate in uncommon and momentous consequences, because the Assassins had retired from the intercourse of mankind, over whom other motives and principles of conduct than justice and benevolence prevail. It would be a difficult matter for men of such a sincere and

simple faith, to estimate the final results of their intentions, among the corrupt and slavish multitude. They
would be perplexed also in their choice of the means,
whereby their intentions might be fulfilled. To produce
immediate pain or disorder for the sake of future benefit,
is consonant, indeed, with the purest religion and philosophy, but never fails to excite invincible repugnance in
the feelings of the many. Against their predilections
and distastes an Assassin, accidentally the inhabitant of
a civilised community, would wage unremitting hostility
from principle. He would find himself compelled to
adopt means which they would abhor, for the sake of
an object which they could not conceive that he should
propose to himself. Secure and self-enshrined in the
magnificence and pre-eminence of his conceptions, spotless as the light of heaven, he would be the victim
among men of calumny and persecution. Incapable
of distinguishing his motives, they would rank him
among the vilest and most atrocious criminals. Great,
beyond all comparison with them, they would despise
him in the presumption of their ignorance. Because
his spirit burned with an unquenchable passion for their
welfare, they would lead him, like his illustrious master,
amidst scoffs, and mockery, and insult, to the remunera-
tion of an ignominious death.

Who hesitates to destroy a venomous serpent that
has crept near his sleeping friend, except the man who
selfishly dreads lest the malignant reptile should turn
its fury on himself? And if the poisoner has assumed
a human shape, if the bane be distinguished only from
the viper's venom by the excess and extent of its
devastation, will the saviour and avenger here retract
and pause, entrenched behind the superstition of the
indefeasible divinity of man? Is the human form,
then, the mere badge of a prerogative for unlicensed
wickedness and mischief? Can the power derived
from the weakness of the oppressed, or the ignorance

of the deceived, confer the right in security to tyrannise and defraud ?

The subject of regular governments, and the disciple of established superstition, dares not to ask this question. For the sake of the eventual benefit, he endures what he esteems a transitory evil, and the moral degradation of man disquiets not his patience. But the religion of an Assassin imposes other virtues than endurance, when his fellow-men groan under tyranny, or have become so bestial and abject that they cannot feel their chains. An Assassin believes that man is eminently man, and only then enjoys the prerogatives of his privileged condition, when his affections and his judgment pay tribute to the God of Nature. The perverse, and vile, and vicious—what were they ? Shapes of some unholy vision, moulded by the spirit of Evil, which the sword of the merciful destroyer should sweep from this beautiful world. Dreamy nothings ; phantasms of misery and mischief, that hold their death-like state on glittering thrones, and in the loathsome dens of poverty. No Assassin would submissively temporise with vice, and in cold charity become a pander to falsehood and desolation. His path through the wilderness of civilized society would be marked with the blood of the oppressor and the ruiner. The wretch, whom nations tremblingly adore, would expiate in his throttling grasp a thousand licensed and venerable crimes.

How many holy liars and parasites, in solemn guise, would his saviour arm drag from their luxurious couches, and plunge in the cold charnel, that the green and many-legged monsters of the slimy grave might eat off at their leisure the lineaments of rooted malignity and detested cunning. The respectable man—the smooth, smiling, polished villain, whom all the city honours ; whose very trade is lies and murder ; who buys his daily bread with the blood and tears of men, would feed the ravens with his limbs. The Assassin would cater nobly for the eyeless worms of earth, and the carrion fowls of heaven.

Yet here, religion and human love had imbued the manners of those solitary people with inexpressible gentleness and benignity. Courage and active virtue, and the indignation against vice, which becomes a hurrying and irresistible passion, slept like the imprisoned earthquake, or the lightning shafts that hang in the golden clouds of evening. They were innocent, but they were capable of more than innocence ; for the great principles of their faith were perpetually acknowledged and adverted to ; nor had they forgotten, in this uninterrupted quiet, the author of their felicity.

Four centuries had thus worn away without producing an event. Men had died, and natural tears had been shed upon their graves, in sorrow that improves the heart. Those who had been united by love had gone to death together, leaving to their friends the bequest of a most sacred grief, and of a sadness that is allied to pleasure. Babes that hung upon their mothers' breasts had become men ; men had died ; and many a wild luxuriant weed that overtopped the habitations of the vale, had twined its roots around their disregarded bones. Their tranquil state was like a summer sea, whose gentle undulations disturb not the reflected stars, and break not the long still line of the rainbow hues of sunrise.

CHAPTER III.

WHERE all is thus calm, the slightest circumstance is recorded and remembered. Before the sixth century had expired one incident occurred, remarkable and strange. A young man, named Albedir, wandering

in the woods, was startled by the screaming of a bird
of prey, and, looking up, saw blood fall, drop by drop,
from among the intertwined boughs of a cedar. Having
climbed the tree, he beheld a terrible and dismaying
spectacle. A naked human body was impaled on the
broken branch. It was maimed and mangled horribly;
every limb bent and bruised into frightful distortion,
and exhibiting a breathing image of the most sickening
mockery of life. A monstrous snake had scented its
prey from among the mountains—and above hovered a
hungry vulture. From amidst this mass of desolated
humanity, two eyes, black and inexpressibly brilliant,
shone with an unearthly lustre. Beneath the blood-
stained eye-brows their steady rays manifested the
serenity of an immortal power, the collected energy
of a deathless mind, spell-secured from dissolution. A
bitter smile of mingled abhorrence and scorn distorted
his wounded lip—he appeared calmly to observe and
measure all around—self-possession had not deserted
the shattered mass of life.

The youth approached the bough on which the
breathing corpse was hung. As he approached, the
serpent reluctantly unwreathed his glittering coils, and
crept towards his dark and loathsome cave. The
vulture, impatient of his meal, fled to the mountain,
that re-echoed with his hoarse screams. The cedar
branches creaked with their agitating weight, faintly, as
the dismal wind arose. All else was deadly silent.

At length a voice issued from the mangled man. It
rattled in hoarse murmurs from his throat and lungs—
his words were the conclusion of some strange mysterious soliloquy. They were broken, and without apparent
connexion, completing wide intervals of inexpressible
conceptions.

"The great tyrant is baffled, even in success. Joy!
joy! to his tortured foe! Triumph to the worm whom
he tramples under his feet! Ha! His suicidal hand

might dare as well abolish the mighty frame of things!
Delight and exultation sit before the closed gates of
death!—I fear not to dwell beneath their black and
ghastly shadow.   Here thy power may not avail!
Thou createst—'tis mine to ruin and destroy.—-I was
thy slave—I am thy equal, and thy foe.—Thousands
tremble before thy throne, who, at my voice, shall dare
to pluck the golden crown from thine unholy head!"
He ceased.   The silence of noon swallowed up his
words.   Albedir clung tighter to the tree—he dared
not for dismay remove his eyes.   He remained mute in
the perturbation of deep and creeping horror.

"Albedir!" said the same voice, "Albedir! in the
name of God, approach.   He that suffered me to fall,
watches thee ;—the gentle and merciful spirits of sweet
human love delight not in agony and horror.   For
pity's sake approach, in the name of thy good God,
approach, Albedir!"   The tones were mild and clear
as the responses of Æolian music.   They floated to
Albedir's ear like the warm breath of June that lingers
in the lawny groves, subduing all to softness.   Tears of
tender affection started into his eyes.   It was as the
voice of a beloved friend.   The partner of his childhood,
the brother of his soul, seemed to call for aid, and
pathetically to remonstrate with delay.   He resisted
not the magic impulse, but advanced towards the spot,
and tenderly attempted to remove the wounded man.
He cautiously descended the tree with his wretched
burthen, and deposited it on the ground.

A period of strange silence intervened.   Awe and
cold horror were slowly succeeding to the softer sensations of tumultuous pity, when again he heard the silver
modulations of the same enchanting voice.   "Weep not
for me, Albedir!   What wretch so utterly lost, but might
inhale peace and renovation from this paradise!   I am
wounded, and in pain ; but having found a refuge in this
seclusion, and a friend in you, I am worthier of envy

II.   L

than compassion. Bear me to your cottage secretly : I would not disturb your gentle partner by my appearance. She must love me more dearly than a brother. I must be the playmate of your children ; already I regard them with a father's love. My arrival must not be regarded as a thing of mystery and wonder. What, indeed, but that men are prone to error and exaggeration, is less inexplicable, than that a stranger, wandering on Lebanon, fell from the rocks into the vale ? Albedir," he continued, and his deepening voice assumed awful solemnity, " in return for the affection with which I cherish thee and thine, thou owest this submission."

Albedir implicitly submitted ; not even a thought had power to refuse its deference. He reassumed his burthen, and proceeded towards the cottage. He watched until Khaled should be absent, and conveyed the stranger into an apartment appropriated for the reception of those who occasionally visited their habitation. He desired that the door should be securely fastened, and that he might not be visited until the morning of the following day.

Albedir waited with impatience for the return of Khaled. The unaccustomed weight of even so transitory a secret hung on his ingenuous and unpractised nature, like a blighting, clinging curse. The stranger's accents had lulled him to a trance of wild and delightful imagination. Hopes, so visionary and aerial, that they had assumed no denomination, had spread themselves over his intellectual frame, and, phantoms as they were, had modelled his being to their shape. Still his mind was not exempt from the visitings of disquietude and perturbation. It was a troubled stream of thought, over whose fluctuating waves unsearchable fate seemed to preside, guiding its unforeseen alternations with an inexorable hand. Albedir paced earnestly the garden of his cottage, revolving every circumstance attendant on the incident of the day. He re-imaged with intense thought the minutest recollections of the scene. In vain—he was the slave of suggestions not to be controlled. Astonishment, horror, and awe—tumultuous sympathy, and a mysterious elevation of soul, hurried away all activity of judgment, and overwhelmed, with stunning force, every attempt at deliberation ɔr inquiry.

His reveries were interrupted at length by the return of Khaled. She entered the cottage, that scene of undisturbed repose, in the confidence that change might as soon overwhelm the eternal world, as disturb this inviolable sanctuary. She started to behold Albedir. Without preface or remark, he recounted with eager haste the occurrences of the day. Khaled's tranquil spirit could hardly keep pace with the breathless rapidity of his narration. She was bewildered with staggering wonder even to hear his confused tones, and behold his agitated countenance.

CHAPTER IV.

ON the following morning Albedir arose at sunrise, and visited the stranger. He found him already risen, and employed in adorning the lattice of his chamber with flowers from the garden. There was something in his attitude and occupation singularly expressive of his entire familiarity with the scene. Albedir's habit: tion seemed to have been his accustomed home. He addressed his host in a tone of gay and affectionate welcome, such as never fails to communicate by sympathy the feelings from which it flows.

"My friend," said he, "the balm of the dew of our vale is sweet ; or is this garden the favoured spot where the winds conspire to scatter the best odours they can find ? Come, lend me your arm awhile, I feel very weak." He motioned to walk forth, but, as if unable to proceed, rested on the seat beside the door. For a few moments they were silent, if the interchange of cheerful and happy looks is to be called silence. At last he observed a spade that rested against the wall. "You have only one spade, brother," said he; "you have only one, I suppose, of any of the instruments of tillage. Your garden ground, too, occupies a certain space which it will be necessary to enlarge. This must be quickly remedied. I cannot earn my supper of to-night, nor of to-morrow; but thenceforward, I do not mean to eat the bread of idleness. I know that you would willingly perform the additional labour which my nourishment would require; I know, also, that you would feel a degree of pleasure in the fatigue arising from this employment, but I shall contest with you such pleasures as these, and such pleasures as these alone." His eyes were somewhat wan, and the tone of his voice languid as he spoke.

As they were thus engaged, Khaled came towards them. The stranger beckoned to her to sit beside him, and taking her hands within his own, looked attentively on her mild countenance. Khaled inquired if he had been refreshed by sleep. He replied by a laugh of careless and inoffensive glee; and placing one of her hands within Albedir's, said, "If this be sleep, here in this odorous vale, where these sweet smiles encompass us, and the voices of those who love are heard—if these be the visions of sleep, sister, those who lie down in misery shall arise lighter than the butterflies. I came from amid the tumult of a world, how different from this! I am unexpectedly among you, in the midst of a scene such as my imagination never dared to promise. I must remain here—I must not depart." Khaled, recovering from the admiration and astonishment caused by the stranger's words and manner, assured him of the happiness which she should feel in such an addition to

her society. Albedir, too, who had been more deeply
impressed than Khaled by the event of his arrival,
earnestly reassured him of the ardour of the affection
with which he had inspired them. The stranger smiled
gently to hear the unaccustomed fervour of sincerity
which animated their address, and was rising to retire,
when Khaled said, " You have not yet seen our children,
Maimuna and Abdallah. They are by the water-side,
playing with their favourite snake. We have only to
cross yonder little wood, and wind down a path cut in
the rock that overhangs the lake, and we shall find them
beside a recess which the shore makes there, and which
a chasm, as it were, among the rocks and woods, encloses. Do you think you could walk there ? " " To
see your children, Khaled ? I think I could, with the
assistance of Albedir's arm, and yours."—So they went
through the wood of ancient cypress, intermingled with
the brightness of many-tinted blooms, which gleamed
like stars through its romantic glens. They crossed the
green meadow, and entered among the broken chasms,
beautiful as they were in their investiture of odoriferous
shrubs. They came at last, after pursuing a path which
wound through the intricacies of a little wilderness, to
the borders of the lake. They stood on the rock which
overhung it, from which there was a prospect of all the
miracles of nature and of art which encircled and
adorned its shores. The stranger gazed upon it with a
countenance unchanged by any emotion, but, as it were,
thoughtfully and contemplatingly. As he gazed, Khaled
ardently pressed his hand, and said, in a low yet eager
voice, " Look, look, lo there ! " He turned towards her,
but her eyes were not on him. She looked below—her
lips were parted by the feelings which possessed her
soul—her breath came and went regularly but inaudibly.
She leaned over the precipice, and her dark hair hanging beside her face, gave relief to its fine lineaments,
animated by such love as exceeds utterance. The

stranger followed her eyes, and saw that her children were in the glen below; then raising his eyes, exchanged with her affectionate looks of congratulation and delight. The boy was apparently eight years old, the girl about two years younger. The beauty of their form and countenance was something so divine and strange, as overwhelmed the senses of the beholder like a delightful dream, with insupportable ravishment. They were arrayed in a loose robe of linen, through which the exquisite proportions of their form appeared. Unconscious that they were observed, they did not relinquish the occupation in which they were engaged. They had constructed a little boat of the bark of trees, and had given it sails of interwoven feathers, and launched it on the water. They sat beside a white flat stone, on which a small snake lay coiled, and when their work was finished, they arose and called to the snake in melodious tones, so that it understood their language. For it unwreathed its shining circles and crept to the boat, into which no sooner had it entered than the girl loosened the band which held it to the shore, and it sailed away. Then they ran round and round the little creek, clapping their hands, and melodiously pouring out wild sounds, which the snake seemed to answer by the restless glancing of his neck. At last a breath of wind came from the shore, and the boat changed its course, and was about to leave the creek, which the snake perceived and leaped into the water, and came to the little children's feet. The girl sang to it, and it leaped into her bosom, and she crossed her fair hands over it, as if to cherish it there. Then the boy answered with a song, and it glided from beneath her hands and crept towards him. While they were thus employed, Maimuna looked up, and seeing her parents on the cliff, ran to meet them up the steep path that wound around it; and Abdallah, leaving his snake, followed joyfully.

ON THE PUNISHMENT OF DEATH.

A Fragment.

THE first law which it becomes a Reformer to propose and support, at the approach of a period of great political change, is the abolition of the punishment of death.

It is sufficiently clear that revenge, retaliation, atonement, expiation, are rules and motives, so far from deserving a place in any enlightened system of political life, that they are the chief sources of a prodigious class of miseries in the domestic circles of society. It is clear that however the spirit of legislation may appear to frame institutions upon more philosophical maxims, it has hitherto, in those cases which are termed criminal, done little more than palliate the spirit, by gratifying a portion of it; and afforded a compromise between that which is best;—the inflicting of no evil upon a sensitive being, without a decisively beneficial result in which he should at least participate;—and that which is worst; that he should be put to torture for the amusement of those whom he may have injured, or may seem to have injured.

Omitting these remoter considerations, let us inquire what *Death* is; that which is applied as a measure of transgressions of indefinite shades of distinction, so soon as they shall have passed that degree and colour of enormity, with which it is supposed no inferior infliction is commensurate.

And first, whether death is good or evil, a punishment or a reward, or whether it be wholly indifferent, no man can take upon himself to assert. That that within us which thinks and feels, continues to think and feel after the dissolution of the body, has been the almost universal opinion of mankind, and the accurate philosophy of what I may be permitted to term the modern Academy, by showing the prodigious depth and extent of our ignorance respecting the causes and nature of sensation, renders probable the affirmative of a proposition, the negative of which it is so difficult to conceive, and the popular arguments against which, derived from what is called the atomic system, are proved to be applicable only to the relation which one object bears to another, as apprehended by the mind, and not to existence itself, or the nature of that essence which is the medium and receptacle of objects.

The popular system of religion suggests the idea that the mind, after death, will be painfully or pleasurably affected according to its determinations during life. However ridiculous and pernicious we must admit the vulgar accessories of this creed to be, there is a certain analogy, not wholly absurd, between the consequences resulting to an individual during life from the virtuous or vicious, prudent or imprudent, conduct of his external actions, to those consequences which are conjectured to ensue from the discipline and order of his internal thoughts, as affecting his condition in a future state. They omit, indeed, to calculate upon the accidents of disease, and temperament, and organisation, and circumstance, together with the multitude of independent agencies which affect the opinions, the conduct, and the happiness of individuals, and produce determinations of the will, and modify the judgment, so as to produce effects the most opposite in natures considerably similar. These are those operations in the order of the whole of nature, tending, we are prone to believe, to some definite mighty end, to which the agencies of our peculiar nature are subordinate ; nor is there any reason to suppose, that in a future state they should become suddenly exempt from that subordination. The philosopher is unable to determine whether our existence in a previous state has affected our present condition, and abstains from deciding whether our present condition would affect us in that which may be future. That, if we continue to exist, the manner of our existence will be such as no inferences nor conjectures, afforded by a consideration of our earthly experience, can elucidate, is sufficiently obvious. The opinion that the vital principle within us, in whatever mode it may continue to exist, must lose that consciousness of definite and individual being which now characterises it, and become a unit in the vast sum of action and of thought which disposes and animates the universe, and is called God, seems to belong to that class of opinion which has been designated as indifferent.

To compel a person to know all that can be known by the dead, concerning that which the living fear, hope, or forget ; to plunge him into the pleasure or pain which there awaits him ; to punish or reward him in a manner and in a degree incalculable and incomprehensible by us; to disrobe him at once from all that intertexture of good and evil with which Nature seems to have clothed every form of individual existence, is to inflict on him the doom of death.

A certain degree of pain and terror usually accompany the infliction of death. This degree is infinitely varied by the infinite variety in the temperament and opinions of the sufferers. As a measure of punishment, strictly so considered, and as an exhibition, which, by its known effects on the sensibility of the sufferer, is intended to intimidate the spectators from incurring a similar liability, it is singularly inadequate.

Firstly,—Persons of energetic character, in whom, as in men who suffer for political crimes, there is a large mixture of enterprise, and fortitude, and disinterestedness, and the elements, though misguided and disarranged, by which the strength and happiness of a nation might have been cemented, die in such a manner, as to make death appear not evil, but good. The death of what is called a traitor, that is, a person who, from whatever motive, would abolish the government of the day, is as often a triumphant exhibition of suffering virtue, as the warning of a culprit. The multitude, instead of departing with a panic-stricken approbation of the laws which exhibited such a spectacle, are inspired with pity, admiration and sympathy ; and the most generous among them feel an emulation to be the authors of such flattering emotions, as they experience stirring in their bosoms. Impressed by what they see and feel, they make no distinction between the motives which incited the criminals to the actions for which they suffer, or the heroic courage with which they turned into good that which their judges awarded to them as evil, or the purpose itself of those actions, though that purpose may happen to be eminently pernicious. The laws in this case lose that sympathy, which it ought to be their chief object to secure, and in a participation of which, consists their chief strength in maintaining those sanctions by which the parts of the social union are bound together, so as to produce, as nearly as possible, the ends for which it is instituted.

Secondly—persons of energetic character, in communities not modelled with philosophical skill to turn all the energies which they contain to the purposes of common good, are prone also to fall into the temptation of undertaking, and are peculiarly fitted for despising the perils attendant upon consummating, the most enormous crimes. Murder, rapes, extensive schemes of plunder, are the actions of persons belonging to this class; and death is the penalty of conviction. But the coarseness of organisation, peculiar to men capable of committing acts wholly selfish, is usually found to be associated with a proportionate insensibility to fear or pain. Their sufferings communicate to those of the spectators, who may be liable to the commission of similar crimes, a sense of the lightness of that event, when closely examined, which at a distance, as uneducated persons are accustomed to do, probably they regarded with horror. But a great majority of the spectators are so bound up in the interests and the habits of social union that no temptation would be sufficiently strong to induce them to a commission of the enormities to which this penalty is assigned. The more powerful, the richer among them, —and a numerous class of little tradesmen are richer and more powerful than those who are employed by them, and the employer, in general, bears this relation to the employed,—regard their own wrongs as, in some degree, avenged, and their own rights secured by this punishment, inflicted as the penalty of whatever crime. In cases of murder or mutilation, this feeling is almost universal. In those, therefore, whom this exhibition does not awaken to the sympathy which extenuates crime and discredits the law which restrains it, it produces feelings more directly at war with the genuine purposes of political society. It excites those emotions which it is the chief object of civilisation to extinguish for ever, and in the extinction of which alone there can be any hope of better institutions than those under which men now misgovern one another. Men feel that their revenge is gratified, and that their security is established, by the extinction and the sufferings of beings, in most respects resembling themselves; and their daily occupations constraining them to a precise form in all their thoughts, they come to connect inseparably the idea of their own advantage with that of the death and torture of others. It is manifest that the object of sane polity is directly the reverse ; and that laws founded upon reason, should accustom the gross vulgar to associate their ideas of security and of interest with the reformation, and the strict restraint, for that purpose alone, of those who might invade it.

The passion of revenge is originally nothing more than an habitual perception of the ideas of the sufferings of the person who inflicts an injury, as connected, as they are in a savage state, or in such portions of society as are yet undisciplined to civilisation, with security that that injury will not be repeated in future. This feeling, engrafted upon superstition and confirmed by habit, at last loses sight of the only object for which it may be supposed to have been implanted, and becomes a passion and a duty to be pursued and fulfilled, even to the destruction of those ends to which it originally tended. The other passions, both good and evil, Avarice, Remorse, Love, Patriotism, present a similar appearance ; and to this principle of the mind over-shooting the mark at which it aims, we owe all that is eminently base or excellent in human nature ; in providing for the nutriment or the extinction of which consists the true art of the legislator.*

* The savage and the illiterate are but faintly aware of the distinction between the future and the past ; they make actions belonging to periods so distinct, the subjects of similar feelings ; they live only in the present, or in the past as it is present. It is in this that the philosopher excels one of the many ; it is this which distinguishes the doctrine of philosophic necessity from fatalism ; and that determination of the will, by which it is the active source of future events, from that liberty or indifference, to which the abstract liability of irremediable actions is attached, according to the notions of the vulgar.

This is the source of the erroneous excesses of Remorse and Revenge ; the one extending itself over the future, and the other over the past ; provinces in which their suggestions can only be the sources of evil. The purpose of a resolution to act more wisely and virtuously in future, and the sense of a necessity of caution in repressing an enemy, are the sources from which the enormous superstitions implied in the words cited have arisen.

Nothing is more clear than that the infliction of punishment in general, in a degree which the reformation and the restraint of those who transgress the laws does not render indispensable, and none more than death, confirms all the inhuman and unsocial impulses of men. It is almost a proverbial remark, that those nations in which the penal code has been particularly mild, have been distinguished from all others by the rarity of crime. But the example is to be admitted to be equivocal. A more decisive argument is afforded by a consideration of the universal connexion of ferocity of manners, and a contempt of social ties, with the contempt of human life. Governments which derive their institutions from the existence of circumstances of barbarism and violence, with some rare exceptions perhaps, are bloody in proportion as they are despotic, and form the manners of their subjects to a sympathy with their own spirit.

The spectators who feel no abhorrence at a public execution, but rather a self-applauding superiority, and a sense of gratified indignation, are surely excited to the most inauspicious emotions. The first reflection of such a one is the sense of his own internal and actual worth, as preferable to that of the victim, whom circumstances have led to destruction. The meanest wretch is impressed with a sense of his own comparative merit. He is one of those on whom the tower of Siloam fell not— he is such a one as Jesus found not in all Samaria, who, in his own soul, throws the first stone at the woman taken in adultery. The popular religion of the country takes its designation from that illustrious person whose beautiful sentiment I have quoted. Any one who has stript from the doctrines of this person the veil of familiarity, will perceive how adverse their spirit is to feelings of this nature.

ON LIFE.

LIFE and the world, or whatever we call that which we are and feel, is an astonishing thing. The mist of familiarity obscures from us the wonder of our being. We are struck with admiration at some of its transient modifications, but it is itself the great miracle. What are changes of empires, the wreck of dynasties, with the opinions which supported them ; what is the birth and the extinction of religious and of political systems, to life ? What are the revolutions of the globe which we inhabit, and the operations of the elements of which it is composed, compared with life ? What is the universe of stars, and suns, of which this inhabited earth is one, and their motions, and their destiny, compared with life ? Life, the great miracle, we admire not, because it is so miraculous. It is well that we are thus shielded by the familiarity of what is at once so certain and so unfathomable, from an astonishment which would otherwise absorb and overawe the functions of that which is its object.

If any artist, I do not say had executed, but had merely conceived in his mind the system of the sun, and the stars, and planets, they not existing, and had painted to us in words, or upon canvas, the spectacle now afforded by the nightly cope of heaven, and illustrated it by the wisdom of astronomy, great would be our admiration. Or had he imagined the scenery of this earth, the

mountains, the seas, and the rivers ; the grass, and the
flowers, and the variety of the forms and masses of the
leaves of the woods, and the colours which attend the
setting and the rising sun, and the hues of the atmosphere, turbid or serene, these things not before existing,
truly we should have been astonished, and it would not
have been a vain boast to have said of such a man,
" Non merita nome di creatore, se non Iddio ed il
Poeta." *. But now these things are looked on with little
wonder, and to be conscious of them with intense delight
is esteemed to be the distinguishing mark of a refined and.
extraordinary person. The multitude of men care not for
them. It is thus with Life—that which includes all.

What is life ? Thoughts and feelings arise, with or
without our will, and we employ words to express them.
We are born, and our birth is unremembered, and our
infancy remembered but in fragments ; we live on, and
in living we lose the apprehension of life. How vain is
it to think that words can penetrate the mystery of our
being ! Rightly used they may make evident our ignorance to ourselves; and this is much. For what are we ?
Whence do we come ? and whither do we go ? Is birth
the commencement, is death the conclusion of our being ?
What is birth and death ?

The most refined abstractions of logic conduct to a
view of life, which, though startling to the apprehension,
is, in fact, that which the habitual sense of its repeated
combinations has extinguished in us. It strips, as it
were, the painted curtain from this scene of things. I
confess that I am one of those who am unable to refuse
my assent to the conclusions of those philosophers who
assert that nothing exists but as it is perceived.

It is a decision against which all our persuasions
struggle, and we must be long convicted before we can
be convinced that the solid universe of external things
is " such stuff as dreams are made of." The shocking

* *Vide supra*, p. 35.—ED.

absurdities of the popular philosophy of mind and matter, its fatal consequences in morals, and their violent dogmatism concerning the source of all things, had early conducted me to materialism. This materialism is a seducing system to young and superficial minds. It allows its disciples to talk, and dispenses them from thinking. But I was discontented with such a view of things as it afforded ; man is a being of high aspirations, "looking both before and after," whose "thoughts wander through eternity," disclaiming alliance with transience and decay; incapable of imagining to himself annihilation ; existing but in the future and the past ; being, not what he is, but what he has been and shall be. Whatever may be his true and final destination, there is a spirit within him at enmity with nothingness and dissolution. This is the character of all life and being. Each is at once the centre and the circumference ; the point to which all things are referred, and the line in which all things are contained. Such contemplations as these, materialism and the popular philosophy of mind and matter alike forbid ; they are only consistent with the intellectual system.

It is absurd to enter into a long recapitulation of arguments sufficiently familiar to those inquiring minds, whom alone a writer on abstruse subjects can be conceived to address. Perhaps the most clear and vigorous statement of the intellectual system is to be found in Sir William Drummond's Academical Questions. After such an exposition, it would be idle to translate into other words what could only lose its energy and fitness by the change. Examined point by point, and word by word, the most discriminating intellects have been able to discern no train of thoughts in the process of reasoning, which does not conduct inevitably to the conclusion which has been stated.

What follows from the admission ? It establishes no new truth, it gives us no additional insight into our hidden nature, neither its action nor itself. Philosophy, impatient as it may be to build, has much work yet remaining as pioneer for the overgrowth of ages. It makes one step towards this object ; it destroys error, and the roots of error. It leaves, what it is too often the duty of the reformer in political and ethical questions to leave, a vacancy. It reduces the mind to that freedom in which it would have acted, but for the misuse of words and signs, the instruments of its own creation. By signs, I would be understood in a wide sense, including what is properly meant by that term, and what I peculiarly mean. In this latter sense, almost all familiar objects are signs, standing, not for themselves, but for others, in their capacity of suggesting one thought which shall lead to a train of thoughts. Our whole life is thus an education of error.

Let us recollect our sensations as children. What a distinct and intense apprehension had we of the world and of ourselves ! Many of the circumstances of social life were then important to us which are now no longer so. But that is not the point of comparison on which I mean to insist. We less habitually distinguished all that we saw and felt, from ourselves. They seemed, as it were, to constitute one mass. There are some persons who, in this respect, are always children. Those who are subject to the state called reverie, feel as if their nature were dissolved into the surrounding universe, or as if the surrounding universe were absorbed into their being. They are conscious of no distinction. And these are states which precede, or accompany, or follow an unusually intense and vivid apprehension of life. As men grow up this power commonly decays, and they become mechanical and habitual agents. Thus feelings and then reasonings are the combined result of a multitude of entangled thoughts, and of a series of what are called impressions, planted by reiteration.

The view of life presented by the most refined deductions of the intellectual philosophy, is that of

M

unity. Nothing exists but as it is perceived. The difference is merely nominal between those two classes of thought, which are vulgarly distinguished by the names of ideas and of external objects. Pursuing the same thread of reasoning, the existence of distinct individual minds, similar to that which is employed in now questioning its own nature, is likewise found to be a delusion. The words *I, you, they*, are not signs of any actual difference subsisting between the assemblage of thoughts thus indicated, but are merely marks employed to denote the different modifications of the one mind.

Let it not be supposed that this doctrine conducts to the monstrous presumption that I, the person who now write and think, am that one mind. I am but a portion of it. The words *I*, and *you*, and *they* are grammatical devices invented simply for arrangement, and totally devoid of the intense and exclusive sense usually attached to them. It is difficult to find terms adequate to express so subtle a conception as that to which the Intellectual Philosophy has conducted us. We are on that verge where words abandon us, and what wonder if we grow dizzy to look down the dark abyss of how little we know !

The relations of *things* remain unchanged, by whatever system. By the word *things* is to be understood any object of thought, that is, any thought upon which any other thought is employed, with an apprehension of distinction. The relations of these remain unchanged ; and such is the material of our knowledge.

What is the cause of life? that is, how was it produced, or what agencies distinct from life have acted or act upon life ? All recorded generations of mankind have wearily busied themselves in inventing answers to this question ; and the result has been,—Religion. Yet, that the basis of all things cannot be, as the popular philosophy alleges, mind, is sufficiently evident. Mind, as far as we have any experience of its properties, and beyond that experience how vain is argument! cannot create, it can only perceive. It is said also to be the cause. But cause is only a word expressing a certain state of the human mind with regard to the manner in which two thoughts are apprehended to be related to each other. If any one desires to know how unsatisfactorily the popular philosophy employs itself upon this great question, they need only impartially reflect upon the manner in which thoughts develop themselves in their minds. It is infinitely improbable that the cause of mind, that is, of existence, is similar to mind.

ON A FUTURE STATE.

IT has been the persuasion of an immense majority of human beings in all ages and nations that we continue to live after death,—that apparent termination of all the functions of sensitive and intellectual existence. Nor has mankind been contented with supposing that species of existence which some philosophers have asserted; namely, the resolution of the component parts of the mechanism of a living being into its elements, and the impossibility of the minutest particle of these sustaining the smallest diminution. They have clung to the idea that sensibility and thought, which they have distinguished from the objects of it, under the several names of spirit and matter, is, in its own nature, less susceptible of division and decay, and that, when the body is resolved into its elements, the principle which animated it will remain perpetual and unchanged. Some philosophers—and those to whom we are indebted for the most stupendous discoveries in physical science, suppose, on the other hand, that intelligence is the mere result of certain combinations among the particles of its objects; and those among them who believe that we live after death, recur to the interposition of a supernatural power, which shall overcome the tendency inherent in all material combinations, to dissipate and be absorbed into other forms.

Let us trace the reasonings which in one and the other have conducted to these two opinions, and endeavour to discover what we ought to think on a question of such momentous interest. Let us analyse the ideas and feelings which constitute the contending beliefs, and watchfully establish a discrimination between words and thoughts. Let us bring the question to the test of experience and fact; and ask ourselves, considering our nature in its entire extent, what light we derive from a sustained and comprehensive view of its component parts, which may enable us to assert, with certainty, that we do or do not live after death.

The examination of this subject requires that it should be stript of all those accessory topics which adhere to it in the common opinion of men. The existence of a God, and a future state of rewards and punishments, are totally foreign to the subject. If it be proved that the world is ruled by a Divine Power, no inference necessarily can be drawn from that circumstance in favour of a future state. It has been asserted, indeed, that as goodness and justice are to be numbered among the attributes of the Deity, he will undoubtedly compensate the virtuous who suffer during life, and that he will make every sensitive being, who does not deserve punishment, happy for ever. But this view of the subject, which it would be tedious as well as superfluous to develop and expose, satisfies no person, and cuts the knot which we now seek to untie. Moreover, should it be proved, on the other hand, that the mysterious principle which regulates the proceedings of the universe, is neither intelligent nor sensitive, yet it is not an inconsistency to suppose at the same time, that the animating power survives the body which it has animated, by laws as independent of any supernatural agent as those through which it first became united with it. Nor, if a future state be clearly proved, does it follow that it will be a state of punishment or reward.

By the word death, we express that condition in which natures resembling ourselves apparently cease to be that which they were. We no longer hear them speak, nor see them move If they have sensations and apprehensions, we no longer participate in them. We know no more than that those external organs, and all that fine texture of material frame, without which we have no experience that life or thought can subsist, are dissolved and scattered abroad. The body is placed under the earth, and after a certain period there remains no vestige even of its form. This is that contemplation of inexhaustible melancholy, whose shadow eclipses the brightness of the world. The common observer is struck with dejection of the spectacle. He contends in vain against the persuasion of the grave, that the dead indeed cease to be. The corpse at his feet is prophetic of his own destiny. Those who have preceded him, and whose voice was delightful to his ear ; whose touch met his like sweet and subtle fire ; whose aspect spread a visionary light upon his path—these he cannot meet again. The organs of sense are destroyed, and the intellectual operations dependent on them have perished with their sources. How can a corpse see or feel? its eyes are eaten out, and its heart is black and without motion. What intercourse can two heaps of putrid clay and crumbling bones hold together ? When you can discover where the fresh colours of the faded flower abide, or the music of the broken lyre, seek life among the dead. Such are the anxious and fearful contemplations of the common observer, though the popular religion often prevents him from confessing them even to himself.

The natural philosopher, in addition to the sensations common to all men inspired by the event of death, believes that he sees with more certainty that it is attended with the annihilation of sentiment and thought. He observes the mental powers increase and fade with those of the body, and even accommodate themselves to the most transitory changes of our physical nature.

Sleep suspends many of the faculties of the vital and intellectual principle; drunkenness and disease will either temporarily or permanently derange them. Madness or idiotcy may utterly extinguish the most excellent and delicate of those powers. In old age the mind gradually withers; and as it grew and was strengthened with the body, so does it together with the body sink into decrepitude. Assuredly these are convincing evidences that so soon as the organs of the body are subjected to the laws of inanimate matter, sensation, and perception, and apprehension, are at an end. It is probable that what we call thought is not an actual being, but no more than the relation between certain parts of that infinitely varied mass, of which the rest of the universe is composed, and which ceases to exist so soon as those parts change their position with regard to each other. Thus colour, and sound, and taste, and odour exist only relatively. But let thought be considered as some peculiar substance, which permeates, and is the cause of, the animation of living beings. Why should that substance be assumed to be something essentially distinct from all others, and exempt from subjection to those laws from which no other substance is exempt? It differs, indeed, from all other substances, as electricity, and light, and magnetism, and the constituent parts of air and earth, severally differ from all others. Each of these is subject to change and to decay, and to conversion into other forms. Yet the difference between light and earth is scarcely greater than that which exists between life, or thought, and fire. The difference between the two former was never alleged as an argument for the eternal permanence of either, in that form under which they first might offer themselves to our notice. Why should the difference between the two latter substances be an argument for the prolongation of the existence of one and not the other, when the existence of both has arrived at their apparent termination? To say that fire exists without manifesting any of the properties of fire, such as light, heat, &c., or that the principle of life exists without consciousness, or memory, or desire, or motive, is to resign, by an awkward distortion of language, the affirmative of the dispute. To say that the principle of life *may* exist in distribution among various forms, is to assert what cannot be proved to be either true or false, but which, were it true, annihilates all hope of existence after death, in any sense in which that event can belong to the hopes and fears of men. Suppose, however, that the intellectual and vital principle differs in the most marked and essential manner from all other known substances; that they have all some resemblance between themselves which it in no degree participates. In what manner can this concession be made an argument for its imperishability? All that we see or know perishes and is changed. Life and thought differ indeed from everything else. But that it survives that period, beyond which we have no experience of its existence, such distinction and dissimilarity affords no shadow of proof, and nothing but our own desires could have led us to conjecture or imagine.

Have we existed before birth? It is difficult to conceive the possibility of this. There is, in the generative principle of each animal and plant, a power which converts the substances by which it is surrounded into a substance homogeneous with itself. That is, the relation between certain elementary particles of matter undergo a change, and submit to new combinations. For when we use the words *principle, power, cause,* &c., we mean to express no real being, but only to class under those terms a certain series of co-existing phenomena; but let it be supposed that this principle is a certain substance which escapes the observation of the chemist and anatomist. It certainly *may be;* though it is sufficiently unphilosophical to allege the possibility of an opinion as a proof of its truth. Does it see, hear, feel, before its combination with those organs on which sensation depends ? Does it reason, imagine, apprehend, without those ideas which sensation alone can communicate? If we have not existed before birth ; if, at the period when the parts of our nature on which thought and life depend, seem to be woven together, they are woven together ; if there are no reasons to suppose that we have existed before that period at which our existence apparently commences, then there are no grounds for supposition that we shall continue to exist after our existence has apparently ceased. So far as thought and life is concerned, the same will take place with regard to us, individually considered, after death, as had place before our birth.

It is said that it is possible that we should continue to exist in some mode totally inconceivable to us at present. This is a most unreasonable presumption. It casts on the adherents of annihilation the burthen of proving the negative of a question, the affirmative of which is not supported by a single argument, and which, by its very nature, lies beyond the experience of the human understanding. It is sufficiently easy, indeed, to form any proposition, concerning which we are ignorant, just not so absurd as not to be contradictory in itself, and defy refutation. The possibility of whatever enters into the wildest imagination to conceive is thus triumphantly vindicated. But it is enough that such assertions should be either contradictory to the known laws of nature, or exceed the limits of our experience, that their fallacy or irrelevancy to our consideration should be demonstrated. They persuade, indeed, only those who desire to be persuaded.

This desire to be for ever as we are ; the reluctance to a violent and unexperienced change, which is common to all the animated and inanimate combinations of the universe, is, indeed, the secret persuasion which has given birth to the opinions of a future state.

SPECULATIONS ON METAPHYSICS.

I. THE MIND.

I. T is an axiom in mental philosophy, that we can think of nothing which we have not perceived. When I say that we can think of nothing, I mean, we can imagine nothing, we can reason of nothing, we can remember nothing, we can foresee nothing. The most astonishing combinations of poetry, the subtlest deductions of logic and mathematics, are no other than combinations which the intellect makes of sensations according to its own laws. A catalogue of all the thoughts of the mind, and of all their possible modifications, is a cyclopædic history of the universe.

But, it will be objected, the inhabitants of the various planets of this and other solar systems ; and the existence of a Power bearing the same relation to all that we perceive and are, as what we call a cause does to what we call effect, were never subjects of sensation, and yet the laws of mind almost universally suggest, according to the various disposition of each, a conjecture, a persuasion, or a conviction of their existence. The reply is simple ; these thoughts are also to be included in the catalogue of existence; they are modes in which thoughts are combined ; the objection only adds force to the conclusion, that beyond the limits of perception and thought nothing can exist.

Thoughts, or ideas, or notions, call them what you will, differ from each other, not in kind, but in force. It has commonly been supposed that those distinct thoughts which affect a number of persons, at regular intervals, during the passage of a multitude of other thoughts, which are called *real*, or *external objects*, are totally different in kind from those which affect only a few persons, and which recur at irregular intervals, and are usually more obscure and indistinct, such as hallucinations, dreams, and the ideas of madness. No essential distinction between any one of these ideas, or any class of them, is founded on a correct observation of the nature of things, but merely on a consideration of what thoughts are most invariably subservient to the security and happiness of life ; and if nothing more were expressed by the distinction, the philosopher might safely accommodate his language to that of the vulgar. But they pretend to assert an essential difference, which has no foundation in truth, and which suggests a narrow and false conception of universal nature, the parent of the most fatal errors in speculation. A specific difference between every thought of the mind is, indeed, a necessary consequence of that law by which it perceives diversity and number ; but a generic and essential difference is wholly arbitrary. The principle of the agreement and similarity of all thoughts, is, that they are all thoughts ; the principle of their disagreement consists in the variety and irregularity of the occasions on which they arise in the mind. That in which they agree, to that in which they differ, is as everything to nothing. Important distinctions, of various degrees of force, indeed, are to be established between them, if they were, as they may be, subjects of ethical and œconomical discussion ; but that is a question altogether distinct.

By considering all knowledge as bounded by perception, whose operations may be indefinitely combined, we arrive at a conception of Nature inexpressibly more magnificent, simple and true, than accords with the ordinary systems of complicated and partial considera- tion.   Nor does a contemplation of the universe, in this comprehensive and synthetical view, exclude the subtlest analysis of its modifications and parts.

A scale might be formed, graduated according to the decrees of a combined ratio of intensity, duration, con- nexion, periods of recurrence, and utility, which would be the standard, according to which all ideas might be measured, and an uninterrupted chain of nicely shadowed distinctions would be observed, from the faintest impres- sion on the senses, to the most distinct combination of those impressions ; from the simplest of those combina- tions, to that mass of knowledge which, including our own nature, constitutes what we call the universe.

We are intuitively conscious of our own existence, and of that connexion in the train of our successive ideas, which we term our identity.   We are conscious also of the existence of other minds ; but not intuitively. Our evidence, with respect to the existence of other minds, is founded upon a very complicated relation of ideas, which it is foreign to the purpose of this treatise to anatomise.   The basis of this relation is, undoubtedly, a periodical recurrence of masses of ideas, which our voluntary determinations have, in one peculiar direction, no power to circumscribe or to arrest, and against the recurrence of which they can only imperfectly provide. The irresistible laws of thought constrain us to believe that the precise limits of our actual ideas are not the actual limits of possible ideas ; the law, according to which these deductions are drawn, is called analogy ; and this is the foundation of all our inferences, from one idea to another, inasmuch as they resemble each other.

We see trees, houses, fields, living beings in our own shape, and in shapes more or less analogous to our own. These are perpetually changing the mode of their existence relatively to us. To express the varieties of these modes, we say, *we move, they move;* and as this motion is continual, though not uniform, we express our conception of the diversities of its course by—*it has been, it is, it shall be.* These diversities are events or objects, and are essential, considered relatively to human identity, for the existence of the human mind. For if the inequalities, produced by what has been termed the operations of the external universe, were levelled by the perception of our being, uniting, and filling up their interstices, motion and mensuration, and time, and space; the elements of the human mind being thus abstracted, sensation and imagination cease. Mind cannot be considered pure.

I.—WHAT METAPHYSICS ARE. ERRORS IN THE USUAL METHODS OF CONSIDERING THEM.

WE do not attend sufficiently to what passes within ourselves. We combine words, combined a thousand times before. In our minds we assume entire opinions ; and in the expression of those opinions, entire phrases, when we would philosophise. Our whole style of expression and sentiment is infected with the tritest plagiarisms. Our words are dead, our thoughts are cold and borrowed.

Let us contemplate facts ; let us, in the great study of ourselves, resolutely compel the mind to a rigid consideration of itself. We are not content with conjecture, and inductions, and syllogisms, in sciences regarding external objects. As in these, let us also, in considering the phenomena of mind, severely collect those facts which cannot be disputed. Metaphysics will thus possess this **conspicuous advantage over every other science, that** each student, by attentively referring to his own mind, may ascertain the authorities, upon which any assertions regarding it are supported. There can thus be no deception, we ourselves being the depositaries of the evidence of the subject which we consider.

Metaphysics may be defined as an inquiry concerning those things belonging to, or connected with, the internal nature of man.

It is said that mind produces motion ; and it might as well have been said, that motion produces mind.

II.—DIFFICULTY OF ANALYSING THE HUMAN MIND.

IF it were possible that a person should give a faithful history of his being, from the earliest epochs of his recollection, a picture would be presented such as the world has never contemplated before. A mirror would be held up to all men in which they might behold their own recollections, and, in dim perspective, their shadowy hopes and fears,—all that they dare not, or that daring and desiring, they could not expose to the open eyes of day. But thought can with difficulty visit the intricate and winding chambers which it inhabits. It is like a river whose rapid and perpetual stream flows outwards ; —like one in dread who speeds through the recesses of some haunted pile, and dares not look behind. The caverns of the mind are obscure, and shadowy ; or pervaded with a lustre, beautifully bright indeed, but shining not beyond their portals. If it were possible to be where we have been, vitally and indeed—if, at the moment of our presence there, we could define the results of our experience,—if the passage from sensation to reflection —from a state of passive perception to voluntary contemplation, were not so dizzying and so tumultuous, this attempt would be less difficult.

III.—HOW THE ANALYSIS SHOULD BE CARRIED ON.

MOST of the errors of philosophers have arisen from considering the human being in a point of view too detailed and circumscribed. He is not a moral, and an intellectual,—but also, and pre-eminently, an imaginative being. His own mind is his law; his own mind is all things to him. If we would arrive at any knowledge which should be serviceable from the practical conclusions to which it leads, we ought to consider the mind of man and the universe as the great whole on which to exercise our speculations. Here, above all, verbal disputes ought to be laid aside, though this has long been their chosen field of battle. It imports little to inquire whether thought be distinct from the objects of thought. The use of the words *external* and *internal*, as applied to the establishment of this distinction, has been the symbol and the source of much dispute. This is merely an affair of words, and as the dispute deserves, to say, that when speaking of the objects of thought, we indeed only describe one of the forms of thought—or that, speaking of thought, we only apprehend one of the operations of the universal system of beings. (1819)

IV.—CATALOGUE OF THE PHENOMENA OF DREAMS, AS CONNECTING SLEEPING AND WAKING.

I. LET us reflect on our infancy, and give as faithfully as possible a relation of the events of sleep.

And first I am bound to present a faithful picture of my own peculiar nature relatively to sleep. I do not doubt that were every individual to imitate me, it would be found that among many circumstances peculiar to their individual nature, a sufficiently general resemblance would be found to prove the connexion existing between those peculiarities and the most universal phenomena. I shall employ caution, indeed, as to the facts which I state, that they contain nothing false or exaggerated. But they contain no more than certain elucidations of my own nature ; concerning the degree in which it resembles, or differs from, that of others, I am by no means accurately aware. It is sufficient, however, to caution the reader against drawing general inferences from particular instances.

I omit the general instances of delusion in fever or delirium, as well as mere dreams considered in themselves. A delineation of this subject, however inexhaustible and interesting, is to be passed over. What is the connexion of sleeping and of waking ?

II. I distinctly remember dreaming three several times, between intervals of two or more years, the same precise dream. It was not so much what is ordinarily called a dream ; the single image, unconnected with all other images, of a youth who was educated at the same school with myself, presented itself in sleep. Even now, after the lapse of many years, I can never hear the name of this youth, without the three places where I dreamed of him presenting themselves distinctly to my mind.

III. In dreams, images acquire associations peculiar to dreaming ; so that the idea of a particular house, when it recurs a second time in dreams, will have relation with the idea of the same house, in the first time, of a nature entirely different from that which the house excites, when seen or thought of in relation to waking ideas.

IV. I have beheld scenes, with the intimate and unaccountable connexion of which with the obscure parts of my own nature, I have been irresistibly impressed.

I have beheld a scene which has produced no unusual effect on my thoughts. After the lapse of many years I have dreamed of this scene. It has hung on my memory, it has haunted my thoughts, at intervals, with the pertinacity of an object connected with human affections. I have visited this scene again. Neither the dream could be dissociated from the landscape, nor the landscape from the dream, nor feelings, such as neither singly could have awakened, from both. But the most remarkable event of this nature, which ever occurred to me, happened five years ago at Oxford. I was walking with a friend, in the neighbourhood of that city, engaged in earnest and interesting conversation. We suddenly turned the corner of a lane, and the view, which its high banks and hedges had concealed, presented itself. The view consisted of a windmill, standing in one among many plashy meadows, inclosed with stone walls; the irregular and broken ground, between the wall and the road on which we stood; a long low hill behind the windmill, and a grey covering of uniform cloud spread over the evening sky. It was that season when the last leaf had just fallen from the scant and stunted ash. The scene surely was a common scene; the season and the hour little calculated to kindle lawless thought; it was a tame uninteresting assemblage of objects, such as would drive the imagination for refuge in serious and sober talk, to the evening fireside, and the dessert of winter fruits and wine. The effect which it produced on me was not such as could have been expected. I suddenly remembered to have seen that exact scene in some dream of long *——

* *Here I was obliged to leave off, overcome by thrilling horror.*— This remark closes this fragment, which was written in 1815. I remember well his coming to me from writing it, pale and agitated, to seek refuge in conversation from the fearful emotions it excited. —[*Note by Mrs. Shelley.*]

FRAGMENTS.

SPECULATIONS ON MORALS.

I.—PLAN OF A TREATISE ON MORALS.

HAT great science which regards nature and the operations of the human mind, is popularly divided into Morals and Metaphysics. The latter relates to a just classification, and the assignment of distinct names to its ideas ; the former regards simply the determination of that arrangement of them which produces the greatest and most solid happiness. It is admitted that a virtuous or moral action is that action which, when considered in all its accessories and consequences, is fitted to produce the highest pleasure to the greatest number of sensitive beings. The laws according to which all pleasure, since it cannot be equally felt by all sensitive beings, ought to be distributed by a voluntary agent, are reserved for a separate chapter.

The design of this little treatise is restricted to the development of the elementary principles of morals. As far as regards that purpose, metaphysical science will be treated merely so far as a source of negative truth ; whilst morality will be considered as a science, respecting which we can arrive at positive conclusions.

The misguided imaginations of men have rendered the ascertaining of what *is not true,* the principal direct service which metaphysical science can bestow upon moral science. Moral science itself is the doctrine of the voluntary actions of man, as a sentient and social being. These actions depend on the thoughts in his mind. But there is a mass of popular opinion, from which the most enlightened persons are seldom wholly free, into the truth or falsehood of which it is incumbent on us to inquire, before we can arrive at any firm conclusions as to the conduct which we ought to pursue in the regulation of our own minds, or towards our fellow-beings ; or before we can ascertain the elementary laws, according to which these thoughts, from which these actions flow, are originally combined.

The object of the forms according to which human society is administered, is the happiness of the individuals composing the communities which they regard, and these forms are perfect or imperfect in proportion to the degree in which they promote this end.

This object is not merely the quantity of happiness enjoyed by individuals as sensitive beings, but the mode in which it should be distributed among them as social beings. It is not enough, if such a coincidence can be conceived as possible, that one person or class of persons should enjoy the highest happiness, whilst another is suffering a disproportionate degree of misery. It is necessary that the happiness produced by the common efforts, and preserved by the common care, should be distributed according to the just claims of each individual; if not, although the quantity produced should be the same, the end of society would remain unfulfilled. The object is in a compound proportion to the quantity of happiness produced, and the correspondence of the mode in which it is distributed, to the elementary feelings of man as a social being.

The disposition in an individual to promote this object is called virtue ; and the two constituent parts of virtue, benevolence and justice, are correlative with these two great portions of the only true object of all voluntary actions of a human being. Benevolence is the desire to be the author of good, and justice the apprehension of the manner in which good ought to be done.

Justice and benevolence result from the elementary laws of the human mind.

CHAPTER I.

ON THE NATURE OF VIRTUE.

SECT. 1. General View of the Nature and Objects of Virtue.—2. The Origin and Basis of Virtue, as founded on the Elementary Principles of Mind.—3. The Laws which flow from the nature of Mind regulating the application of those principles to human actions. —4. Virtue, a possible attribute of man.

WE exist in the midst of a multitude of beings like ourselves, upon whose happiness most of our actions exert some obvious and decisive influence.

The regulation of this influence is the object of moral science.

We know that we are susceptible of receiving painful or pleasurable impressions of greater or less intensity and duration. That is called good which produces pleasure ; that is called evil which produces pain. These are general names, applicable to every class of causes, from which an overbalance of pain or pleasure may result. But when a human being is the active instrument of generating or diffusing happiness, the principle through which it is most effectually instrumental to that purpose, is called virtue. And benevolence, or the desire to be the author of good, united with justice, or an apprehension of the manner in which that good is to be done, constitutes virtue.

But, wherefore should a man be benevolent and just? The immediate emotions of his nature, especially in its most inartificial state, prompt him to inflict pain, and to arrogate dominion. He desires to heap superfluities to his own store, although others perish with famine. He is propelled to guard against the smallest invasion of his own liberty, though he reduces others to a condition of the most pitiless servitude. He is revengeful, proud, and selfish. Wherefore should he curb these propensities?

It is inquired for what reason a human being should engage in procuring the happiness, or refrain from producing the pain of another? When a reason is required to prove the necessity of adopting any system of conduct, what is it that the objector demands? He requires proof of that system of conduct being such as will most effectually promote the happiness of mankind. To demonstrate this, is to render a moral reason. Such is the object of Virtue.

A common sophism, which, like many others, depends on the abuse of a metaphorical expression to a literal purpose, has produced much of the confusion which has involved the theory of morals. It is said that no person is bound to be just or kind, if, on his neglect, he should fail to incur some penalty. Duty is obligation. There can be no obligation without an obliger. Virtue is a law, to which it is the will of the lawgiver that we should conform; which will we should in no manner be bound to obey, unless some dreadful punishment were attached to disobedience. This is the philosophy of slavery and superstition.

In fact, no person can be *bound* or *obliged*, without some power preceding to bind and oblige. If I observe a man bound hand and foot, I know that some one bound him. But if I observe him returning self-satisfied from the performance of some action, by which he has been the willing author of extensive benefit, I do not infer that the anticipation of hellish agonies,

or the hope of heavenly reward, has constrained him
to such an act.   *   *   *   *

It remains to be stated in what manner the sensations which constitute the basis of virtue originate in
the human mind ; what are the laws which it receives
there ; how far the principles of mind allow it to be an
attribute of a human being ; and, lastly, what is the
probability of persuading mankind to adopt it as a
universal and systematic motive of conduct.

BENEVOLENCE.

THERE is a class of emotions which we instinctively
avoid. A human being, such as is man considered
in his origin, a child a month old, has a very imperfect
consciousness of the existence of other natures resembling itself. All the energies of its being are directed to
the extinction of the pains with which it is perpetually
assailed. At length it discovers that it is surrounded
by natures susceptible of sensations similar to its own.
It is very late before children attain to this knowledge.
If a child observes, without emotion, its nurse or its
mother suffering acute pain, it is attributable rather to
ignorance than insensibility. So soon as the accents
and gestures, significant of pain, are referred to the
feelings which they express, they awaken in the mind
of the beholder a desire that they should cease. Pain
is thus apprehended to be evil for its own sake, without
any other necessary reference to the mind by which its
existence is perceived, than such as is indispensable
to its perception. The tendencies of our original
sensations, indeed, all have for their object the preservation of our individual being. But these are passive

* A leaf of manuscript is wanting here, manifestly treating of
self-love and disinterestedness.—[*Note by Mrs. Shelley.*]

SPECULATIONS ON MORALS. 199

and unconscious. In proportion as the mind acquires an active power, the empire of these tendencies becomes limited. Thus an infant, a savage, and a solitary beast, is selfish, because its mind is incapable of receiving an accurate intimation of the nature of pain as existing in beings resembling itself. The inhabitant of a highly civilised community will more acutely sympathise with the sufferings and enjoyments of others, than the inhabitant of a society of a less degree of civilisation. He who shall have cultivated his intellectual powers by familiarity with the highest specimens of poetry and philosophy, will usually sympathise more than one engaged in the less refined functions of manual labour. Every one has experience of the fact, that to sympathise with the sufferings of another, is to enjoy a transitory oblivion of his own.

The mind thus acquires, by exercise, a habit, as it were, of perceiving and abhorring evil, however remote from the immediate sphere of sensations with which that individual mind is conversant. Imagination or mind employed in prophetically imaging forth its objects, is that faculty of human nature on which every gradation of its progress, nay, every, the minutest, change, depends. Pain or pleasure, if subtly analysed, will be found to consist entirely in prospect. The only distinction between the selfish man and the virtuous man is, that the imagination of the former is confined within a narrow limit, whilst that of the latter embraces a comprehensive circumference. In this sense, wisdom and virtue may be said to be inseparable, and criteria of each other. Selfishness is the offspring of ignorance and mistake; it is the portion of unreflecting infancy, and savage solitude, or of those whom toil or evil occupations have blunted or rendered torpid; disinterested benevolence is the product of a cultivated imagination, and has an intimate connexion with all the arts which add ornament, or dignity, or power, or stability to the social state of man. Virtue is thus entirely a refinement of civilised life ; a creation of the human mind ; or, rather, a combination which it has made, according to elementary rules contained within itself, of the feelings suggested by the relations established between man and man.

All the theories which have refined and exalted humanity, or those which have been devised as alleviations of its mistakes and evils, have been based upon the elementary emotions of disinterestedness, which we feel to constitute the majesty of our nature. Patriotism, as it existed in the ancient republics, was never, as has been supposed, a calculation of personal advantages. When Mutius Scævola thrust his hand into the burning coals, and Regulus returned to Carthage, and Epicharis sustained the rack silently, in the torments of which she knew that she would speedily perish, rather than betray the conspirators to the tyrant ; * these illustrious persons certainly made a small estimate of their private interest. If it be said that they sought posthumous fame ; instances are not wanting in history which prove that men have even defied infamy for the sake of good. But there is a great error in the world with respect to the selfishness of fame. It is certainly possible that a person should seek distinction as a medium of personal gratification. But the love of fame is frequently no more than a desire that the feelings of others should confirm, illustrate, and sympathise with, our own. In this respect it is allied with all that draws us out of ourselves. It is the "last infirmity of noble minds." Chivalry was likewise founded on the theory of self-sacrifice. Love possesses so extraordinary a power over the human heart, only because disinterestedness is united with the natural propensities. These propensities themselves are comparatively impotent in cases where the imagination of pleasure to be given, as well as to be

* Tacitus.

received, does not enter into the account. Let it not be objected that patriotism, and chivalry, and sentimental love, have been the fountains of enormous mischief. They are cited only to establish the proposition that, according to the elementary principles of mind, man is capable of desiring and pursuing good for its own sake.

JUSTICE.

THE benevolent propensities are thus inherent in the human mind. We are impelled to seek the happiness of others. We experience a satisfaction in being the authors of that happiness. Everything that lives is open to impressions of pleasure and pain. We are led by our benevolent propensities to regard every human being indifferently with whom we come in contact. They have preference only with respect to those who offer themselves most obviously to our notice. Human beings are indiscriminating and blind; they will avoid inflicting pain, though that pain should be attended with eventual benefit; they will seek to confer pleasure without calculating the mischief that may result. They benefit one at the expense of many.

There is a sentiment in the human mind that regulates benevolence in its application as a principle of action. This is the sense of justice. Justice, as well as benevolence, is an elementary law of human nature. It is through this principle that men are impelled to distribute any means of pleasure which benevolence may suggest the communication of to others, in equal portions among an equal number of applications. If ten men are shipwrecked on a desert island, they distribute whatever subsistence may remain to them into equal portions among themselves. If six of them conspire to deprive the remaining four of their share, their conduct is termed unjust.

The existence of pain has been shown to be a circumstance which the human mind regards with dissatisfaction, and of which it desires the cessation. It is equally according to its nature to desire that the advantages to be enjoyed by a limited number of persons should be enjoyed equally by all. This proposition is supported by the evidence of indisputable facts. Tell some ungarbled tale of a number of persons being made the victims of the enjoyments of one, and he who would appeal in favour of any system which might produce such an evil to the primary emotions of our nature, would have nothing to reply. Let two persons, equally strangers, make application for some benefit in the possession of a third to bestow, and to which he feels that they have an equal claim. They are both sensitive beings ; pleasure and pain affect them alike.

*   *   *   *   *

CHAPTER II.

IT is foreign to the general scope of this little treatise to encumber a simple argument by controverting any of the trite objections of habit or fanaticism. But there are two ; the first, the basis of all political mistake, and the second, the prolific cause and effect of religious error, which it seems useful to refute.

First, it is inquired, " Wherefore should a man be benevolent and just ? " The answer has been given in the preceding chapter.

If a man persists to inquire why he ought to promote the happiness of mankind, he demands a mathematical or metaphysical reason for a moral action. The absurdity of this scepticism is more apparent, but not less real, than the exacting a moral reason for a mathematical or metaphysical fact. If any person should refuse to admit that all the radii of a circle are of equal length, or that human actions are necessarily determined by motives, until it could be proved that these radii and these actions uniformly tended to the production of the greatest general good, who would not wonder at the unreasonable and capricious association of his ideas?

The writer of a philosophical treatise may, I imagine, at this advanced era of human intellect, be held excused from entering into a controversy with those reasoners, if such there are, who would claim an exemption from its decrees in favour of any one among those diversified systems of obscure opinion respecting morals, which, under the name of religions, have in various ages and countries prevailed among mankind. Besides that if, as these reasoners have pretended, eternal torture or happiness will ensue as the consequence of certain actions, we should be no nearer the possession of a standard to determine what actions were right and wrong, even if this pretended revelation, which is by no means the case, had furnished us with a complete catalogue of them. The character of actions as virtuous or vicious would by no means be determined alone by the personal advantage or disadvantage of each moral agent in-dividually considered. Indeed, an action is often virtuous in proportion to the greatness of the personal calamity which the author willingly draws upon him-self by daring to perform it. It is because an action produces an overbalance of pleasure or pain to the greatest number of sentient beings, and not merely because its consequences are beneficial or injurious to the author of that action, that it is good or evil. Nay, this latter consideration has a tendency to pollute the purity of virtue, inasmuch as it consists in the motive rather than in the consequences of an action. A person who should labour for the happiness of mankind lest he should be tormented eternally in Hell, would with reference to that motive possess as little claim to the epithet of virtuous, as he who should torture, imprison, and burn them alive, a more usual and natural consequence of such principles, for the sake of the enjoyments of Heaven.

My neighbour, presuming on his strength, may direct me to perform or to refrain from a particular action ; indicating a certain arbitrary penalty in the event of disobedience within his power to inflict. My action, if modified by his menaces, can in no degree participate in virtue. He has afforded me no criterion as to what is right or wrong. A king, or an assembly of men, may publish a proclamation affixing any penalty to any particular action, but that is not immoral because such penalty is affixed. Nothing is more evident than that the epithet of virtue is inapplicable to the refraining from that action on account of the evil arbitrarily attached to it. If the action is in itself beneficial, virtue would rather consist in not refraining from it, but in firmly defying the personal consequences attached to its performance.

Some usurper of supernatural energy might subdue the whole globe to his power ; he might possess new and unheard-of resources for induing his punishments with the most terrible attributes of pain. The torments of his victims might be intense in their degree, and protracted to an infinite duration. Still the " will of the lawgiver " would afford no surer criterion as to what actions were right or wrong. It would only increase the possible virtue of those who refuse to become the instruments of his tyranny.

II.—MORAL SCIENCE CONSISTS IN CONSIDERING THE DIFFERENCE, NOT THE RESEMBLANCE, OF PERSONS.

THE internal influence, derived from the constitution of the mind from which they flow, produces that peculiar modification of actions, which makes them intrinsically good or evil.

To attain an apprehension of the importance of this distinction, let us visit, in imagination, the proceedings of some metropolis. Consider the multitude of human beings who inhabit it, and survey, in thought, the actions of the several classes into which they are divided. Their obvious actions are apparently uniform: the stability of human society seems to be maintained sufficiently by the uniformity of the conduct of its members, both with regard to themselves and with regard to others. The labourer arises at a certain hour, and applies himself to the task enjoined him. The functionaries of government and law are regularly employed in their offices and courts. The trader holds a train of conduct from which he never deviates. The ministers of religion employ an accustomed language, and maintain a decent and equable regard. The army is drawn forth, the motions of every soldier are such as they were expected to be ; the general commands, and his words are echoed from troop to troop. The domestic actions of men are, for the most part, undistinguishable one from the other, at a superficial glance. The actions which are classed under the general appellation of marriage, education, friendship, &c., are perpetually going on, and to a superficial glance, are similar one to the other.

But, if we would see the truth of things, they must be stripped of this fallacious appearance of uniformity. In truth, no one action has, when considered in its whole extent, any essential resemblance with any other. Each individual, who composes the vast multitude which we have been contemplating, has a peculiar frame of mind, which, whilst the features of the great mass of his actions remain uniform, impresses the minuter lineaments with its peculiar hues. Thus, whilst his life, as a whole, is like the lives of other men, in detail it is most unlike ; and the more subdivided the actions become, that is,

the more they enter into that class which have a vital
influence on the happiness of others and his own, so
much the more are they distinct from those of other
men.

> " Those little nameless unremember'd acts
> Of kindness and of love," *

as well as those deadly outrages which are inflicted by
a look, a word—or less—the very refraining from some
faint and most evanescent expression of countenance ;
these flow from a profounder source than the series of
our habitual conduct, which, it has been already said,
derives its origin from without.   These are the actions,
and such as these, which make human life what it is,
and are the fountains of all the good and evil with which
its entire surface is so widely and impartially overspread ;
and though they are called minute, they are called so in
compliance with the blindness of those who cannot estimate their importance.   It is in the due appreciating the
general effects of their peculiarities, and in cultivating
the habit of acquiring decisive knowledge respecting the
tendencies arising out of them in particular cases, that
the most important part of moral science consists.   The
deepest abyss of these vast and multitudinous caverns,
it is necessary that we should visit.

  This is the difference between social and individual
man.   Not that this distinction is to be considered
definite, or characteristic of one human being as compared with another ; it denotes rather two classes of
agency, common in a degree to every human being.
None is exempt, indeed, from that species of influence
which affects, as it were, the surface of his being, and
gives the specific outline to his conduct.   Almost all
that is ostensible submits to that legislature created by
the general representation of the past feelings of mankind—imperfect as it is from a variety of causes, as it

* Wordsworth, *Tintern Abbey.*—Ed.

exists in the government, the religion, and domestic habits. Those who do not nominally, yet actually, submit to the same power. The external features of their conduct, indeed, can no more escape it, than the clouds can escape from the stream of the wind ; and his opinion, which he often hopes he has dispassionately secured from all contagion of prejudice and vulgarity, would be found, on examination, to be the inevitable excrescence of the very usages from which he vehemently dissents. Internally all is conducted otherwise ; the efficiency, the essence, the vitality of actions, derives its colour from what is no ways contributed to from any external source. Like the plant, which while it derives the accident of its size and shape from the soil in which it springs, and is cankered, or distorted, or inflated, yet retains those qualities which essentially divide it from all others ; so that hemlock continues to be poison, and the violet does not cease to emit its odour in whatever soil it may grow.

We consider our own nature too superficially. We look on all that in ourselves with which we can discover a resemblance in others ; and consider those resemblances as the materials of moral knowledge. It is in the differences that it actually consists.

GHOST STORIES.

Geneva, Sunday, 18th August 1816.

EE Apollo's Sexton,* who tells us many mysteries of his trade. We talk of Ghosts. Neither Lord Byron nor M. G. L. seem to believe in them; and they both agree, in the very face of reason, that none could believe in ghosts without believing in God. I do not think that all the persons who profess to discredit these visitations, really discredit them; or, if they do in the daylight, are not admonished by the approach of loneliness and midnight, to think more respectfully of the world of shadows.

Lewis recited a poem, which he had composed at the request of the Princess of Wales. The Princess of Wales, he premised, was not only a believer in ghosts, but in magic and witchcraft, and asserted, that prophecies made in her youth had been accomplished since. The tale was of a lady in Germany.

This lady, Minna, had been exceedingly attached to

---

* Matthew Gregory Lewis—so named in *English Bards and Scotch Reviewers.* When Lewis first saw Lord Byron, he asked him earnestly,—" Why did you call me Apollo's sexton?" The noble poet found it difficult to reply to this categorical species of reproof. The above stories have, some of them, appeared in print; but, as a ghost story depends entirely on the mode in which it is told, I think the reader will be pleased to read these, written by Shelley, fresh from their relation by Lewis.—[*Note by Mrs. Shelley.*]

her husband, and they had made a vow that the one who died first, should return after death to visit the other as a ghost. She was sitting one day alone in her chamber, when she heard an unusual sound of footsteps on the stairs. The door opened, and her husband's spectre, gashed with a deep wound across the forehead, and in military habiliments, entered. She appeared startled at the apparition ; and the ghost told her, that when he should visit her in future, she would hear a passing bell toll, and these words distinctly uttered close to her ear, " Minna, I am here." On inquiry, it was found that her husband had fallen in battle on the very day she was visited by the vision. The intercourse between the ghost and the woman continued for some time, until the latter laid aside all terror, and indulged herself in the affection which she had felt for him while living. One evening she went to a ball, and permitted her thoughts to be alienated by the attentions of a Florentine gentleman, more witty, more graceful, and more gentle, as it appeared to her, than any person she had ever seen. As he was conducting her through the dance, a death bell tolled. Minna, lost in the fascination of the Florentine's attentions, disregarded, or did not hear the sound. A second peal, louder and more deep, startled the whole company, when Minna heard the ghost's accustomed whisper, and raising her eyes, saw in an opposite mirror the reflection of the ghost, standing over her. She is said to have died of terror.

Lewis told four other stories—all grim.

I.

A YOUNG man who had taken orders, had just been presented with a living, on the death of the incumbent. It was in the Catholic part of Germany. He arrived at the parsonage on a Saturday night ; it was summer, and waking about three o'clock in the morning, and it being broad day, he saw a venerable-looking man, but with an aspect exceedingly melancholy, sitting at a desk in the window, reading, and two beautiful boys standing near him, whom he regarded with looks of the profoundest grief. Presently he rose from his seat, the boys followed him, and they were no more to be seen. The young man, much troubled, arose, hesitating whether he should regard what he had seen as a dream, or a waking phantasy. To divert his dejection, he walked towards the church, which the sexton was already employed in preparing for the morning service. The first sight that struck him was a portrait, the exact resemblance of the man whom he had seen sitting in his chamber. It was the custom in this district to place the portrait of each minister, after his death, in the church.

He made the minutest inquiries respecting his predecessor, and learned that he was universally beloved, as a man of unexampled integrity and benevolence; but that he was the prey of a secret and perpetual sorrow. His grief was supposed to have arisen from an attachment to a young lady, with whom his situation did not permit him to unite himself. Others, however, asserted, that a connexion did subsist between them, and that even she occasionally brought to his house two beautiful boys, the offspring of their connexion.— Nothing further occurred until the cold weather came, and the new minister desired a fire to be lighted in the stove of the room where he slept. A hideous stench arose from the stove as soon as it was lighted, and, on examining it, the bones of two male children were found within.

II.

LORD LYTTELTON and a number of his friends were joined during the chase by a stranger. He was excellently mounted, and displayed such courage, or, rather so much desperate rashness, that no other person in the hunt could follow him. The gentlemen, when the chase was concluded, invited the stranger to dine with them. His conversation was something of a wonderful kind. He astonished, he interested, he commanded the attention of the most inert. As night came on, the company, being weary, began to retire one by one, much later than the usual hour : the most intellectual among them were retained latest by the stranger's fascination. As he perceived that they began to depart, he redoubled his efforts to retain them. At last, when few remained, he entreated them to stay with him ; but all pleaded the fatigue of a hard day's chase, and all at last retired. They had been in bed about an hour, when they were awakened by the most horrible screams, which issued from the stranger's room. Every one rushed towards it. The door was locked. After a moment's deliberation they burst it open, and found the stranger stretched on the ground, writhing with agony, and weltering in blood. On their entrance he arose, and collecting himself, apparently with a strong effort, entreated them to leave him—not to disturb him, that he would give every possible explanation in the morning. They complied. In the morning, his chamber was found vacant, and he was seen no more.

III.

MILES ANDREWS, a friend of Lord Lyttelton, was sitting one night alone when Lord Lyttelton came in, and informed him that he was dead, and that this was his ghost which he saw before him. Andrews pettishly told him not to play any ridiculous tricks upon him, for he was not in a temper to bear them. The ghost then departed. In the morning Andrews asked his servant at what hour Lord Lyttelton had arrived. The servant said he did not know that he had arrived, but that he would inquire. On inquiry it was found that Lord Lyttelton had not arrived, nor had the door been opened to any one during the whole night. Andrews sent to Lord Lyttelton, and discovered, that he had died precisely at the hour of the apparition.

IV.

A GENTLEMAN on a visit to a friend who lived on the skirts of an extensive forest in the east of Germany, lost his way. He wandered for some hours among the trees, when he saw a light at a distance. On approaching it, he was surprised to observe, that it proceeded from the interior of a ruined monastery. Before he knocked he thought it prudent to look through the window. He saw a multitude of cats assembled round a small grave, four of whom were letting down a coffin with a crown upon it. The gentleman, startled at this unusual sight, and imagining that he had arrived among the retreats of fiends or witches, mounted his horse and rode away with the utmost precipitation. He arrived at his friend's house at a late hour, who had sat up for him. On his arrival his friend questioned as to the cause of the traces of trouble visible in his face. He began to recount his adventure, after much difficulty, knowing that it was scarcely possible that his friends should give faith to his relation. No sooner had he mentioned the coffin with a crown upon it, than his friend's cat, who seemed to have been lying asleep before the fire, leaped up, saying—"Then I am the King of the Cats!" and scrambled up the chimney, and was seen no more.

Thursday, 29th August.—We depart from Geneva, at nine in the morning. The Swiss are very slow drivers; besides which we have Jura to mount; we, therefore, go a very few posts to-day. The scenery is very beautiful, and we see many magnificent views. We pass Les Rousses, which, when we crossed in the spring, was deep in snow. We sleep at Morrez.

Friday, 30th.—We leave Morrez, and arrive in the evening at Dole, after a various day.

Saturday, 31st.—From Dole we go to Rouvray, where we sleep. We pass through Dijon; and, after Dijon, take a different route than that which we followed on the two other occasions. The scenery has some beauty and singularity in the line of the mountains which surround the Val de Suzon. Low, yet precipitous hills, covered with vines or woods, and with streams, meadows, and poplars, at the bottom.

Sunday, September 1st. — Leave Rouvray, pass Auxerre, where we dine; a pretty town, and arrive, at two o'clock, at Villeneuve le Guiard.

Monday, 2d.—From Villeneuve le Guiard, we arrive at Fontainebleau. The scenery around this palace is wild and even savage. The soil is full of rocks, apparently granite, which on every side break through the ground. The hills are low, but precipitous and rough. The valleys, equally wild, are shaded by forests. In the midst of this wilderness stands the palace. Some of the apartments equal in magnificence anything that I could conceive. The roofs are fretted with gold, and the canopies of velvet. From Fontainebleau we proceed to Versailles, in the route towards Rouen. We arrive at Versailles at nine.

Tuesday, 3d.—We saw the palace and gardens of Versailles and le Grand et Petit Trianon. They surpass Fontainebleau. The gardens are full of statues, vases, fountains, and colonnades. In all that essentially belongs to a garden they are extraordinarily deficient. The orangery is a stupid piece of expense. There was one orange-tree, not apparently so old, sown in 1442. We saw only the gardens and the theatre at the Petit Trianon. The gardens are in the English taste, and extremely pretty. The Grand Trianon was open. It is a summer palace, light, yet magnificent. We were unable to devote the time it deserved to the gallery of paintings here. There was a portrait of Madame de la Vallière, the repentant mistress of Louis XIV. She was melancholy, but exceedingly beautiful, and was represented as holding a skull, and sitting before a crucifix, pale, and with downcast eyes.

We then went to the great palace. The apartments are unfurnished, but even with this disadvantage, are more magnificent than those of Fontainebleau. They are lined with marble of various colours, whose pedestals and capitals are gilt, and the ceiling is richly gilt with compartments of painting. The arrangement of these materials has in them, it is true, something effeminate and royal. Could a Grecian architect have commanded all the labour and money which was expended on Versailles, he would have produced a fabric which the whole world has never equalled. We saw the Hall of Hercules, the balcony where the King and the Queen exhibited themselves to the Parisian mob. The people who showed us through the palace, obstinately refused to say anything about the Revolution. We could not even find out in which chamber the rioters of the 10th August found the king. We saw the Salle d'Opera, where are now preserved the portraits of the kings. There was the race of the house of Orleans, with the exception of Egalité, all extremely handsome. There was Madame de Maintenon, and beside her a beautiful little girl, the daughter of La Vallière. The pictures had been hidden during the Revolution. We saw the Library of Louis XVI. The librarian had held some place in the ancient court near Marie Antoinette. He returned with the Bourbons, and was waiting for some better situation. He showed us a book which he had preserved during the Revolution. It was a book of paintings, representing a Tournament at the Court of Louis XIV. ; and it seemed that the present desolation of France, the fury of the injured people, and all the horrors to which they abandoned themselves, stung by their long sufferings, flowed naturally enough from expenditures so immense, as must have been demanded by the magnificence of this tournament. The vacant rooms of this palace imaged well the hollow show of monarchy. After seeing these things we departed toward Havre, and slept at Auxerre.

Wednesday, 4th.—We passed through Rouen, and saw the cathedral, an immense specimen of the most costly and magnificent gothic. The interior of the church disappoints. We saw the burial-place of Richard Cœur de Lion and his brother. The altar of the church is a fine piece of marble. Sleep at Yvetot.

Thursday, 5th.—We arrive at Havre, and wait for the packet—wind contrary.

FRAGMENT FROM JOURNAL.

Thursday, March 26, 1818.

In a brief journal I kept at that time, I find a few pages in Shelley's handwriting, descriptive of the passage over the mountains of Les Eschelles.—[*Note by Mrs. Shelley.*]

March 26, Thursday.—We travel towards the mountains, and begin to enter the valleys of the Alps. The

country becomes covered again with verdure and cultivation, and white chateaux and scattered cottages
among woods of old oak and walnut trees. The vines
are here peculiarly picturesque ; they are trellised upon
immense stakes, and the trunks of them are moss-
covered and hoary with age. Unlike the French
vines, which creep lowly on the ground, they form
rows of interlaced bowers, which, when the leaves are
green and the red grapes are hanging among those
hoary branches, will afford a delightful shadow to those
who sit upon the moss underneath. The vines are
sometimes planted in the open fields, and sometimes
among lofty orchards of apple and pear-trees, the twigs
of which were just becoming purple with the bursting
blossoms.

We dined at Les Eschelles, a village at the foot of the
mountain of the same name, the boundaries of France
and Savoy. Before this we had been stopped at Pont
Bonvoisin, where the legal limits of the French and
Sardinian territories are placed. We here heard that a
Milanese had been sent back all the way to Lyons, because his passport was unauthorised by the Sardinian
Consul, a few days before, and that we should be subjected to the same treatment. We, in respect to the
character of our nation I suppose, were suffered to pass.
Our books, however, were, after a long discussion, sent
to Chambery, to be submitted to the censor ; a priest,
who admits nothing of Rousseau, Voltaire, &c., into the
dominions of the King of Sardinia. All such books are
burned.

After dinner we ascended Les Eschelles, winding
along a road, cut through perpendicular rocks, of immense elevation, by Charles Emanuel, Duke of Savoy,
in 1582. The rocks, which cannot be less than a
thousand feet in perpendicular height, sometimes overhang the road on each side, and almost shut out the
sky. The scene is like that described in the Prometheus

of Æschylus. Vast rifts and caverns in the granite precipices, wintry mountains with ice and snow above ; the loud sounds of unseen waters within the caverns, and walls of toppling rocks, only to be scaled as he describes, by the winged chariot of the ocean nymphs.

Under the dominion of this tyranny, the inhabitants of the fertile valleys, bounded by these mountains, are in a state of most frightful poverty and disease. At the foot of this ascent, were cut into the rocks at several places, stories of the misery of the inhabitants, to move the compassion of the traveller. One old man, lame and blind, crawled out of a hole in the rock, wet with the perpetual melting of the snows of above, and dripping like a shower-bath.

The country, as we descended to Chambéry, continued as beautiful ; though marked with somewhat of a softer character than before ; we arrived a little after night-fall.

LETTERS FROM ITALY.

LETTERS FROM ITALY.

TO THOMAS LOVE PEACOCK.

Milan, April, 1818.

MY DEAR PEACOCK,

EHOLD us arrived at length at the end of our journey—that is, within a few miles of it—because we design to spend the summer on the shore of the Lake of Como. Our journey was somewhat painful from the cold—and in no other manner interesting until we passed the Alps : of course I except the Alps themselves ; but no sooner had we arrived at Italy, than the loveliness of the earth and the serenity of the sky made the greatest difference in my sensations. I depend on these things for life ; for in the smoke of cities, and the tumult of human kind, and the chilling fogs and rain of our own country, I can hardly be said to live. With what delight did I hear the woman, who conducted us to see the triumphal arch of Augustus at Susa, speak the clear and complete language of Italy, though half unintelligible to me, after that nasal and abbreviated cacophony of the French ! A ruined arch of magnificent proportions, in the Greek taste, standing in a kind of road of green lawn, overgrown with violets and prim-roses, and in the midst of stupendous mountains, and a *blonde* woman, of light and graceful manners, something in the style of Fuseli's Eve, were the first things we met in Italy.

This city is very agreeable. We went to the opera last night—which is a most splendid exhibition. The opera itself was not a favourite, and the singers very inferior to our own. But the ballet, or rather a kind of melodrame or pantomimic drama, was the most splendid spectacle I ever saw. We have no Miss Melanie here—in every other respect, Milan is unquestionably superior. The manner in which language is translated into gesture, the complete and full effect of the whole as illustrating the history in question, the unaffected self-possession of each of the actors, even to the children, made this choral drama more impressive than I could have conceived possible. The story is *Othello,* and strange to say, it left no disagreeable impression.

I write, but I am not in the humour to write, and you must expect longer, if not more entertaining, letters soon —that is, in a week or so—when I am a little recovered from my journey. Pray tell us all the news with regard to our own offspring, whom we left at nurse in England ; as well as those of our friends. Mention Cobbett and politics too — and Hunt—to whom Mary is now writing—and particularly your own plans and yourself. You shall hear more of me and my plans soon. My health is improved already— and my spirits something— and I have many literary schemes, and one in particular—which I thirst to be settled that I may begin. I have ordered Ollier to send you some sheets &c. for revision.

Adieu.—Always faithfully yours,

P. B. S.

TO THOMAS LOVE PEACOCK.

Milan, April 20, 1818.

My DEAR PEACOCK,

I HAD no conception that the distance between us, measured by time in respect of letters, was so great. I have but just received yours dated the 2d—and when you will receive mine written from this city somewhat later than the same date, I cannot know. I am sorry to hear that you have been obliged to remain at Marlow ; a certain degree of society being almost a necessity of life, particularly as we are not to see you this summer in Italy. But this, I suppose, must be as it is. I often revisit Marlow in thought. The curse of this life is, that whatever is once known, can never be unknown. You inhabit a spot, which before you inhabit it, is as indifferent to you as any other spot upon earth, and when, persuaded by some necessity, you think to leave it, you leave it not ; it clings to you—and with memories of things, which, in your experience of them, gave no such promise, revenges your desertion. Time flows on, places are changed ; friends who were with us, are no longer with us ; yet what has been seems yet to be, but barren and stripped of life. See, I have sent you a study for Nightmare Abbey.

Since I last wrote to you we have been to. Como, looking for a house. This lake exceeds any thing I ever beheld in beauty, with the exception of the arbutus islands of Killarney. It is long and narrow, and has the appearance of a mighty river winding among the mountains and the forests. We sailed from the town of Como to a tract of country called the Tremezina, and saw the various aspects presented by that part of the lake. The mountains between Como and that village, or rather cluster of villages, are covered on high with chesnut forests (the eating chesnuts, on which the in-

habitants of the country subsist in time of scarcity),
which sometimes descend to the very verge of the lake,
overhanging it with their hoary branches.   But usually
the immediate border of this shore is composed of laurel-
trees, and bay, and myrtle, and wild-fig trees, and olives,
which grow in the crevices of the rocks, and overhang
the caverns, and shadow the deep glens, which are
filled with the flashing light of the waterfalls.   Other
flowering shrubs, which I cannot name, grow there also.
On high, the towers of village churches are seen white
among the dark forests.   Beyond, on the opposite shore,
which faces the south, the mountains descend less precipitously to the lake, and although they are much
higher, and some covered with perpetual snow, there
intervenes between them and the lake a range of lower
hills, which have glens and rifts opening to the other,
such as I should fancy the *abysses* of Ida or Parnassus.
Here are plantations of olive, and orange, and lemon-
trees, which are now so loaded with fruit, that there is
more fruit than leaves,—and vineyards.   This shore
of the lake is one continued village, and the Milanese
nobility have their villas here.   The union of culture
and the untameable profusion and loveliness of nature
is here so close, that the line where they are divided
can hardly be discovered.   But the finest scenery is
that of the Villa Pliniana ; so called from a fountain
which ebbs and flows every three hours, described by
the younger Pliny, which is in the court-yard.   This
house, which was once a magnificent palace, and is now
half in ruins, we are endeavouring to procure.   It is
built upon terraces *raised from* the bottom of the lake,
together with its garden, at the foot of a semi-circular
precipice, overshadowed by profound forests of chesnut.
The scene from the colonnade is the most extraordinary,
at once, and the most lovely that eye ever beheld.   On
one side is the mountain, and immediately over you
are clusters of cypress-trees of an astonishing height,

which seem to pierce the sky. Above you, from among
the clouds, as it were, descends a waterfall of immense
size, broken by the woody rocks into a thousand channels
to the lake. On the other side is seen the blue extent
of the lake and the mountains, speckled with sails and
spires. The apartments of the Pliniana are immensely
large, but ill furnished and antique. The terraces,
which overlook the lake, and conduct under the shade
of such immense laurel-trees as deserve the epithet of
Pythian, are most delightful. We stayed at Como two
days, and have now returned to Milan, waiting the issue
of our negotiation about a house. Como is only six
leagues from Milan, and its mountains are seen from
the cathedral.

This cathedral is a most astonishing work of art. It
is built of white marble, and cut into pinnacles of
immense height, and the utmost delicacy of workmanship, and loaded with sculpture. The effect of it,
piercing the solid blue with those groups of dazzling
spires, relieved by the serene depth of this Italian
heaven, or by moonlight when the stars seem gathered
among those clustered shapes, is beyond any thing I
had imagined architecture capable of producing. The
interior, though very sublime, is of a more earthly
character, and with its stained glass and massy granite
columns overloaded with antique figures, and the silver
lamps, that burn forever under the canopy of black cloth
beside the brazen altar and the marble fretwork of the
dome, give it the aspect of some gorgeous sepulchre.
There is one solitary spot among those aisles, behind
the altar, where the light of day is dim and yellow under
the storied window, which I have chosen to visit, and
read Dante there.

I have devoted this summer, and indeed the next
year, to the composition of a tragedy on the subject
of Tasso's madness, which I find upon inspection is,
if properly treated, admirably dramatic and poetical.

II.   P

But, you will say, I have no dramatic talent; very true, in a certain sense; but I have taken the resolution to see what kind of a tragedy a person without dramatic talent could write. It shall be better morality than *Fazio*, and better poetry than *Bertram*, at least. You tell me nothing of *Rhododaphne*, a book from which, I confess, I expected extraordinary success.

Who lives in my house at Marlow now, or what is to be done with it? I am seriously persuaded that the situation was injurious to my health, or I should be tempted to feel a very absurd interest in who is to be its next possessor. The expense of our journey here has been very considerable—but we are now living at the hotel here, in a kind of pension, which is very reasonable in respect of price, and when we get into a ménage of our own, we have every reason to expect that we shall experience something of the boasted cheapness of Italy. The finest bread, made of a sifted flour, the whitest and the best I ever tasted, is only *one English penny* a pound. All the necessaries of life bear a proportional relation to this. But then the luxuries, tea, &c., are very dear,—and the English, as usual, are cheated in a way that is quite ridiculous, if they have not their wits about them. We do not know a single human being, and the opera, until last night, has been always the same. Lord Byron, we hear, has taken a house for three years, at Venice; whether we shall see him or not, I do not know. The number of English who pass through this town is very great. They ought to be in their own country in the present crisis. Their conduct is wholly inexcusable. The people here, though inoffensive enough, seem both in body and soul a miserable race. The men are hardly men; they look like a tribe of stupid and shrivelled slaves, and I do not think that I have seen a gleam of intelligence in the countenance of man since I passed the Alps. The women in enslaved countries are always better than the men; but they have tight-laced

figures, and figures and mien which express (O how unlike
the French !) a mixture of the coquette and prude, which
reminds me of the worst characteristics of the English.
Everything but humanity is in much greater perfection
here than in France. The cleanliness and comfort of
the inns is something quite English. The country is
beautifully cultivated ; and altogether, if you can, as one
ought always to do, find your happiness in yourself, it is
a most delightful and commodious place to live in.

Adieu.—Your affectionate friend,

P. B. S.

TO THOMAS LOVE PEACOCK.

Milan, April 30th, 1818.

MY DEAR PEACOCK,

I WRITE, simply to tell you, to direct your next letters,
Poste Restante, Pisa. We have engaged a vetturino for
that city, and leave Milan to-morrow morning. Our
journey will occupy six or seven days.

Pisa is not six miles from the Mediterranean, with
which it communicates by the river Arno. We shall
pass by Piacenza, Parma, Bologna, the Apennines, and
Florence, and I will endeavour to tell you something of
these celebrated places in my next letter ; but I cannot
promise much, for, though my health is much improved,
my spirits are unequal, and seem to desert me when I
attempt to write.

Pisa, they say, is uninhabitable in the midst of
summer—we shall do, therefore, what other people do,
retire to Florence, or to the mountains. But I will
write to you our plans from Pisa, when I shall understand them better myself.

You may easily conjecture the motives which led us
to forego the divine solitude of Como. To me, whose

chief pleasure in life is the contemplation of nature, you may imagine how great is this loss.

Let us hear from you *once a fortnight.* Do not forget those who do not forget you.

Adieu.—Ever most sincerely yours,

P. B. SHELLEY.

TO THOMAS LOVE PEACOCK.

Livorno, June 5, 1818.

MY DEAR PEACOCK,

WE have not heard from you since the middle of April—that is, we have received only *one* letter from you since our departure from England. It necessarily follows that some accident has intercepted them. Address, in future, to the care of Mr. Gisborne, Livorno — and I shall receive them, though sometimes somewhat circuitously, yet always securely.

We left Milan on the first of May, and travelled across the Apennines to Pisa. This part of the Apennine is far less beautiful than the Alps; the mountains are wide and wild, and the whole scenery broad and undetermined —the imagination cannot find a home in it. The plain of the Milanese, and that of Parma, is exquisitely beautiful—it is like one garden, or rather cultivated wilderness; because the corn and the meadow-grass grow under high and thick trees, festooned to one another by regular festoons of vines. On the seventh day we arrived at Pisa, where we remained three or four days. A large disagreeable city, almost without inhabitants. We then proceeded to this great trading town, where we have remained a month, and which, in a few days, we leave for the Bagni di Lucca, a kind of watering-place situated in the depth of the Apennines; the scenery surrounding this village is very fine.

We have made some acquaintance with a very amiable

and acccomplished lady, Mrs. Gisborne, who is the sole attraction in this most unattractive of cities. We had no idea of spending a month here, but she has made it even agreeable. We shall see something of Italian society at the Bagni di Lucca, where the most fashionable people resort.

When you send my parcel—which, by-the-bye, I should request you to direct to Mr. Gisborne—I wish you could contrive to enclose the two last parts of Clarke's Travels, relating to Greece, and belonging to Hookham. You know I subscribe there still—and I have determined to take the *Examiner* here. You would, therefore, oblige me, by sending it weekly, after having read it yourself, to the same direction, and so clipped, as to make as little weight as possible.

I write as if writing where perhaps my letter may never arrive.

With every good wish from all of us,
Believe me most sincerely yours,
P. B. S.

TO MR. AND MRS. GISBORNE

(LEGHORN).

Bagni di Lucca, July 10th, 1818.

YOU cannot know, as some friends in England do, to whom my silence is still more inexcusable, that this silence is no proof of forgetfulness or neglect.

I have, in truth, nothing to say, but that I shall be happy to see you again, and renew our delightful walks, until the desire or the duty of seeing new things hurries us away. We have spent a month here in our accustomed solitude, with the exception of one night at the Casino ; and the choice society of all ages, which I took care to pack up in a large trunk before we left England,

have revisited us here.   I am employed just now, having
little better to do, in translating into my fainting and
inefficient periods, the divine eloquence of Plato's Symposium ; only as an exercise, or, perhaps, to give Mary
some idea of the manners and feelings of the Athenians
—so different on many subjects from that of any other
community that ever existed.

We have almost finished Ariosto—who is entertaining and graceful, and *sometimes* a poet.   Forgive me,
worshippers of a more equal and tolerant divinity in
poetry, if Ariosto pleases me less than you.   Where
is the gentle seriousness, the delicate sensibility, the
calm and sustained energy, without which true greatness
cannot be ?   He is so cruel, too, in his descriptions ;
his most prized virtues are vices almost without disguise.
He constantly vindicates and embellishes revenge in its
grossest form ; the most deadly superstition that ever
infested the world.   How different from the tender and
solemn enthusiasm of Petrarch—or even the delicate
moral sensibility of Tasso, though somewhat obscured
by an assumed and artificial style.

We read a good deal here—and we read little in
Livorno.   We have ridden, Mary and I, once only, to
a place called Prato Fiorito, on the top of the mountains : the road, winding through forests, and over
torrents, and on the verge of green ravines, affords
scenery magnificently fine.   I cannot describe it to you,
but bid you, though vainly, come and see.   I take great
delight in watching the changes of the atmosphere here,
and the growth of the thunder showers with which the
noon is often overshadowed, and which break and fade
away towards evening into flocks of delicate clouds.
Our fire-flies are fading away fast; but there is the
planet Jupiter, who rises majestically over the rift in
the forest-covered mountains to the south, and the pale
summer lightning which is spread out every night, at
intervals, over the sky.   No doubt Providence has con-

trived these things, that, when the fire-flies go out, the low-flying owl may see her way home.

Remember me kindly to the Machinista.

With the sentiment of impatience until we see you again in the autumn,

I am, yours most sincerely,

P. B. SHELLEY.

TO WILLIAM GODWIN.

Bagni di Lucca, July 25th, 1818.

MY DEAR GODWIN,

WE have, as yet, seen nothing of Italy which marks it to us as the habitation of departed greatness.   The serene sky, the magnificent scenery, the delightful pro- ductions of the climate, are known to us, indeed, as the same with those which the ancients enjoyed.   But Rome and Naples—even Florence, are yet to see ; and if we were to write you at present a history of our impressions, it would give you no idea that we lived in Italy.

I am exceedingly delighted with the plan you propose of a book, illustrating the character of our calumniated republicans.   It is precisely the subject for Mary, and I imagine, that, but for the fear of being excited to refer to books not within her reach, she would attempt to begin it here, and order the works you notice.   I am unfortunately little skilled in English history, and the interest which it excites in me is so feeble, that I find it a duty to attain merely to that general knowledge of it which is indispensable.

Mary has just finished Ariosto with me, and, indeed, has attained a very competent knowledge of Italian. She is now reading Livy.   I have been constantly . occupied in literature, but have written little—except some translations from Plato, in which I exercised myself, in the despair of producing anything original.

The Symposium of Plato seems to me one of the most valuable pieces of all antiquity, whether we consider the intrinsic merit of the composition, or the light which it throws on the inmost state of manners and opinions among the ancient Greeks. I have occupied myself in translating this, and it has excited me to attempt an Essay upon the cause of some differences in sentiment between the Ancients and Moderns, with respect to the subject of the dialogue.

Two things give us pleasure in your last letters,—the resumption of Malthus, and the favourable turn of the general election. If Ministers do not find some means, totally inconceivable to me, of plunging the nation in war, do you imagine that they can subsist? Peace is all that a country, in the present state of England, seems to require, to afford it tranquillity and leisure for attempting some remedy not to the universal evils of all constituted society, but to the peculiar system of misrule under which those evils have been exasperated now. I wish that I had health or spirits that would enable me to enter into public affairs, or that I could find words to express all that I feel and know.

The modern Italians seem a miserable people, without sensibility, or imagination, or understanding. Their outside is polished, and an intercourse with them seems to proceed with much facility, though it ends in nothing, and produces nothing. The women are particularly empty, and though possessed of the same kind of superficial grace, are devoid of every cultivation and refinement. They have a ball at the Casino here every Sunday, which we attend—but neither Mary nor C*** dance. I do not know whether they refrain from philosophy or protestantism.

I hear that poor Mary's book is attacked most violently in the Quarterly Review. We have heard some praise of it, and among others, an article of Walter Scott's in Blackwood's Magazine.

If you should have anything to send us—and, I assure you, anything relating to England is interesting to us— commit it to the care of Ollier the bookseller, or P***— they send me a parcel every quarter.

My health is, I think, better, and, I imagine, continues to improve ; but I still have busy thoughts and dispiriting cares, which I would shake off—and it is now summer.——A thousand good wishes to yourself and your undertakings.

Ever most affectionately yours,

P. B. S.

TO MRS. SHELLEY

(BAGNI DI LUCCA).

Florence, Thursday, 11 *o'clock.*
(*20th August,* 1818.)

DEAREST MARY,

WE have been delayed in this city four hours, for the Austrian minister's passport, but are now on the point of setting out with a vetturino, who engages to take us on the third day to Padua ; that is, we shall only sleep three nights on the road. * * * * * * Yesterday's journey, performed in a one-horse cabriolet, almost without springs, over a rough road, was excessively fatiguing.   *** suffered most from it ; for, as to myself, there are occasions in which fatigue seems a useful medicine, as I have felt no pain in my side—a most delightful respite—since I left you.   The country was various and exceedingly beautiful.   Sometimes there were those low cultivated lands, with their vine festoons, and large bunches of grapes just becoming purple—at others we passed between high mountains, crowned with some of the most majestic Gothic ruins I ever saw, which frowned from the bare precipices, or were half

seen among the olive copses. As we approached
Florence, the country became cultivated to a very high
degree, the plain was filled with the most beautiful
villas, and, as far as the eye could reach, the mountains
were covered with them ; for the plains are bounded on
all sides by blue and misty mountains. The vines are
here trailed on low trellises of reeds interwoven into
crosses to support them, and the grapes, now almost
ripe, are exceedingly abundant. You everywhere meet
those teams of beautiful white oxen, which are now
labouring the little vine-divided fields with their Virgilian
ploughs and carts. Florence itself, that is the Lung'
Arno (for I have seen no more), I think is the most
beautiful city I have yet seen. It is surrounded with
cultivated hills, and from the bridge which crosses the
broad channel of the Arno, the view is the most animated
and elegant I ever saw. You see three or four bridges,
one apparently supported by Corinthian pillars, and the
white sails of the boats, relieved by the deep green of
the forest, which comes to the water's edge, and the
sloping hills covered with bright villas on every side.
Domes and steeples rise on all sides, and the cleanliness
is remarkably great. On the other side there are the
foldings of the Vale of Arno above ; first the hills of
olive and vine, then the chesnut woods, and then the
blue and misty pine forests, which invest the aerial
Apennines, that fade in the distance. I have seldom
seen a city so lovely at first sight as Florence.

We shall travel hence within a few hours, with the
speed of the post, since the distance is 190 miles, and
we are to do it in three days, besides the half day, which
is somewhat more than sixty miles a day. We have
now got a comfortable carriage and two mules, and,
thanks to Paolo, have made a very decent bargain,
comprising everything, to Padua. I should say we
had delightful fruit for breakfast,—figs, very fine—and
peaches, unfortunately gathered before they were ripe,

whose smell was like what one fancies of the wakening of Paradise flowers.

Well, my dearest Mary, are you very lonely ? Tell me truth, my sweetest, do you ever cry ? I shall hear from you once at Venice, and once on my return here. If you love me you will keep up your spirits—and, at all events, tell me truth about it ; for, I assure you, I am not of a disposition to be flattered by your sorrow, though I should be by your cheerfulness ; and, above all, by seeing such fruits of my absence as were produced when we were at Geneva. What acquaintances have you made ? I might have travelled to Padua with a German, who had just come from Rome, and had scarce recovered from a malaria fever, caught in the Pontine Marshes, a week or two since ; and I conceded to ***'s entreaties—and to *your* absent suggestions, and omitted the opportunity, although I have no great faith in such species of contagion. It is not very hot—not at all too much so for my sensations, and the only thing that incommodes me are the gnats at night, who roar like so many humming tops in one's ear—and I do not always find zanzariere. How is Willmouse and little Clara ? They must be kissed for me—and you must particularly remember to speak my name to William, and see that he does not quite forget me before I return. Adieu—my dearest girl, I think that we shall soon meet. I shall write again from Venice. Adieu, dear Mary !

I have been reading the " Noble Kinsmen," in which, with the exception of that lovely scene, to which you added so much grace in reading to me, I have been disappointed. The Jailor's Daughter is a poor imitation, and deformed. The whole story wants moral discrimination and modesty. I do not believe Shake-speare wrote a word of it.

TO MRS. SHELLEY

(BAGNI DI LUCCA).

Venice, Sunday morning.
(August 23rd, 1818.)

MY DEAREST MARY,

WE arrived here last night at twelve o'clock, and it is now before breakfast the next morning. I can, of course, tell you nothing of the future ; and though I shall not close this letter till post time, yet I do not know exactly when that is. Yet, if you are very impatient, look along the letter and you will see another date, when I may have something to relate.

I came from Padua hither in a gondola, and the gondoliere, among other things, without any hint on my part, began talking of Lord Byron. He said he was a *giovinotto Inglese*, with a *nome stravagante*, who lived very luxuriously, and spent great sums of money. This man, it seems, was one of Lord Byron's gondolieri. No sooner had we arrived at the inn, than the waiter began talking about him — said, that* he frequented Mrs. H.'s *conversazioni* very much.

Our journey from Florence to Padua contained nothing which may not be related another time. At Padua, as I said, we took a gondola—and left it at three o'clock. These gondolas are the most beautiful and convenient boats in the world. They are finely carpeted and furnished with black, and painted black. The couches on which you lean are extraordinarily soft, and are so disposed as to be the most comfortable to those who lean or sit. The windows have at will either venetian plate-glass flowered, or venetian blinds, or blinds of black cloth to shut out the light. The weather here is extremely cold—indeed, sometimes very painfully so, and yesterday it began to rain. We passed the laguna in the middle of the night in a most violent storm of wind, rain, and lightning. It was very curious to observe the elements above in a state of such tremendous convulsion, and the surface of the water almost calm; for these lagunas, though five miles broad, a space enough in a storm to sink a gondola, are so shallow that the boatmen drive the boat along with a pole. The sea-water, furiously agitated by the wind, shone with sparkles like stars. Venice, now hidden and now disclosed by the driving rain, shone dimly with its lights. We were all this while safe and comfortable. Well, adieu, dearest: I shall, as Miss Byron says,* resume the pen in the evening.

Sunday Night, 5 o'clock in the Morning.

Well, I will try to relate everything in its order.

*   *   *   *   *

At three o'clock I called on Lord Byron: he was delighted to see me.

He took me in his gondola across the laguna to a long sandy island, which defends Venice from the Adriatic. When we disembarked, we found his horses waiting for us, and we rode along the sands of the sea, talking. Our conversation consisted in histories of his wounded feelings, and questions as to my affairs, and great professions of friendship and regard for me. He said, that if he had been in England at the time of the Chancery affair, he would have moved heaven and earth to have prevented such a decision. We talked of literary matters, his Fourth Canto, which, he says, is very good, and indeed repeated some stanzas of great energy to me. When we returned to his palace—which,

* * * (*The letter is here torn.*)

The Hoppners are the most amiable people I ever knew. They are much attached to each other, and

* *i.e.,* Harriet Byron, in Richardson's novel of *Sir Charles Grandison.*—ED.

have a nice little boy, seven months old. Mr. H. paints beautifully, and this excursion, which he has just put off, was an expedition to the Julian Alps, in this neighbourhood—for the sake of sketching, to procure winter employment. He has only a fortnight's leisure, and he has sacrificed two days of it to strangers whom he never saw before. Mrs. H. has hazel eyes and sweet looks.

(*Paper torn.*)

Well, but the time presses, I am now going to the banker's to send you money for the journey, which I shall address to you at Florence, Post-office. Pray come instantly to Este, where I shall be waiting in the utmost anxiety for your arrival. You can pack up directly you get this letter, and employ the next day on that. The day after, get up at four o'clock, and go post to Lucca, where you will arrive at six. Then take a vetturino for Florence to arrive the same evening. From Florence to Este is three days' vetturino journey —and you could not, I think, do it quicker by the post. Make Paolo take you to good inns, as we found very bad ones, and pray avoid the Tre Mori at Bologna, *perche vi sono cose inespressibili nei letti.* I do not think you can, but *try* to get from Florence to Bologna in one day. Do not take the post, for it is not much faster, and very expensive. I have been obliged to decide on all these things without you : I have done for the best – and, my own beloved Mary, you must soon come and scold me if I have done wrong, and kiss me if I have done right—for, I am sure, I do not know which—and it is only the event that can show. We shall at least be saved the trouble of introduction, and have formed acquaintance with a lady who is so good, so beautiful, so angelically mild, that were she as wise too, she would be quite a ***. Her eyes are like a reflection of yours. Her manners are like yours when you know and like a person.

Do you know, dearest, how this letter was written ? By scraps and patches, and interrupted every minute. The gondola is now come to take me to the banker's. Este is a little place, and the house found without diffi- culty. I shall count four days for this letter : one day for packing, four for coming here—and on the ninth or tenth day we shall meet.

I am too late for the post—but I send an express to overtake it. Enclosed is an order for fifty pounds. If you knew all that I had to do !—

Dearest love, be well, be happy, come to me—con- fide in your own constant and affectionate

P. B. S.

Kiss the blue-eyed darlings for me, and do not let William forget me. Clara cannot recollect me.

TO MRS. SHELLEY

(*I Cappuccini—Este*).

Padua, mezzogiorno.
(*Sept.* 22, 1818.)

MY BEST MARY,

I FOUND at Mount Selice a favourable opportunity for going to Venice, where I shall try to make some arrangement for you and little Ca.* to come for some days, and shall meet you, if I do not write anything in the mean time, at Padua, on Thursday morning. C. says she is obliged to come to see the Medico, whom we missed this morning, and who has appointed as the only hour at which he can be at leisure—half-past eight in the morning. You must, therefore, arrange matters so that you should come to the Stella d'Oro a little

* Clara, born at Marlow, Sept. 3, 1817.—ED.

before that hour—a thing to be accomplished only by setting out at half-past three in the morning. You will by this means arrive at Venice very early in the day, and avoid the heat, which might be bad for the babe, and take the time, when she would at least sleep great part of the time. C. will return with the return carriage, and I shall meet you, or send to you at Padua.

Meanwhile remember Charles the First—and do you be prepared to bring at least *some* of Myrra translated ; bring the book also with you, and the sheets of " Prometheus Unbound," which you will find numbered from one to twenty-six on the table of the pavilion. My poor little Clara, how is she to-day? Indeed I am somewhat uneasy about her, and though I feel secure that there is no danger, it would be very comfortable to have some reasonable person's opinion about her. The Medico at Padua is certainly a man in great practice, but I confess he does not satisfy me.

Am I not like a wild swan to be gone so suddenly? But, in fact, to set off alone to Venice required an exertion. I felt myself capable of making it, and I knew that you desired it. What will not be—if so it is destined the lonely journey through that wide, cold France? But we shall see.

Adieu, my dearest love—remember Charles I. and Myrra. I have been already imagining how you will conduct some scenes. The second volume of " St Leon " begins with this proud and true sentiment— " There is nothing which the human mind can conceive, which it may not execute." Shakespeare was only a human being.

Adieu till Thursday.   Your ever affectionate

P. B. S.

TO THOMAS LOVE PEACOCK.

Este, October 8, 1818.

MY DEAR PEACOCK,

I HAVE not written to you, I think, for six weeks. But I have been on the point of writing many times, and have often felt that I had many things to say. But I have not been without events to disturb and distract me, amongst which is the death of my little girl. She died of a disorder peculiar to the climate. We have all had bad spirits enough, and I, in addition, bad health. I *intend* to be better soon : there is no malady, bodily or mental, which does not either kill or is killed.

We left the Baths of Lucca, I think, the day after I wrote to you—on a visit to Venice—partly for the sake of seeing the city. We made a very delightful acquaintance there with a Mr. and Mrs. Hoppner, the gentleman an Englishman, and the lady a Swissesse, mild and beautiful, and unprejudiced, in the best sense of the word. The kind attentions of these people made our short stay at Venice very pleasant. I saw Lord Byron, and really hardly knew him again ; he is changed into the liveliest and happiest-looking man I ever met. He read me the first canto of his " Don Juan "—a thing in the style of Beppo, but infinitely better, and dedicated to Southey, in ten or a dozen stanzas, more like a mixture of wormwood and verdigris than satire. Venice is a wonderfully fine city. The approach to it over the laguna, with its domes and turrets glittering in a long line over the blue waves, is one of the finest architectural delusions in the world. It seems to have—and literally it has—its foundations in the sea. The silent streets are paved with water, and you hear nothing but the dashing of the oars, and the occasional cries of the gondolieri. I heard nothing of Tasso. The gondolas themselves

are things of a most romantic and picturesque appearance ; I can only compare them to moths of which a
coffin might have been the chrysalis.   They are hung
with black, and painted black, and carpeted with grey ;
they curl at the prow and stern, and at the former there
is a nondescript beak of shining steel, which glitters at
the end of its long black mass.

The Doge's palace, with its library, is a fine monument of aristocratic power.   I saw the dungeons, where
these scoundrels used to torment their victims.   They
are of three kinds—one adjoining the place of trial,
where the prisoners destined to immediate execution
were kept.   I could not descend into them, because the
day on which I visited it, was festa.   Another under the
leads of the palace, where the sufferers were roasted to
death or madness by the ardours of an Italian sun : and
others called the Pozzi—or wells, deep underneath, and
communicating with those on the roof by secret passages
—where the prisoners were confined sometimes half up
to their middles in stinking water.   When the French
came here, they found only one old man in the dungeons,
and he could not speak.   But Venice, which was once
a tyrant, is now the next worse thing, a slave ; for in
fact it ceased to be free, or worth our regret as a nation,
from the moment that the oligarchy usurped the rights
of the people.   Yet, I do not imagine that it was ever
so degraded as it has been since the French, and
especially the Austrian yoke.   The Austrians take sixty
per cent. in taxes, and impose free quarters on the
inhabitants.   A horde of German soldiers, as vicious
and more disgusting than the Venetians themselves,
insult these miserable people.   I had no conception
of the excess to which avarice, cowardice, superstition,
ignorance, passionless lust, and all the inexpressible
brutalities which degrade human nature, could be
carried, until I had passed a few days at Venice.

We have been living this last month near the little

town from which I date this letter, in a very pleasant villa which has been lent to us, and we are now on the point of proceeding to Florence, Rome, and Naples—at which last city we shall spend the winter, and return northwards in the spring.   Behind us here are the Euganean hills, not so beautiful as those of the Bagni di Lucca, with Arquà, where Petrarch's house and tomb are religiously preserved and visited.   At the end of our garden is an extensive Gothic castle, now the habitation of owls and bats, where the Medici family resided before they came to Florence.   We see before us the wide flat plains of Lombardy, in which we see the sun and moon rise and set, and the evening star, and all the golden magnificence of autumnal clouds.   But I reserve wonder for Naples.

I have been writing—and indeed have just finished the first act of a lyric and classical drama, to be called "Prometheus Unbound."   Will you tell me what there is in Cicero about a drama supposed to have been written by Æschylus under this title?

I ought to say that I have just read Malthus in a French translation.   Malthus is a very clever man, and the world would be a great gainer if it would seriously take his lessons into consideration, if it were capable of attending seriously to anything but mischief—but what on earth does he mean by some of his inferences?

Yours ever faithfully,
P. B. S.

I will write again from Rome and Florence—in better spirits, and to more agreeable purpose, I hope.   You saw those beautiful stanzas in the fourth canto * about the Nymph Egeria.   Well, I did not whisper a word about nympholepsy : I hope you acquit me—and I hope you will not carry delicacy so far as to let this suppress anything nympholeptic.

* Of *Childe Harold.*—Ed.

TO THOMAS LOVE PEACOCK.

Ferrara, Nov. 8th, 1818.

MY DEAR PEACOCK,

WE left Este yesterday on our journey towards
Naples. The roads were particularly bad; we have,
therefore, accomplished only two days' journey, of
eighteen and twenty-four miles each, and you may
imagine that our horses must be tolerably good ones, to
drag our carriage, with five people and heavy luggage,
through deep and clayey roads. The roads are, however, good during the rest of the way.

The country is flat, but intersected by lines of wood,
trellised with vines, whose broad leaves are now stamped
with the redness of their decay. Every here and there
one sees people employed in agricultural labours, and
the plough, the harrow, or the cart, drawn by long
teams of milk-white or dove-coloured oxen of immense
size and exquisite beauty. This, indeed, might be the
country of Pasiphaes. In one farm-yard I was shown
sixty-three of these lovely oxen, tied to their stalls, in
excellent condition. A farm-yard in this part of Italy
is somewhat different from one in England. First, the
house, which is large and high, with strange-looking
unpainted window-shutters, generally closed, and dreary
beyond conception. The farm-yard and out-buildings,
however, are usually in the neatest order. The thresh-
ing-floor is not under cover, but like that described in
the Georgics, usually flattened by a broken column, and
neither the mole, nor the toad, nor the ant, can find on
its area a crevice for their dwelling. Around it, at this
season, are piled the stacks of the leaves and stalks of
Indian corn, which has lately been threshed and dried
upon its surface. At a little distance are vast heaps of
many-coloured zucchi or pumpkins, some of enormous
size, piled as winter food for the hogs. There are

turkeys, too, and fowls wandering about, and two or three dogs, who bark with a sharp hylactism. The people who are occupied with the care of these things seem neither ill-clothed nor ill-fed, and the blunt in-civility of their manners has an English air with it, very discouraging to those who are accustomed to the im-pudent and polished lying of the inhabitants of the cities. I should judge the agricultural resources of this country to be immense, since it can wear so flourishing an appearance, in spite of the enormous discouragements which the various tyranny of the governments inflicts on it. I ought to say that one of the farms belongs to a Jew banker at Venice, another Shylock.—We arrived late at the inn where I now write; it was once the palace of a Venetian nobleman, and is now an excellent inn. To-morrow we are going to see the sights of Ferrara.

Nov. 9.

We have had heavy rain and thunder all night; and the former still continuing, we went in the carriage about the town. We went first to look at the cathedral, but the beggars very soon made us sound a retreat; so, whether, as it is said, there is a copy of a picture of Michael Angelo there or no, I cannot tell. At the public library we were more successful. This is, indeed, a magnificent establishment, containing, as they say, 160,000 volumes. We saw some illuminated manu-scripts of church music, with the verses of the psalms interlined between the square notes, each of which consisted of the most delicate tracery, in colours incon-ceivably vivid. They belonged to the neighbouring convent of Certolda, and are three or four hundred years old; but their hues are as fresh as if they had been executed yesterday. The tomb of Ariosto occupies one end of the largest saloon of which the library is composed; it is formed of various marbles, surmounted by an expressive bust of the poet, and subscribed with a few Latin verses, in a less miserable taste than those usually employed for similar purposes. But the most interesting exhibitions here, are the writings, &c., of Ariosto and Tasso, which are preserved, and were concealed from the undistinguishing depredations of the French with pious care. There is the arm-chair of Ariosto, an old plain wooden piece of furniture, the hard seat of which was once occupied by, but has now survived its cushion, as it has its master. I could fancy Ariosto sitting in it ; and the satires in his own handwriting which they unfold beside it, and the old bronze inkstand, loaded with figures, which belonged also to him. assists the willing delusion. This inkstand has an antique, rather than an ancient appearance. Three nymphs lean forth from the circumference, and on the top of the lid stands a cupid, winged and looking up, with a torch in one hand, his bow in the other, and his quiver beside him. A medal was bound round the skeleton of Ariosto, with his likeness impressed upon it. I cannot say I think it had much native expression, but, perhaps, the artist was in fault. On the reverse is a hand, cutting with a pair of scissors the tongue from a serpent, upraised from the grass, with this legend —*Pro bono malum.* What this reverse of the boasted Christian maxim means, or how it applies to Ariosto, either as a satirist or a serious writer, I cannot exactly tell. The cicerone attempted to explain, and it is to his commentary that my bewildering is probably due—if, indeed, the meaning be very plain, as is possibly the case.

There is here a manuscript of the entire Gerusalemme Liberata, written by Tasso's own hand ; a manuscript of some poems, written in prison, to the Duke Alfonso ; and the satires of Ariosto, written also by his own hand ; and the Pastor Fido of Guarini. The Gerusalemme, though it had evidently been copied and recopied, is interlined, particularly towards the end, with numerous corrections. The handwriting of Ariosto is a small, firm, and pointed character, expressing, as I should say, a strong and keen, but circumscribed energy of mind ; that of Tasso is large, free, and flowing, except that there is a checked expression in the midst of its flow, which brings the letters into a smaller compass than one expected from the beginning of the word. It is the symbol of an intense and earnest mind, exceeding at times its own depth, and admonished to return by the chillness of the waters of oblivion striking upon its adventurous feet. You know I always seek in what I see the manifestation of something beyond the present and tangible object ; and as we do not agree in physiognomy, so we may not agree now. But my business is to relate my own sensations, and not to attempt to inspire others with them. Some of the MSS. of Tasso were sonnets to his persecutor, which contain a great deal of what is called flattery. If Alfonso's ghost were asked how he felt those praises now, I wonder what he would say. But to me there is much more to pity than to condemn in these entreaties and praises of Tasso. It is as a bigot prays to and praises his god, whom he knows to be the most remorseless, capricious, and inflexible of tyrants, but whom he knows also to be omnipotent. Tasso's situation was widely different from that of any persecuted being of the present day ; for, from the depth of dungeons, public opinion might now at length be awakened to an echo that would startle the oppressor. But then there was no hope. There is something irresistibly pathetic to me in the sight of Tasso's own handwriting, moulding expressions of adulation and entreaty to a deaf and stupid tyrant, in an age when the most heroic virtue would have exposed its possessor to hopeless persecution, and—such is the alliance between virtue and genius—which unoffending genius could not escape.

We went afterwards to see his prison in the hospital of Sant' Anna, and I enclose you a piece of the wood of the very door, which for seven years and three months divided this glorious being from the air and the light which had nourished in him those influences which he has communicated, through his poetry, to thousands. The dungeon is low and dark, and, when I say that it is really a very decent dungeon, I speak as one who has seen the prisons in the Doge's palace of Venice. But it is a horrible abode for the coarsest and meanest thing that ever wore the shape of man, much more for one of delicate susceptibilities and elevated fancies. It is low, and has a grated window, and being sunk some feet below the level of the earth, is full of unwholesome damps. In the darkest corner is a mark in the wall where the chains were rivetted, which bound him hand and foot. After some time, at the instance of some Cardinal, his friend, the Duke allowed his victim a fireplace ; the mark where it was walled up yet remains.

At the entrance of the Liceo, where the library is, we were met by a penitent ; his form was completely enveloped in a ghost-like drapery of white flannel ; his bare feet were sandalled ; and there was a kind of net-work visor drawn over his eyes, so as entirely to conceal his face. I imagine that this man had been adjudged to suffer this penance for some crime known only to himself and his confessor, and this kind of exhibition is a striking instance of the power of the Catholic superstition over the human mind. He passed, rattling his wooden box for charity.

Adieu.—You will hear from me again before I arrive at Naples.

Yours, ever sincerely,

P. B. S.

TO THOMAS LOVE PEACOCK.

Bologna, Monday, Nov. 9th, 1818.

MY DEAR PEACOCK,

I HAVE seen a quantity of things here—churches, palaces, statues, fountains, and pictures ; and my brain is at this moment like a portfolio of an architect, or a print-shop, or a common-place book. I will try to re-collect something of what I have seen ; for, indeed, it requires, if it will obey, an act of volition. First, we went to the cathedral, which contains nothing remark-able, except a kind of shrine, or rather a marble canopy, loaded with sculptures, and supported on four marble columns. We went then to a palace—I am sure I forget the name of it—where we saw a large gallery of pictures. Of course, in a picture gallery you see three hundred pictures you forget, for one you remember. I remember, however, an interesting picture by Guido, of the Rape of Proserpine, in which Proserpine casts back her languid and half-unwilling eyes, as it were, to the flowers she had left ungathered in the fields of Enna. There was an exquisitely executed piece of Correggio, about four saints, one of whom seemed to have a pet dragon in a leash. I was told that it was the devil who was bound in that style—but who can make anything of four saints ? For what can they be supposed to be about? There was one painting, indeed, by this master, Christ beatified, inexpressibly fine. It is a half figure, seated on a mass of clouds, tinged with an ethereal, rose-like lustre ; the arms are expanded ; the whole frame seems dilated with expression ; the countenance is heavy, as it were, with the weight of the rapture of the spirit ; the lips parted, but scarcely parted, with the breath of intense but regulated passion ; the eyes are calm and benignant ; the whole features harmonised in majesty and sweetness. The hair is parted on the forehead, and falls in heavy locks on each side. It is motionless, but seems as if the faintest breath would move it. The colouring, I suppose, must be very good, if I could remark and understand it. The sky is of a pale aerial orange, like the tints of latest sunset ; it does not seem painted around and beyond the figure, but everything seems to have absorbed, and to have been penetrated by its hues. I do not think we saw any other of Correggio, but this specimen gives me a very exalted idea of his powers.

We went to see heaven knows how many more palaces—Ranuzzi, Marriscalchi, Aldobrandi. If you want Italian names for any purpose, here they are ; I should be glad of them if I was writing a novel. I saw many more of Guido. One, a Samson drinking water out of an ass's jaw-bone, in the midst of the slaughtered Philistines. Why he is supposed to do this, God, who gave him this jaw-bone, alone knows—but certain it is, that the painting is a very fine one. The figure of Samson stands in strong relief in the foreground, coloured, as it were, in the hues of human life, and full of strength and elegance. Round him lie the Philistines in all the attitudes of death. One prone, with the slight convulsion of pain just passing from his forehead, whilst on his lips and chin death lies as heavy as sleep. Another leaning on his arm, with his hand, white and motion-less, hanging out beyond. In the distance, more dead bodies ; and, still further beyond, the blue sea and the blue mountains, and one white and tranquil sail.

There is a Murder of the Innocents, also, by Guido, finely coloured, with much fine expression—but the subject is very horrible, and it seemed deficient in strength—at least, you require the highest ideal energy, the most poetical and exalted conception of the subject, to reconcile you to such a contemplation. There was a Jesus Christ crucified, by the same, very fine. One gets tired, indeed, whatever may be the conception and execution of it, of seeing that monotonous and agonised form for ever exhibited in one prescriptive attitude of torture. But the Magdalen, clinging to the cross, with the look of passive and gentle despair beaming from beneath her bright flaxen hair, and the figure of St. John, with his looks uplifted in passionate compassion ; his hands clasped, and his fingers twisting themselves together, as it were, with involuntary anguish ; his feet almost writhing up from the ground with the same sympathy ; and the whole of this arrayed in colours of a diviner nature, yet most like nature's self. Of the contemplation of this one would never weary.

There was a " Fortune " too, of Guido ; a piece of mere beauty. There was the figure of Fortune on a globe, eagerly proceeding onwards, and Love was trying to catch her back by the hair, and her face was half turned towards him ; her long chesnut hair was floating in the stream of the wind, and threw its shadow over her fair forehead. Her hazel eyes were fixed on her pursuer, with a meaning look of playfulness, and a light smile was hovering on her lips. The colours which arrayed her delicate limbs were ethereal and warm.

But, perhaps, the most interesting of all the pictures of Guido which I saw, was a Madonna Lattante. She is leaning over her child, and the maternal feelings with which she is pervaded are shadowed forth on her soft and gentle countenance, and in her simple and affectionate gestures—there is what an unfeeling observer would call a dulness in the expression of her face ; her eyes are almost closed ; her lip depressed ; there is a serious, and even a heavy relaxation, as it were, of all the muscles which are called into action by ordinary emotions ; but it is only as if the spirit of love, almost insupportable from its intensity, were brooding over and weighing down the soul, or whatever it is, without which the material frame is inanimate and inexpressive.

There is another painter here, called Franceschini, a

Bolognese, who, though certainly very inferior to Guido, is yet a person of excellent powers. One entire church, that of Santa Catarina, is covered by his works. I do not know whether any of his pictures have ever been seen in England. His colouring is less warm than that of Guido, but nothing can be more clear and delicate, it is as if he could have dipped his pencil in the hues of some serenest and star-shining twilight. His forms have the same delicacy and aerial loveliness ; their eyes are all bright with innocence and love ; their lips scarce divided by some gentle and sweet emotion. His winged children are the loveliest ideal beings ever created by the human mind. These are generally, whether in the capacity of Cherubim or Cupid, accessories to the rest of the picture ; and the underplot of their lovely and infantine play is something almost pathetic, from the excess of its unpretending beauty. One of the best of his pieces is an Annunciation of the Virgin ; the Angel is beaming in beauty ; the Virgin, soft, retiring, and simple.

We saw besides one picture of Raphael—St. Cecilia : this is in another and higher style ; you forget that it is a picture as you look at it ; and yet it is most unlike any of those things which we call reality. It is of the inspired and ideal kind, and seems to have been conceived and executed in a similar state of feeling to that which produced among the ancients those perfect specimens of poetry and sculpture which are the baffling models of succeeding generations. There is a unity and a perfection in it of an incommunicable kind. The central figure, St. Cecilia, seems rapt in such inspiration as produced her image in the painter's mind ; her deep, dark, eloquent eyes lifted up ; her chesnut hair flung back from her forehead—she holds an organ in her hands—her countenance, as it were, calmed by the depth of its passion and rapture, and penetrated throughout with the warm and radiant light of life. She is listening to the music of heaven, and, as I

imagine, has just ceased to sing, for the four figures
that surround her evidently point, by their attitudes,
towards her; particularly St. John, who, with a tender
yet impassioned gesture, bends his countenance towards
her, languid with the depth of his emotion. At her
feet lie various instruments of music, broken and un-
strung. Of the colouring I do not speak; it eclipses
nature, yet it has all her truth and softness.

We saw some pictures of Domenichino, Carracci,
Albano, Guercino, Elisabetta Sirani. The two former,
remember, I do not pretend to taste—I cannot admire.
Of the latter there are some beautiful Madonnas. There
are several of Guercino, which they said were very fine.
I dare say they were, for the strength and complication of his figures made my head turn round. One,
indeed, was certainly powerful. It was the representation
of the founder of the Carthusians exercising his austerities
in the desert, with a youth as his attendant, kneeling
beside him at an altar : on another altar stood a skull
and a crucifix; and around were the rocks and the trees
of the wilderness. I never saw such a figure as this
fellow. His face was wrinkled like a dried snake's skin,
and drawn in long hard lines : his very hands were
wrinkled. He looked like an animated mummy. He
was clothed in a loose dress of death-coloured flannel,
such as you might fancy a shroud might be, after it had
wrapt a corpse a month or two. It had a yellow, putre-
fied, ghastly hue, which it cast on all the objects around,
so that the hands and face of the Carthusian and his
companion were jaundiced by this sepulchral glimmer.
Why write books against religion, when we may hang
up such pictures? But the world either will not or
cannot see. The gloomy effect of this was softened,
and, at the same time, its sublimity diminished, by the
figure of the Virgin and Child in the sky, looking down
with admiration on the monk, and a beautiful flying
figure of an angel.

Enough of pictures. I saw the place where Guido and his mistress, Elisabetta Sirani, were buried. This lady was poisoned at the age of twenty-six, by another lover, a rejected one, of course. Our guide said she was very ugly, and that we might see her portrait to-morrow.

Well, good-night, for the present. "To-morrow to fresh fields and pastures new."

Nov. 10.

To-day we first went to see those divine pictures of Raffael and Guido again, and then rode up the mountains, behind this city, to visit a chapel dedicated to the Madonna. It made me melancholy to see that they had been varnishing and restoring some of these pictures, and that even some had been pierced by the French bayonets. These are symptoms of the mortality of man ; and, perhaps, few of his works are more evanescent than paintings. Sculpture retains its freshness for twenty centuries—the Apollo and the Venus are as they were. But books are perhaps the only productions of man coeval with the human race. Sophocles and Shakespeare can be produced and reproduced for ever. But how evanescent are paintings, and must necessarily be. Those of Zeuxis and Apelles are no more, and perhaps they bore the same relation to Homer and Æschylus, that those of Guido and Raffael bear to Dante and Petrarch. There is one refuge from the despondency of this contemplation. The material part, indeed, of their works must perish, but they survive in the mind of man, and the remembrances connected with them are transmitted from generation to generation. The poet embodies them in his creations ; the systems of philosophers are modelled to gentleness by their contemplation ; opinion, that legislator, is infected with their influence ; men become better and wiser ; and the unseen seeds are perhaps thus sown, which shall produce a plant more excellent even than that from which they fell. But all this might as well be said or thought at Marlow as Bologna. The chapel of the Madonna is a very pretty Corinthian building—very beautiful, indeed. It commands a fine view of these fertile plains, the many-folded Apennines, and the city. I have just returned from a moonlight walk through Bologna. It is a city of colonnades, and the effect of moonlight is strikingly picturesque. There are two towers here—one 400 feet high —ugly things, built of brick, which lean both different ways ; and with the delusion of moonlight shadows, you might almost fancy that the city is rocked by an earthquake. They say they were built so on purpose ; but I observe in all the plain of Lombardy the church towers lean.

Adieu.—God grant you patience to read this long letter, and courage to support the expectation of the next. Pray part them from the *Cobbetts* on your breakfast table—they may fight it out in your mind.

Yours ever, most sincerely,

P. B. S.

TO THOMAS LOVE PEACOCK.

Rome, November 20th, 1818.

MY DEAR PEACOCK,

BEHOLD me in the capital of the vanished world. But I have seen nothing except St. Peter's and the Vatican, overlooking the city in the mist of distance, and the Dogana, where they took us to have our luggage examined, which is built between the ruins of a temple to Antoninus Pius. The Corinthian columns rise over the dwindled palaces of the modern town, and the wrought cornice is changed on one side, as it were, to masses of wave-worn precipice, which overhang you, far, far on high.

I take advantage of this rainy evening, and before Rome has effaced all other recollections, to endeavour to recall the vanished scenes through which we have passed. We left Bologna, I forget on what day, and passing by Rimini, Fano, and Foligno, along the Via Flaminia and Terni, have arrived at Rome after ten days' somewhat tedious, but most interesting, journey. The most remarkable things we saw were the Roman excavations in the rock, and the great waterfall of Terni. Of course you have heard that there are a Roman bridge and a triumphal arch at Rimini, and in what excellent taste they are built. The bridge is not unlike the Strand bridge, but more bold in proportion, and of course infinitely smaller. From Fano we left the coast of the Adriatic, and entered the Apennines, following the course of the Metaurus, the banks of which were the scene of the defeat of Asdrubal : and it is said (you can refer to the book) that Livy has given a very exact and animated description of it. I forget all about it, but shall look as soon as our boxes are opened. Following the river, the vale contracts, the banks of the river become steep and rocky, the forests of oak and ilex which overhang its emerald-coloured stream, cling to their abrupt precipices. About four miles from Fossombrone, the river forces for itself a passage between the walls and toppling precipices of the loftiest Apennines, which are here rifted to their base, and undermined by the narrow and tumultuous torrent. It was a cloudy morning, and we had no conception of the scene that awaited us. Suddenly the low clouds were struck by the clear north wind, and like curtains of the finest gauze, removed one by one, were drawn from before the mountain, whose heaven-cleaving pinnacles and black crags overhanging one another, stood at length defined in the light of day. The road runs parallel to the river, at a considerable height, and is carried through the mountain by a vaulted cavern. The marks of the chisel of the legionaries of the Roman Consul are yet evident.

We passed on day after day, until we came to Spoleto, I think the most romantic city I ever saw. There is here an aqueduct of astonishing elevation, which unites two rocky mountains,—there is the path of a torrent below, whitening the green dell with its broad and barren track of stones, and above there is a castle, apparently of great strength and of tremendous magnitude, which overhangs the city, and whose marble bastions are perpendicular with the precipice. I never saw a more impressive picture ; in which the shapes of nature are of the grandest order, but over which the creations of man, sublime from their antiquity and greatness, seem to predominate. The castle was built by Belisarius or Narses, I forget which, but was of that epoch.

From Spoleto we went to Terni, and saw the cataract of the Velino. The glaciers of Montanvert and the source of the Arveiron is the grandest spectacle I ever saw. This is the second. Imagine a river sixty feet in breadth, with a vast volume of waters, the outlet of a great lake among the higher mountains, falling 300 feet into a sightless gulf of snow-white vapour, which bursts up for ever and for ever from a circle of black crags, and thence leaping downwards, makes five or six other cataracts, each fifty or a hundred feet high, which exhibit, on a smaller scale, and with beautiful and sublime variety, the same appearances. But words (and far less could painting) will not express it. Stand upon the brink of the platform of cliff, which is directly oppo-site. You see the ever-moving water stream down. It comes in thick and tawny folds, flaking off like solid snow gliding down a mountain. It does not seem hollow within, but without it is unequal, like the folding of linen thrown carelessly down ; your eye follows it,

and it is lost below ; not in the black rocks which gird
it around, but in its own foam and spray, in the cloud-
like vapours boiling up from below, which is not like
rain, nor mist, nor spray, nor foam, but water, in a
shape wholly unlike anything I ever saw before. It is
as white as snow, but thick and impenetrable to the
eye. The very imagination is bewildered in it. A
thunder comes up from the abyss wonderful to hear ;
for, though it ever sounds, it is never the same, but,
modulated by the changing motion, rises and falls
intermittingly ; we passed half an hour in one spot
looking at it, and thought but a few minutes had gone
by. The surrounding scenery is, in its kind, the
loveliest and most sublime that can be conceived. In
our first walk we passed through some olive groves,
of large and ancient trees, whose hoary and twisted
trunks leaned in all directions. We then crossed a
path of orange trees by the river side, laden with their
golden fruit, and came to a forest of ilex of a large
size, whose evergreen and acorn-bearing boughs were
intertwined over our winding path. Around, hemming
in the narrow vale, were pinnacles of lofty mountains
of pyramidical rock clothed with all evergreen plants
and trees ; the vast pine whose feathery foliage trembled
in the blue air, the ilex, that ancestral inhabitant of
these mountains, the arbutus with its crimson-coloured
fruit and glittering leaves. After an hour's walk, we
came beneath the cataract of Terni, within the distance
of half a mile ; nearer you cannot approach, for the
Nar, which has here its confluence with the Velino,
bars the passage. We then crossed the river formed
by this confluence, over a narrow natural bridge of
rock, and saw the cataract from the platform I first
mentioned. We think of spending some time next
year near this waterfall. The inn is very bad, or we
should have stayed there longer.

We came from Terni last night to a place called

Nepi, and to-day arrived at Rome across the much-belied Campagna di Roma, a place I confess infinitely to my taste. It is a flattering picture of Bagshot Heath. But then there are the Apennines on one side, and Rome and St. Peter's on the other, and it is intersected by perpetual dells clothed with arbutus and ilex.

Adieu—very faithfully yours,

P. B. S.

TO THOMAS LOVE PEACOCK.

Naples, December 22, 1818.

MY DEAR PEACOCK

I HAVE received a letter from you here, dated November 1st; you see the reciprocation of letters from the term of our travels is more slow. I entirely agree with what you say about *Childe Harold.* The spirit in which it is written is, if insane, the most wicked and mischievous insanity that ever was given forth. It is a kind of obstinate and self-willed folly, in which he hardens himself. I remonstrated with him in vain on the tone of mind from which such a view of things alone arises. For its real root is very different from its apparent one. Nothing can be less sublime than the true source of these expressions of contempt and desperation. The fact is, that first, the Italian women with whom he associates, are perhaps the most contemptible of all who exist under the moon—the most ignorant, the most disgusting, the most bigoted; * * * * an ordinary Englishman cannot approach them. Well, Lord Byron is familiar with the lowest sort of these women, the people his gondolieri pick up in the streets. He associates with wretches who seem almost to have lost the gait and physiognomy of man, and who do not scruple to avow practices, which are

not only not named, but I believe seldom even conceived in England. He says he disapproves, but he
endures. He is heartily and deeply discontented with
himself; and contemplating in the distorted mirror
of his own thoughts the nature and the destiny of
man, what can he behold but objects of contempt
and despair? But that he is a great poet, I think
the address to Ocean proves. And he has a certain
degree of candour while you talk to him, but unfortunately it does not outlast your departure. No,
I do not doubt, and, for his sake, I ought to hope,
that his present career must end soon in some violent
circumstance.

Since I last wrote to you, I have seen the ruins of
Rome, the Vatican, St. Peter's, and all the miracles of
ancient and modern art contained in that majestic city.
The impression of it exceeds anything I have ever
experienced in my travels. We stayed there only a
week, intending to return at the end of February, and
devote two or three months to its mines of inexhaustible
contemplation, to which period I refer you for a minute
account of it. We visited the Forum and the ruins of
the Coliseum every day. The Coliseum is unlike any
work of human hands I ever saw before. It is of
enormous height and circuit, and the arches built of
massy stones are piled on one another, and jut into the
blue air, shattered into the forms of overhanging rocks.
It has been changed by time into the image of an
amphitheatre of rocky hills overgrown by the wild olive,
the myrtle, and the fig-tree, and threaded by little paths,
which wind among its ruined stairs and immeasurable
galleries: the copse-wood overshadows you as you
wander through its labyrinths, and the wild weeds of
this climate of flowers bloom under your feet. The
arena is covered with grass, and pierces, like the skirts
of a natural plain, the chasms of the broken arches
around. But a small part of the exterior circumference

remains—it is exquisitely light and beautiful ; and the effect of the perfection of its architecture, adorned with ranges of Corinthian pilasters, supporting a bold cornice, is such, as to diminish the effect of its greatness. The interior is all ruin. I can scarcely believe that when encrusted with Dorian marble and ornamented by columns of Egyptian granite its effect could have been so sublime and so impressive as in its present state. It is open to the sky, and it was the clear and sunny weather of the end of November in this climate when we visited it, day after day.

Near it is the arch of Constantine, or rather the arch of Trajan ; for the servile and avaricious senate of degraded Rome ordered that the monument of his predecessor should be demolished in order to dedicate one to the Christian reptile, who had crept among the blood of his murdered family to the supreme power. It is exquisitely beautiful and perfect. The Forum is a plain in the midst of Rome, a kind of desert full of heaps of stones and pits, and though so near the habitations of men, is the most desolate place you can conceive. The ruins of temples stand in and around it, shattered columns and ranges of others complete, supporting cornices of exquisite workmanship, and vast vaults of shattered domes distinct with regular compartments, once filled with sculptures of ivory or brass. The temples of Jupiter, and Concord, and Peace, and the Sun, and the Moon, and Vesta, are all within a short distance of this spot. Behold the wrecks of what a great nation once dedicated to the abstractions of the mind ! Rome is a city, as it were, of the dead, or rather of those who cannot die, and who survive the puny generations which inhabit and pass over the spot which they have made sacred to eternity. In Rome, at least in the first enthusiasm of your recognition of ancient time, you see nothing of the Italians. The nature of the city assists the delusion, for its vast and antique walls describe a circumference of sixteen miles, and thus the population is thinly scattered over this space, nearly as great as London. Wide wild fields are enclosed within it, and there are grassy lanes and copses winding among the ruins, and a great green hill, lonely and bare, which overhangs the Tiber. The gardens of the modern palaces are like wild woods of cedar, and cypress, and pine, and the neglected walks are overgrown with weeds. The English burying-place is a green slope near the walls, under the pyramidal tomb of Cestius, and is, I think, the most beautiful and solemn cemetery I ever beheld. To see the sun shining on its bright grass, fresh, when we first visited it, with the autumnal dews, and hear the whispering of the wind among the leaves of the trees which have overgrown the tomb of Cestius, and the soil which is stirring in the sun-warm earth, and to mark the tombs, mostly of women and young people who were buried there, one might, if one were to die, desire the sleep they seem to sleep. Such is the human mind, and so it peoples with its wishes vacancy and oblivion.

I have told you little about Rome; but I reserve the Pantheon, and St. Peter's, and the Vatican, and Raphael, for my return. About a fortnight ago I left Rome, and Mary and C—— followed in three days, for it was necessary to procure lodgings here without alighting at an inn. From my peculiar mode of travelling I saw little of the country, but could just observe that the wild beauty of the scenery and the barbarous ferocity of the inhabitants progressively increased. On entering Naples, the first circumstance that engaged my attention was an assassination. A youth ran out of a shop, pursued by a woman with a bludgeon, and a man armed with a knife. The man overtook him, and with one blow in the neck laid him dead in the road. On my expressing the emotions of horror and indignation which I felt, a Calabrian priest, who travelled with me, laughed heartily, and

attempted to quiz me, as what the English call a flat.
I never felt such an inclination to beat any one. Heaven
knows I have little power, but he saw that I looked
extremely displeased, and was silent. This same man,
a fellow of gigantic strength and stature, had expressed
the most frantic terror of robbers on the road ; he cried
at the sight of my pistol, and it had been with great difficulty that the joint exertions of myself and the vetturino
had quieted his hysterics.

But external nature in these delightful regions con-
trasts with and compensates for the deformity and
degradation of humanity. We have a lodging divided
from the sea by the royal gardens, and from our windows we see perpetually the blue waters of the bay,
forever changing, yet forever the same, and encompassed by the mountainous island of Capreæ, the lofty
peaks which overhang Salerno, and the woody hill of
Posilipo, whose promontories hide from us Misenum and
the lofty isle Inarime,* which, with its divided summit,
forms the opposite horn of the bay. From the pleasant
walks of the garden we see Vesuvius ; a smoke by day
and a fire by night is seen upon its summit, and the
glassy sea often reflects its light or shadow. The
climate is delicious. We sit without a fire, with the
windows open, and have almost all the productions of
an English summer. The weather is usually like what
Wordsworth calls " the first fine day of March ; " sometimes very much warmer, though perhaps it wants that
" each minute sweeter than before," which gives an in-
toxicating sweetness to the awakening of the earth from
its winter's sleep in England. We have made two
excursions, one to Baiæ and one to Vesuvius, and we
propose to visit, successively, the islands, Pæstum,
Pompeii, and Beneventum.

We set off an hour after sunrise one radiant morning
in a little boat ; there was not a cloud in the sky, nor a

* The ancient name of Ischia.—[*Note by Mrs. Shelley.*]

wave upon the sea, which was so translucent that you
could see the hollow caverns clothed with the glaucous
sea-moss, and the leaves and branches of those delicate
weeds that pave the unequal bottom of the water. As
noon approached, the heat, and especially the light,
became intense. We passed Posilipo, and came first
to the eastern point of the bay of Puzzoli, which is within
the great bay of Naples, and which again encloses that
of Baiæ. Here are lofty rocks and craggy islets, with
arches and portals of precipice standing in the sea, and
enormous caverns, which echoed faintly with the murmur of the languid tide. This is called La Scuola di
Virgilio. We then went directly across to the promontory of Misenum, leaving the precipitous island of Nisida
on the right. Here we were conducted to see the Mare
Morto, and the Elysian fields ; the spot on which Virgil
places the scenery of the Sixth Æneid. Though extremely beautiful, as a lake, and woody hills, and this
divine sky must make it, I confess my disappointment.
The guide showed us an antique cemetery, where the
niches used for placing the cinerary urns of the dead
yet remain. We then coasted the bay of Baiæ to the
left, in which we saw many picturesque and interesting
ruins ; but I have to remark that we never disembarked
but we were disappointed—while from the boat the
effect of the scenery was inexpressibly delightful. The
colours of the water and the air breathe over all things
here the radiance of their own beauty. After passing
the bay of Baiæ, and observing the ruins of its antique
grandeur standing like rocks in the transparent sea
under our boat, we landed to visit lake Avernus. We
passed through the cavern of the Sibyl (not Virgil's
Sibyl), which pierces one of the hills which circumscribe
the lake, and came to a calm and lovely basin of water,
surrounded by dark woody hills, and profoundly solitary.
Some vast ruins of the·temple of Pluto stand on a lawny
hill on one side of it, and are reflected in its windless

mirror. It is far more beautiful than the Elysian fields
—but there are all the materials for beauty in the latter,
and the Avernus was once a chasm of deadly and pesti-
lential vapours. About half a mile from Avernus, a
high hill, called Monte Novo, was thrown up by volcanic
fire.

Passing onward we came to Pozzoli, the ancient
Dicæarchea, where there are the columns remaining
of a temple to Serapis, and the wreck of an enormous
amphitheatre, changed, like the Coliseum, into a natural
hill of the overteeming vegetation. Here also is the
Solfatara, of which there is a poetical description in the
Civil War of Petronius, beginning—" Est locus," * and
in which the verses of the poet are infinitely finer than
what he describes, for it is not a very curious place.
After seeing these things we returned by moonlight to
Naples in our boat. What colours there were in the
sky, what radiance in the evening star, and how the
moon was encompassed by a light unknown to our
regions !

Our next excursion was to Vesuvius. We went to
Resina in a carriage, where Mary and I mounted mules,
and C—— was carried in a chair on the shoulders of
four men, much like a member of parliament after he
has gained his election, and looking, with less reason,
quite as frightened. So we arrived at the hermitage of
San Salvador, where an old hermit, belted with rope, set
forth the plates for our refreshment.

Vesuvius is, after the glaciers, the most impressive
exhibition of the energies of nature I ever saw. It
has not the immeasurable greatness, the overpowering
magnificence, nor, above all, the radiant beauty of the

[* Est locus exciso penitus demersus hiatu,
   Parthenopem inter, magnæque Dicarchidos arva,
   Cocytia perfusus aqua, nam spiritus, extra
   Qui furit, effusus funesto spargitur æstu, &c.
                    PETRONII ARBITRI *Satyricon.*]

glaciers; but it has all their character of tremendous and irresistible strength. From Resina to the hermitage you wind up the mountain, and cross a vast stream of hardened lava, which is an actual image of the waves of the sea, changed into hard black stone by enchantment. The lines of the boiling flood seem to hang in the air, and it is difficult to believe that the billows which seem hurrying down upon you are not actually in motion. This plain was once a sea of liquid fire. From the hermitage we crossed another vast stream of lava, and then went on foot up the cone—this is the only part of the ascent in which there is any difficulty, and that difficulty has been much exaggerated. It is composed of rocks of lava, and declivities of ashes; by ascending the former and descending the latter, there is very little fatigue. On the summit is a kind of irregular plain, the most horrible chaos that can be imagined; riven into ghastly chasms, and heaped up with tumuli of great stones and cinders, and enormous rocks blackened and calcined, which had been thrown from the volcano upon one another in terrible confusion. In the midst stands the conical hill from which volumes of smoke, and the fountains of liquid fire, are rolled forth forever. The mountain is at present in a slight state of eruption; and a thick heavy white smoke is perpetually rolled out, interrupted by enormous columns of an impenetrable black bituminous vapour, which is hurled up, fold after fold, into the sky with a deep hollow sound, and fiery stones are rained down from its darkness, and a black shower of ashes fell even where we sat. The lava, like the glacier, creeps on perpetually, with a crackling sound as of suppressed fire. There are several springs of lava; and in one place it gushes precipitously over a high crag, rolling down the half-molten rocks and its own overhanging waves; a cataract of quivering fire. We approached the extremity of one of the rivers of lava; it is about twenty feet in breadth and ten in height; and as the inclined plane was not rapid, its motion was very slow. We saw the masses of its dark exterior surface detach themselves as it moved, and betray the depth of the liquid flame. In the day the fire is but slightly seen ; you only observe a tremulous motion in the air, and streams and fountains of white sulphurous smoke.

At length we saw the sun sink between Capreæ and Inarime, and, as the darkness increased, the effect of the fire became more beautiful. We were, as it were, surrounded by streams and cataracts of the red and radiant fire ; and in the midst, from the column of bituminous smoke shot up into the air, fell the vast masses of rock, white with the light of their intense heat, leaving behind them through the dark vapour trains of splendour. We descended by torch-light, and I should have enjoyed the scenery on my return, but they conducted me, I know not how, to the hermitage in a state of intense bodily suffering, the worst effect of which was spoiling the pleasure of Mary and C——. Our guides on the occasion were complete savages. You have no idea of the horrible cries which they suddenly utter, no one knows why, the clamour, the vociferation, the tumult. C—— in her palanquin suffered most from it ; and when I had gone on before, they threatened to leave her in the middle of the road, which they would have done had not my Italian servant promised them a beating, after which they became quiet. Nothing, however, can be more picturesque than the gestures and the physiognomies of these savage people. And when, in the darkness of night, they unexpectedly begin to sing in chorus some fragments of their wild but sweet national music, the effect is exceedingly fine.

Since I wrote this I have seen the museum of this city. Such statues ! There is a Venus ; an ideal shape of the most winning loveliness. A Bacchus, more sublime than any living being. A Satyr, making love to a youth, in which the expressed life of the sculpture, and the inconceivable beauty of the form of the youth, overcome one's repugnance to the subject. There are multitudes of wonderfully fine statues found in Herculaneum and Pompeii. We are going to see Pompeii the first day that the sea is waveless. Herculaneum is almost filled up; no more excavations are made; the king bought the ground and built a palace upon it.

You don't see much of Hunt. I wish you could contrive to see him when you go to town, and ask him what he means to answer to Lord Byron's invitation. He has now an opportunity, if he likes, of seeing Italy. What do you think of joining his party, and paying us a visit next year; I mean as soon as the reign of winter is dissolved? Write to me your thoughts upon this. I cannot express to you the pleasure it would give me to welcome such a party.

I have depression enough of spirits and not good health, though I believe the warm air of Naples does me good. We see absolutely no one here.

> Adieu, my dear Peacock,
> affectionately your friend,
> P. B. S.

TO THOMAS LOVE PEACOCK.

Naples, Jan. 26th, 1819.

MY DEAR PEACOCK,

YOUR two letters arrived within a few days of each other, one being directed to Naples, and the other to Livorno. They are more welcome visitors to me than mine can be to you. I writing as from sepulchres, you from the habitations of men yet unburied; though the sexton, Castlereagh, after having dug their grave, stands with his spade in his hand, evidently doubting whether he will not be forced to occupy it himself.

Your news about the bank-note trials is excellent good.
Do I not recognise in it the influence of Cobbett ?   You
don't tell me what occupies Parliament.   I know you
will laugh at my demand, and assure me that it is in
different.   Your pamphlet I want exceedingly to see.
Your calculations in the letter are clear, but require
much oral explanation.   You know I am an infernal
arithmetician.   If none but me had contemplated
"lucentemque globum lunæ, Titaniaque astra," the
world would yet have doubted whether they were many
hundred feet higher than the mountain tops.

In my accounts of pictures and things, I am more
pleased to interest you than the many ; and this is
fortunate, because, in the first place, I have no idea of
attempting the latter, and if I did attempt it, I should
assuredly fail.   A perception of the beautiful charac-
terizes those who differ from ordinary men, and those
who can perceive it would not buy enough to pay
the printer.   Besides, I keep no journal, and the only
records of my voyage will be the letters I send you.
The bodily fatigue of standing for hours in galleries
exhausts me ; I believe that I don't see half that I
ought, on that account.   And, then, we know nobody,
and the common Italians are so sullen and stupid, it's
impossible to get information from them.   At Rome,
where the people seem superior to any in Italy, I cannot fail to stumble on something more.   O, if I had
health, and strength, and equal spirits, what boundless
intellectual improvement might I not gather in this
wonderful country !   At present I write little else but
poetry, and little of that.   My first act of Prometheus
is complete, and I think you would like it.   I consider
poetry very subordinate to moral and political science,
and if I were well, certainly I would aspire to the latter,
for I can conceive a great work, embodying the discoveries of all ages, and harmonizing the contending
creeds by which mankind have been ruled.   Far from

me is such an attempt, and I shall be content, by exercising my fancy, to amuse myself, and perhaps some others, and cast what weight I can into the scale of that balance, which the Giant of Arthegall holds.

Since you last heard from me, we have been to see Pompeii, and are waiting now for the return of spring weather, to visit, first, Pæstum, and then the islands ; after which we shall return to Rome. I was astonished at the remains of this city ; I had no conception of anything so perfect yet remaining. My idea of the mode of its destruction was this :—First, an earthquake shattered it, and unroofed almost all its temples, and split its columns ; then a rain of light, small pumice-stones fell ; then torrents of boiling water, mixed with ashes, filled up all its crevices. A wide, flat hill, from which the city was excavated, is now covered by thick woods, and you see the tombs and the theatres, the temples and the houses, surrounded by the uninhabited wilderness. We entered the town from the side towards the sea, and first saw two theatres ; one more magnificent than the other, strewn with the ruins of the white marble which formed their seats and cornices, wrought with deep, bold sculpture. In the front, between the stage and the seats, is the circular space, occasionally occupied by the chorus. The stage is very narrow, but long, and divided from this space by a narrow enclosure parallel to it, I suppose for the orchestra. On each side are the consuls' boxes, and below, in the theatre at Herculaneum, were found two equestrian statues of admirable workmanship, occupying the same place as the great bronze lamps did at Drury Lane. The smallest of the theatres is said to have been comic, though I should doubt. From both you see, as you sit on the seats, a prospect of the most wonderful beauty.

You then pass through the ancient streets ; they are very narrow, and the houses rather small, but all con-structed on an admirable plan, especially for this climate

The rooms are built round a court, or sometimes two,
according to the extent of the house. In the midst is
a fountain, sometimes surrounded with a portico, supported on fluted columns of white stucco ; the floor is
paved with mosaic, sometimes wrought in imitation of
vine leaves, sometimes in quaint figures, and more or
less beautiful, according to the rank of the inhabitant.
There were paintings on all, but most of them have
been removed to decorate the royal museums. Little
winged figures, and small ornaments of exquisite elegance,
yet remain. There is an ideal life in the forms of these
paintings of an incomparable loveliness, though most
are evidently the work of very inferior artists. It seems
as if, from the atmosphere of mental beauty which surrounded them, every human being caught a splendour
not his own. In one house you see how the bed-rooms
were managed ;—a small sofa was built up, where the
cushions were placed ; two pictures, one representing
Diana and Endymion, the other Venus and Mars, decorate the chamber ; and a little niche, which contains
the statue of a domestic god. The floor is composed
of a rich mosaic of the rarest marbles, agate, jasper,
and porphyry ; it looks to the marble fountain and the
snow-white columns, whose entablatures strew the floor
of the portico they supported. The houses have only
one story, and the apartments, though not large, are
very lofty. A great advantage results from this, wholly
unknown in our cities. The public buildings, whose
ruins are now forests as it were of white fluted columns,
and which then supported entablatures, loaded with
sculptures, were seen on all sides over the roofs of the
houses. This was the excellence of the ancients. Their
private expenses were comparatively moderate ; the
dwelling of one of the chief senators of Pompeii is
elegant indeed, and adorned with most beautiful specimens of art, but small. But their public buildings are
everywhere marked by the bold and grand designs of

an unsparing magnificence. In the little town of Pompeii, (it contained about twenty thousand inhabitants,) it is wonderful to see the number and the grandeur of their public buildings. Another advantage, too, is that, in the present case, the glorious scenery around is not shut out, and that, unlike the inhabitants of the Cimmerian ravines of modern cities, the ancient Pompeians could contemplate the clouds and the lamps of heaven ; could see the moon rise high behind Vesuvius, and the sun set in the sea, tremulous with an atmosphere of golden vapour, between Inarime and Misenum.

We next saw the temples. Of the temple of Æsculapius little remains but an altar of black stone, adorned with a cornice imitating the scales of a serpent. His statue, in terra-cotta, was found in the cell. The temple of Isis is more perfect. It is surrounded by a portico of fluted columns, and in the area around it are two altars, and many ceppi for statues ; and a little chapel of white stucco, as hard as stone, of the most exquisite proportion ; its panels are adorned with figures in bas relief, slightly indicated, but of a workmanship the most delicate and perfect that can be conceived. They are Egyptian subjects, executed by a Greek artist, who has harmonized all the unnatural extravagances of the original conception into the supernatural loveliness of his country's genius. They scarcely touch the ground with their feet, and their wind-uplifted robes seem in the place of wings. The temple in the midst, raised on a high platform, and approached by steps, was decorated with exquisite paintings, some of which we saw in the museum at Portici. It is small, of the same materials as the chapel, with a pavement of mosaic, and fluted Ionic columns of white stucco, so white that it dazzles you to look at it.

Thence through other porticos and labyrinths of walls and columns, (for I cannot hope to detail everything to you,) we came to the Forum. This is a large square,

surrounded by lofty porticos of fluted columns, some
broken, some entire, their entablatures strewed under
them. The temple of Jupiter, of Venus, and another
temple, the Tribunal, and the Hall of Public Justice,
with their forests of lofty columns, surround the Forum.
Two pedestals or altars of an enormous size, (for,
whether they supported equestrian statues, or were
the altars of the temple of Venus, before which they
stand, the guide could not tell,) occupy the lower end
of the Forum. At the upper end, supported on an
elevated platform, stands the temple of Jupiter. Under
the colonnade of its portico we sat, and pulled out our
oranges, and figs, and bread, and medlars, (sorry fare,
you will say,) and rested to eat. Here was a magnificent spectacle. Above and between the multitudinous
shafts of the sunshining columns was seen the sea, re-
flecting the purple heaven of noon above it, and supporting, as it were, on its line the dark lofty mountains
of Sorrento, of a blue inexpressibly deep, and tinged
towards their summits with streaks of new-fallen snow.
Between was one small green island. To the right was
Capreæ, Inarime, Prochyta, and Misenum. Behind
was the single summit of Vesuvius, rolling forth volumes
of thick white smoke, whose foam-like column was sometimes darted into the clear dark sky, and fell in little
streaks along the wind. Between Vesuvius and the
nearer mountains, as through a chasm, was seen the
main line of the loftiest Apennines, to the east. The
day was radiant and warm. Every now and then we
heard the subterranean thunder of Vesuvius; its distant
deep peals seemed to shake the very air and light of
day, which interpenetrated our frames, with the sullen
and tremendous sound. This scene was what the
Greeks beheld (Pompeii, you know, was a Greek city).
They lived in harmony with nature; and the interstices
of their incomparable columns were portals, as it were,
to admit the spirit of beauty which animates this glorious

II.   S

universe to visit those whom it inspired. If such is Pompeii, what was Athens? What scene was exhibited from the Acropolis, the Parthenon, and the temples of Hercules, and Theseus, and the Winds? The islands and the Ægean sea, the mountains of Argolis, and the peaks of Pindus and Olympus, and the darkness of the Bœotian forests interspersed?

From the Forum we went to another public place; a triangular portico, half inclosing the ruins of an enormous temple. It is built on the edge of the hill overlooking the sea. Δ That black point is the temple. In the apex of the triangle stands an altar and a fountain, and before the altar once stood the statue of the builder of the portico. Returning hence, and following the consular road, we came to the eastern gate of the city. The walls are of enormous strength, and inclose a space of three miles. On each side of the road beyond the gate are built the tombs. How unlike ours! They seem not so much hiding-places for that which must decay, as voluptuous chambers for immortal spirits. They are of marble, radiantly white; and two, especially beautiful, are loaded with exquisite bas reliefs. On the stucco-wall that incloses them are little emblematic figures of a relief exceedingly low, of dead and dying animals, and little winged genii, and female forms bending in groups in some funeral office. The higher reliefs represent, one a nautical subject, and the other a Bacchanalian one. Within the cell stand the cinerary urns, sometimes one, sometimes more. It is said that paintings were found within; which are now, as has been everything moveable in Pompeii, removed, and scattered about in royal museums. These tombs were the most impressive things of all. The wild woods surround them on either side; and along the broad stones of the paved road which divides them, you hear the late leaves of autumn shiver and rustle in the stream of the inconstant wind, as it were, like the step of ghosts.

The radiance and magnificence of these dwellings of the dead, the white freshness of the scarcely finished marble, the impassioned or imaginative life of the figures which adorn them, contrast strangely with the simplicity of the houses of those who were living when Vesuvius overwhelmed them.

I have forgotten the amphitheatre, which is of great magnitude, though much inferior to the Coliseum. I now understand why the Greeks were such great poets ; and, above all, I can account, it seems to me, for the harmony, the unity, the perfection, the uniform excellence, of all their works of art. They lived in a perpetual commerce with external nature, and nourished themselves upon the spirit of its forms. Their theatres were all open to the mountains and the sky. Their columns, the ideal types of a sacred forest, with its roof of interwoven tracery, admitted the light and wind ; the odour and the freshness of the country penetrated the cities. Their temples were mostly upaithric ; and the flying clouds, the stars, or the deep sky, were seen above. O, but for that series of wretched wars which terminated in the Roman conquest of the world ; but for the Christian religion, which put the finishing stroke on the ancient system ; but for those changes that conducted Athens to its ruin,—to what an eminence might not humanity have arrived !

In a short time I hope to tell you something of the museum of this city.

You see how ill I follow the maxim of Horace, at least in its literal sense : " nil admirari "—which I should say, " prope res est una "—to prevent there ever being anything admirable in the world. Fortunately Plato is of my opinion ; and I had rather err with Plato than be right with Horace.

At this moment I have received your letter indicating that you are removing to London. I am very much interested in the subject of this change, and beg you would write me all the particulars of it. You will be able now to give me perhaps a closer insight into the politics of the times than was permitted you at Marlow. Of H—— I have a very slight opinion. There are rumours here of a revolution in Spain. A ship came in twelve days from Catalonia, and brought a report that the king was massacred ; that eighteen thousand insurgents surrounded Madrid ; but that before the popular party gained head enough seven thousand were murdered by the inquisition. Perhaps you know all by this time. The old king of Spain is dead here. Cobbett is a fine ʽυμενοποιος—does his influence increase or diminish? What a pity that so powerful a genius should be combined with the most odious moral qualities.

We have reports here of a change in the English ministry—to what does it amount ? for, besides my national interest in it, I am on the watch to vindicate my most sacred rights, invaded by the chancery court.

I suppose now we shall not see you in Italy this spring, whether Hunt comes or not. It's probable I shall hear nothing from him for some months, particularly if he does not come. Give me *ses nouvelles.*

I am under an English surgeon here, who says I have a disease of the liver, which he will cure. We keep horses, as this kind of exercise is absolutely essential to my health. Elise * has just married our Italian servant, and has quitted us ; the man was a great rascal, and cheated enormously : this event was very much against our advice.

I have scarcely been out since I wrote last.

Adieu ! yours most faithfully,

P. B. S.

* A Swiss girl whom we had engaged as nursery-maid two years before, at Geneva.—[*Note by Mrs. Shelley.*]

TO THOMAS LOVE PEACOCK.

Rome, March 23d, 1819.

MY DEAR PEACOCK,

I WROTE to you the day before our departure from
Naples. We came by slow journeys, with our own
horses, to Rome, resting one day at Mola di Gaeta, at
the inn called Villa di Cicerone, from being built on the
ruins of his Villa, whose immense substructions overhang
the sea, and are scattered among the orange-groves.
Nothing can be lovelier than the scene from the terraces
of the inn. On one side precipitous mountains, whose
bases slope into an inclined plane of olive and orange-
copses—the latter forming, as it were, an emerald sky of
leaves, starred with innumerable globes of their ripening
fruit, whose rich splendour contrasted with the deep
green foliage ; on the other the sea—bounded on one
side by the antique town of Gaeta, and the other by
what appears to be an island, the promontory of Circe.
From Gaeta to Terracina the whole scenery is of the
most sublime character. At Terracina precipitous
conical crags of immense height shoot into the sky and
overhang the sea. At Albano we arrived again in sight
of Rome. Arches after arches in unending lines stretch-
ing across the uninhabited wilderness, the blue defined
line of the mountains seen between them ; masses of
nameless ruin standing like rocks out of the plain ; and
the plain itself, with its billowy and unequal surface,
announced the neighbourhood of Rome. And what shall
I say to you of Rome ? If I speak of the inanimate ruins,
the rude stones piled upon stones, which are the sepulchres of the fame of those who once arrayed them with
the beauty which has faded, will you believe me insensible
to the vital, the almost breathing creations of genius yet
subsisting in their perfection ? What has become, you

will ask, of the Apollo, the Gladiator, the Venus of the
Capitol ?   What of the Apollo di Belvedere, the Laocoon ?
What of Raffaelle and Guido ?   These things are best
spoken of when the mind has drunk in the spirit of their
forms ; and little indeed can I, who must devote no more
than a few months to the contemplation of them, hope
to know or feel of their profound beauty.

I think I told you of the Coliseum, and its impressions
on me on my first visit to this city.   The next most
considerable relic of antiquity, considered as a ruin, is
the Thermæ of Caracalla.   These consist of six enormous
chambers, above 200 feet in height, and each inclosing
a vast space like that of a field.   There are, in addition,
a number of towers and labyrinthine recesses, hidden
and woven over by the wild growth of weeds and ivy.
Never was any desolation more sublime and lovely.
The perpendicular wall of ruin is cloven into steep
ravines filled up with flowering shrubs, whose thick
twisted roots are knotted in the rifts of the stones;   At
every step the aerial pinnacles of shattered stone group
into new combinations of effect, and tower above the
lofty yet level walls, as the distant mountains change
their aspect to one travelling rapidly along the plain.
The perpendicular walls resemble nothing more than
that cliff of Bisham wood, that is overgrown with wood,
and yet is stony and precipitous—you know the one I
mean ; not the chalk-pit, but the spot that has the pretty
copse of fir-trees and privet-bushes at its base, and
where H * * and I scrambled up, and you, to my infinite
discontent, would go home.   These walls surround green
and level spaces of lawn, on which some elms have
grown, and which are interspersed towards their skirts
by masses of the fallen ruin, overtwined with the broad
leaves of the creeping weeds.   The blue sky canopies
it, and is as the everlasting roof of these enormous
halls.

But the most interesting effect remains.   In one of

the buttresses, that supports an immense and lofty
arch, which "bridges the very winds of heaven," are
the crumbling remains of an antique winding staircase,
whose sides are open in many places to the precipice.
This you ascend, and arrive on the summit of these
piles. There grow on every side thick entangled
wildernesses of myrtle, and the myrletus, and bay, and
the flowering laurustinus, whose white blossoms are
just developed, the wild fig, and a thousand nameless
plants sown by the wandering winds. These woods
are intersected on every side by paths, like sheep
tracks through the copse-wood of steep mountains,
which wind to every part of the immense labyrinth.
From the midst rise those pinnacles and masses, themselves like mountains, which have been seen from below.
In one place you wind along a narrow strip of weed-
grown ruin, on one side is the immensity of earth and
sky, on the other a narrow chasm, which is bounded
by an arch of enormous size, fringed by the many-
coloured foliage and blossoms, and supporting a lofty
and irregular pyramid, overgrown like itself with the
all-prevailing vegetation. Around rise other crags and
other peaks, all arrayed, and the deformity of their vast
desolation softened down, by the undecaying investiture
of nature. Come to Rome. It is a scene by which
expression is overpowered; which words cannot convey.
Still further, winding up one-half of the shattered pyramids, by the path through the blooming copsewood,
you come to a little mossy lawn, surrounded by the
wild shrubs; it is overgrown with anemones, wall-
flowers, and violets, whose stalks pierce the starry
moss, and with radiant blue flowers, whose names I
know not, and which scatter through the air the divinest
odour, which, as you recline under the shade of the
ruin, produces sensations of voluptuous faintness, like
the combinations of sweet music. The paths still wind
on, threading the perplexed windings, other labyrinths,

other lawns, and deep dells of wood, and lofty rocks, and terrific chasms. When I tell you that these ruins cover several acres, and that the paths above penetrate at least half their extent, your imagination will fill up all that I am unable to express of this astonishing scene.

I speak of these things not in the order in which I visited them, but in that of the impression which they made on me, or perhaps chance directs. The ruins of the ancient Forum are so far fortunate that they have not been walled up in the modern city. They stand in an open, lonesome place, bounded on one side by the modern city, and the other by the Palatine Mount, covered with shapeless masses of ruin. The tourists tell you all about these things, and I am afraid of stumbling on their language when I enumerate what is so well known. There remain eight granite columns of the Ionic order, with their entablature, of the temple of Concord, founded by Camillus. I fear that the immense expense demanded by these columns forbids us to hope that they are the remains of any edifice dedicated by that most perfect and virtuous of men. It is supposed to have been repaired under the Eastern Emperors ; alas, what a contrast of recollections ! Near them stand those Corinthian fluted columns, which supported the angle of a temple ; the architrave and entablature are worked with delicate sculpture. Beyond, to the south, is another solitary column ; and still more distant, three more, supporting the wreck of an entablature. Descending from the Capitol to the Forum, is the triumphal arch of Septimius Severus, less perfect than that of Constantine, though from its pro- portions and magnitude, a most impressive monument. That of Constantine, or rather of Titus, (for the relief and sculpture, and even the colossal images of Dacian captives, were torn by a decree of the senate from an arch dedicated to the latter, to adorn that of this stupid

and wicked monster, Constantine, one of whose chief
merits consists in establishing a religion, the destroyer
of those arts which would have rendered so base a
spoliation unnecessary) is the most perfect. It is an
admirable work of art. It is built of the finest marble,
and the outline of the reliefs is in many parts as perfect as if just finished. Four Corinthian fluted columns
support, on each side, a bold entablature, whose bases
are loaded with reliefs of captives in every attitude of
humiliation and slavery. The compartments above
express in bolder relief the enjoyment of success ; the
conqueror on his throne, or in his chariot, or nodding
over the crushed multitudes, who writhe under his
horses' hoofs, as those below express the torture and
abjectness of defeat. There are three arches, whose
roofs are panelled with fretwork, and their sides
adorned with similar reliefs. The keystone of these
arches is supported each by two winged figures of
Victory, whose hair floats on the wind of their own
speed, and whose arms are outstretched, bearing
trophies, as if impatient to meet. They look, as it
were, borne from the subject extremities of the earth,
on the breath which is the exhalation of that battle and
desolation, which it is their mission to commemorate.
Never were monuments so completely fitted to the
purpose for which they were designed, of expressing
that mixture of energy and error which is called a
triumph.

I walk forth in the purple and golden light of an
Italian evening, and return by star or moonlight, through
this scene. The elms are just budding, and the warm
spring winds bring unknown odours, all sweet, from the
country. I see the radiant Orion through the mighty
columns of the temple of Concord, and the mellow
fading light softens down the modern buildings of the
Capitol, the only ones that interfere with the sublime
desolation of the scene. On the steps of the Capitol

itself, stand two colossal statues of Castor and Pollux, each with his horse, finely executed, though far inferior to those of Monte Cavallo, the cast of one of which you know we saw together in London. This walk is close to our lodging, and this is my evening walk.

What shall I say of the modern city? Rome is yet the capital of the world. It is a city of palaces and temples, more glorious than those which any other city contains, and of ruins more glorious than they. Seen from any of the eminences that surround it, it exhibits domes beyond domes, and palaces, and colonnades interminably, even to the horizon; interspersed with patches of desert, and mighty ruins which stand girt by their own desolation, in the midst of the fanes of living religions and the habitations of living men, in sublime loneliness. St. Peter's is, as you have heard, the loftiest building in Europe. Externally it is inferior in architectural beauty to St. Paul's, though not wholly devoid of it; internally it exhibits littleness on a large scale, and is in every respect opposed to antique taste. You know my propensity to admire; and I tried to persuade myself out of this opinion—in vain; the more I see of the interior of St. Peter's, the less impression as a whole does it produce on me. I cannot even think it lofty, though its dome is considerably higher than any hill within fifty miles of London; and when one reflects, it is an astonishing monument of the daring energy of man. Its colonnade is wonderfully fine, and there are two fountains, which rise in spire-like columns of water to an immense height in the sky, and falling on the porphyry vases from which they spring, fill the whole air with a radiant mist, which at noon is thronged with innumerable rainbows. In the midst stands an obelisk. In front is the palace-like façade of St. Peter's, certainly magnificent; and there is produced, on the whole, an architectural combination unequalled in the world. But the dome of the temple is concealed, except at a very

great distance, by the façade and the inferior part of
the building, and that diabolical contrivance they call
an attic.

The effect of the Pantheon is totally the reverse of
that of St. Peter's. Though not a fourth part of the
size, it is, as it were, the visible image of the universe;
in the perfection of its proportions, as when you regard
the unmeasured dome of heaven, the idea of magnitude
is swallowed up and lost. It is open to the sky, and
its wide dome is lighted by the ever-changing illumina-
tion of the air. The clouds of noon fly over it, and at
night the keen stars are seen through the azure darkness, hanging immoveably, or driving after the driving
moon among the clouds. We visited it by moonlight;
it is supported by sixteen columns, fluted and Corinthian,
of a certain rare and beautiful yellow marble, exquisitely
polished, called here *giallo antico*. Above these are the
niches for the statues of the twelve gods. This is the
only defect of this sublime temple; there ought to have
been no interval between the commencement of the
dome and the cornice, supported by the columns. Thus
there would have been no diversion from the magnificent simplicity of its form. This improvement is alone
wanting to have completed the unity of the idea.

The fountains of Rome are, in themselves, magnificent combinations of art, such as alone it were worth
coming to see. That in the Piazza Navona, a large
square, is composed of enormous fragments of rock,
piled on each other, and penetrated, as by caverns.
This mass supports an Egyptian obelisk of immense
height. On the four corners of the rock recline, in
different attitudes, colossal figures representing the four
divisions of the globe. The water bursts from the
crevices beneath them. They are sculptured with great
spirit; one impatiently tearing a veil from his eyes;
another with his hands stretched upwards. The Fontana
di Trevi is the most celebrated, and is rather a waterfall

than a fountain ; gushing out from masses of rock, with
a gigantic figure of Neptune ; and below are two river
gods, checking two winged horses, struggling up from
among the rocks and waters.   The whole is not ill-con-
ceived nor executed ; but you know not how delicate
the imagination becomes by dieting with antiquity day
after day.   The only things that sustain the comparison
are Raphael, Guido, and Salvator Rosa.

The fountain on the Quirinal, or rather the group
formed by the statues, obelisk and the fountain, is, however, the most admirable of all.   From the Piazza
Quirinale, or rather Monte Cavallo, you see the boundless ocean of domes, spires, and columns, which is the
City, Rome.   On a pedestal of white marble rises an
obelisk of red granite, piercing the blue sky.   Before
it is a vast basin of porphyry, in the midst of which
rises a column of the purest water, which collects into
itself all the overhanging colours of the sky, and breaks
them into a thousand prismatic hues and graduated
shadows—they fall together with its dashing water-drops
into the outer basin.   The elevated situation of this
fountain produces, I imagine, this effect of colour.   On
each side, on an elevated pedestal, stand the statues of
Castor and Pollux, each in the act of taming his horse,
which are said, but I believe wholly without authority,
to be the work of Phidias and Praxiteles.   These figures
combine the irresistible energy with the sublime and
perfect loveliness supposed to have belonged to their
divine nature.   The reins no longer exist, but the position of their hands and the sustained and calm command
of their regard, seem to require no mechanical aid to
enforce obedience.   The countenances at so great a
height are scarcely visible, and I have a better idea of
that of which we saw a cast together in London, than
of the other.   But the sublime and living majesty of
their limbs and mien, the nervous and fiery animation
of the horses they restrain, seen in the blue sky of Italy,

and overlooking the city of Rome, surrounded by the light and the music of that crystalline fountain, no cast can communicate.

These figures were found at the Baths of Constantine, but, of course, are of remote antiquity. I do not acquiesce, however, in the practice of attributing to Phidias, or Praxiteles, or Scopas, or some great master, any admirable work that may be found. We find little of what remained, and perhaps the works of these were such as greatly surpassed all that we conceive of most perfect and admirable in what little has escaped the *deluge.* If I am too jealous of the honour of the Greeks, our masters, and creators, the gods whom we should worship,—pardon me.

I have said what I feel without entering into any critical discussions of the *ruins* of Rome, and the mere outside of this inexhaustible mine of thought and feeling. Hobhouse, Eustace, and Forsyth, will tell all the shew-knowledge about it—"the common stuff of the earth." By-the-bye, Forsyth is worth reading, as I judge from a chapter or two I have seen. I cannot get the book here.

I ought to have observed that the central arch of the triumphal arch of Titus yet subsists, more perfect in its proportions, they say, than any of a later date. This I did not remark. The figures of Victory, with unfolded wings, and each spurning back a globe with outstretched feet, are, perhaps, more beautiful than those on either of the others. Their lips are parted : a delicate mode of indicating the fervour of their desire to arrive at the destined resting-place, and to express the eager respiration of their speed. Indeed, so essential to beauty were the forms expressive of the exercise of the imagination and the affections considered by *Greek* artists, that no ideal figure of antiquity, not destined to some representation directly exclusive of such a character, is to be found with closed lips. Within this arch are two panelled alto relievos, one representing a train of people bearing in procession the instruments of Jewish worship, among which is the holy candlestick with seven branches ; on the other, Titus standing in a quadriga, with a winged Victory. The grouping of the horses, and the beauty, correctness and energy of their delineation, is remarkable, though they are much destroyed.

TO THOMAS LOVE PEACOCK.

Rome, April 6th, 1819.

MY DEAR PEACOCK,

I SENT you yesterday a long letter, all about antique Rome, which you had better keep for some leisure day. I received yours, and one of Hunt's, yesterday.—So, you know the B——s ? I could not help considering Mrs. B., when I knew her, as the most admirable speci-men of a human being I had ever seen. Nothing earthly ever appeared to me more perfect than her character and manners. It is improbable that I shall ever meet again the person whom I so much esteemed, and still admire. I wish, however, that when you see her, you would tell her that I have not forgotten her, nor any of the amiable circle once assembled round her ; and that I desire such remembrances to her, as an exile and a *Pariah* may be permitted to address to an acknow-ledged member of the community of mankind. I hear they dined at your lodgings. But no mention of A * * * and his wife—where were they ? C * * *, though so young when I saw her, gave indications of her mother's excellences ; and, certainly less fascinating, is, I doubt not, equally amiable, and more sincere. It was hardly possible for a person of the extreme subtlety and delicacy of Mrs. B——'s understanding and affections, to be quite sincere and constant.

I am all anxiety about your I. H. affair. There are few who will feel more hearty satisfaction at your success, in this or any other enterprise, than I shall. Pray let me have the earliest intelligence.

When shall I return to England? The Pythia has ascended the tripod, but she replies not. Our present plans—and I know not what can induce us to alter them—lead us back to Naples in a month or six weeks, where it is almost decided that we should remain until the commencement of 1820. You may imagine when we receive such letters as yours and Hunt's, what this resolution costs us—but these are not our only communications from England. My health is materially better. My spirits not the most brilliant in the world; but that we attribute to our solitary situation, and, though happy, how should I be lively? We see something of Italian society indeed. The Romans please me much, especially the women ; who, though totally devoid of every kind of information, or culture of the imagination, or affections, or understanding—and, in this respect, a kind of gentle savages—yet contrive to be interesting. Their extreme innocence and *naïveté*, the freedom and gentleness of their manners ; the total absence of affectation, makes an intercourse with them very like an intercourse with uncorrupted children, whom they resemble in loveliness as well as simplicity. I have seen two women in society here of the highest beauty ; their brows and lips, and the moulding of the face modelled with sculptural exactness, and the dark luxuriance of their hair floating over their fine complexions—and the lips—you must hear the commonplaces which escape from them before they cease to be dangerous. The only inferior part are the eyes, which, though good and gentle, want the mazy depth of colour behind colour, with which the intellectual women of England and Germany entangle the heart in soul-inwoven labyrinths.

This is holy week, and Rome is quite full. The Emperor of Austria is here, and Maria Louisa is coming. On their journey through the other cities of Italy, she was greeted with loud acclamations, and vivas of Napoleon. Idiots and slaves ! Like the frogs in the fable, because they are discontented with the log, they call upon the stork, who devours them. Great festas, and magnificent funzioni here—we cannot get tickets to all. There are five thousand strangers in Rome, and only room for five hundred, at the celebration of the famous Miserere, in the Sistine chapel, the only thing I regret we shall not be present at. After all, Rome is eternal, and were all that *is* extinguished, that which *has been*, the ruins and the sculptures, would remain, and Raffaelle and Guido be alone regretted.

In the square of St. Peter's there are about three hundred fettered criminals at work, hoeing out the weeds that grow between the stones of the pavement. Their legs are heavily ironed, and some are chained two by two. They sit in long rows, hoeing out the weeds, dressed in parti-coloured clothes. Near them sit or saunter, groups of soldiers, armed with loaded muskets. The iron discord of those innumerable chains clanks up into the sonorous air, and produces, contrasted with the musical dashing of the fountains, and the deep azure beauty of the sky, and the magnificence of the architecture around, a conflict of sensations allied to madness. It is the emblem of Italy—moral degradation contrasted with the glory of nature and the arts.

We see no English society here ; it is not probable that we could if we desired it, and I am certain that we should find it insupportable. The manners of the rich English are wholly insupportable, and they assume pretences which they would not venture upon in their own country.—I am yet ignorant of the event of Hobhouse's election. I saw the last numbers were—Lamb, 4200 ; and Hobhouse, 3900—14th day. There is little hope.

That mischievous Cobbett has divided and weakened the interest of the popular party, so that the factions that prey upon our country have been able to coalesce to its exclusion. The N——s you have not seen. I am curious to know what kind of a girl Octavia becomes ; she promised well. Tell H—— his Melpomene is in the Vatican, and that her attitude and drapery surpass, if possible, the graces of her countenance.

My " Prometheus Unbound " is just finished, and in a month or two I shall send it. It is a drama, with characters and mechanism of a kind yet unattempted ; and I think the execution is better than any of my former attempts. By-the-bye, have you seen Ollier ? I never hear from him, and am ignorant whether some verses I sent him from Naples, entitled, I think, " Lines on the Euganean hills," have reached him in safety or not. As to the Reviews, I suppose there is nothing but abuse ; and this is not hearty or sincere enough to amuse me. As to the poem now printing,* I lay no stress on it one way or the other. The concluding lines are natural.

I believe, my dear Peacock, that you wish us to come back to England. How is it possible ? Health, competence, tranquillity—all these Italy permits, and England takes away. I am regarded by all who know or hear of me, except, I think, on the whole, five individuals, as a rare prodigy of crime and pollution, whose look even might infect. This is a large computation, and I don't think I could mention more than three. Such is the spirit of the English abroad as well as at home.

Few compensate, indeed, for all the rest, and if I were *alone* I should laugh ; or if I were rich enough to do all things, which I shall never be. Pity me for my absence from those social enjoyments which England might afford me, and which I know so well how to

* Rosalind and Helen.

II.   T

appreciate.   S†ill, I shall returń some fine morning, out
of pure weakness of heart.

My dear Peacock, most faithfully yours,
P. B. SHELLEY.

TO MR. AND MRS. GISBORNE

(LEGHORN).

Rome, April 6th, 1819.

MY DEAR FRIENDS,

A COMBINATION of circumstances, which Mary will
explain to you, leads us back to Naples in June, or
rather the end of May, where we shall remain until the
ensuing winter.   We shall take a house at Portici, or
Castel a Mare, until late in the autumn.

The object of this letter is to ask you to spend this
period with us.   There is no society which we have
regretted or desired so much as yours, and in our solitude the benefit of your concession would be greater
than I can express.   What is a sail to Naples?   It is
the season of tranquil weather and prosperous winds.
If I knew the magic that lay in any given form of words,
I would employ them to persuade ; but I fear that all I
can say is, as you know with truth, we desire that you
would come—we wish to see you.   You came to see
Mary at Lucca, directly I had departed to Venice.   It
is not our custom, when we can help it, any more than
it is yours, to divide our pleasures.

What shall I say to entice you?   We shall have a
piano, and some books, and—little else, beside ourselves.
But what will be most inviting to you, you will give
much, though you may receive but little pleasure.

But whilst I write this with more desire than hope,
yet some of that, perhaps the project may fall into your

designs.   It is intolerable to think of your being buried
at Livorno.   The success assured by Mr. Reveley's
talents requires another scene.   You may have decided
to take this summer to consider—and why not with us
at Naples, rather than at Livorno ?

I could address, with respect to Naples, the words of
Polypheme in Theocritus, to all the friends I wish to see,
and you especially :

'Εξένθοις, Γαλάτεια, καὶ ἐξενθοῖσα λάθοιο,
Ὥσπερ ἐγὼ νῦν ᾧδε καθήμενος, οἴκαδ' ἀπενθεῖν.

> Most sincerely yours,
> P. B. SHELLEY.

TO THOMAS LOVE PEACOCK.

Livorno, July, 1819.

MY DEAR PEACOCK,

WE still remain, and shall remain nearly two months
longer, at Livorno.   Our house is a melancholy one,*
and only cheered by letters from England.   I got your
note, in which you speak of three letters having been
sent to Naples, which I have written for.   I have heard
also from H——, who confirms the news of your success,
an intelligence most grateful to me.

The object of the present letter is to ask a favour of
you.   I have written a tragedy, on the subject of a story
well known in Italy, and, in my conception, eminently
dramatic.†   I have taken some pains to make my play
fit for representation, and those who have already seen

---

* We had lost our eldest, and, at that time, only child, the preceding month at Rome.—[*Note by Mrs. Shelley.*]
    † This refers of course (as the sequel shows still more fully) to
The Cenci.—ED.

it judge favourably. It is written without any of the peculiar feelings and opinions which characterise my other compositions; I having attended simply to the impartial development of such characters, as it is probable the persons represented really were, together with the greatest degree of popular effect to be produced by such a development. I send you a translation of the Italian manuscript on which my play is founded, the chief subject of which I have touched very delicately; for my principal doubt, as to whether it would succeed as an acting play, hangs entirely on the question, as to whether such a thing as incest in this shape, however treated, would be admitted on the stage. I think, however, it will form no objection; considering, first, that the facts are matter of history; and, secondly, the peculiar delicacy with which I have treated it.

I am exceedingly interested in the question of whether this attempt of mine will succeed or no. I am strongly inclined to the affirmative at present, founding my hopes on this, that, as a composition, it is certainly not inferior to any of the modern plays that have been acted, with the exception of " Remorse ;" * that the interest of its plot is incredibly greater and more real; and that there is nothing beyond what the multitude are contented to believe that they can understand, either in imagery, opinion, or sentiment. I wish to preserve a complete incognito, and can trust to you, that whatever else you do, you will, at least, favour me on this point. Indeed, this is essential, deeply essential, to its success. After it had been acted, and successfully, (could I hope such a thing,) I would own it if I pleased, and use the celebrity it might acquire to my own purposes.

What I want you to do is, to procure for me its presentation at Covent Garden. The principal char-

* Coleridge's tragedy of *Remorse,* performed at Drury Lane in 1813.—ED.

acter, Beatrice, is precisely fitted for Miss O'Neil, and it might even seem written for her, (God forbid that I should ever see her play it—it would tear my nerves to pieces,) and, in all respects, it is fitted only for Covent Garden. The chief male character, I confess, I should be very unwilling that any one but Kean should play—that is impossible, and I must be contented with an inferior actor. I think you know some of the people of that theatre, or, at least, some one who knows them, and when you have read the play, you may say enough perhaps to induce them not to reject it without consideration—but of this, perhaps, if I may judge from the tragedies which they have accepted, there is no danger at any rate.

Write to me as soon as you can on this subject, because it is necessary that I should present it, or, if rejected by the theatre, print it this coming season ; lest somebody else should get hold of it, as the story, which now exists only in manuscript, begins to be generally known among the English. The translation which I send you, is to be prefixed to the play, together with a print of Beatrice. I have a copy of her picture by Guido, now in the Colonna palace at Rome—the most beautiful creature you can conceive.

Of course, you will not show the manuscript to any one—and write to me by return of post, at which time the play will be ready to be sent.

*   *   *   *   *

I expect soon to write again, and it shall be a less selfish letter. As to Ollier, I don't know what has been published, or what has arrived at his hands.—My " Prometheus," though ready, I do not send till I know more.

Ever yours, most faithfully,

P. B. S.

TO LEIGH HUNT.*

Livorno, Sept. 27th, 1819.
MY DEAR FRIEND,

WE are now on the point of leaving this place for Florence, where we have taken pleasant apartments for six months, which brings us to the first of April, the season at which new flowers and new thoughts spring forth upon the earth and in the mind. What is then our destination is yet undecided. I have not yet seen Florence, except as one sees the outside of the streets ; but its *physiognomy* indicates it to be a city, which, though the ghost of a republic, yet possesses most amiable qualities. I wish you could meet us there in the spring, and we would try to muster up a "lièta brigata," which, leaving behind them the pestilence of remembered misfortunes, might act over again the pleasures of the Interlocutors in Boccaccio. I have been lately reading this most divine writer. He is, in a high sense of the word, a poet, and his language has the rhythm and harmony of verse. I think him not equal certainly to Dante or Petrarch, but far superior to Tasso and Ariosto, the children of a later and of a colder day. I consider the three first as the productions of the vigour of the infancy of a new nation—as rivulets from the same spring as that which fed the greatness of the republics of Florence and Pisa, and which checked the influence of the German emperors ; and from which, through obscurer channels, Raffaelle and Michael Angelo drew the light and the harmony of their inspiration. When the second-rate poets of Italy wrote, the corrupting blight of tyranny was already hanging on every bud of

* Only a mutilated fragment of this letter was published by Leigh Hunt : it is accordingly given here as printed for the first time in its entirety by Mrs. Shelley.—ED.

genius. Energy, and simplicity, and unity of idea, were
no more. In vain do we seek, in the finest passages
of Ariosto and Tasso, any expression which at all
approaches in this respect to those of Dante and
Petrarch. How much do I admire Boccaccio! What
descriptions of nature are those in his little introductions
to every new day ! It is the morning of life stripped of
that mist of familiarity which makes it obscure to us.
Boccaccio seems to me to have possessed a deep sense
of the fair ideal of human life, considered in its social
relations. His more serious theories of love agree
especially with mine. He often expresses things lightly
too, which have serious meanings of a very beautiful
kind. He is a moral casuist, the opposite of the
Christian, stoical, ready-made, and worldly system of
morals. Do you remember one little remark, or rather
maxim of his, which might do some good to the
common narrow-minded conceptions of love,—"Bocca
bacciata non perde ventura ; anzi rinnuova, come fa la
luna"?

We expect Mary to be confined towards the end of
October. The birth of a child will probably retrieve her
from some part of her present melancholy depression.

It would give me much pleasure to know Mr. Lloyd.
Do you know, when I was in Cumberland, I got Southey
to borrow a copy of Berkeley from him, and I remember
observing some pencil notes in it, probably written by
Lloyd, which I thought particularly acute. One, especially, struck me as being the assertion of a doctrine, of
which even then I had long been persuaded, and on
which I had founded much of my persuasions, as regarded the imagined cause of the universe—"Mind
cannot create, it can only perceive." Ask him if he
remembers having written it. Of Lamb you know my
opinion, and you can bear witness to the regret which I
felt, when I learned that the calumny of an enemy had
deprived me of his society whilst in England.—Ollier
told me that the Quarterly are going to review me. I

suppose it will be a pretty   ,* and as I am acquiring
a taste for humour and drollery, I confess I am curious
to see it.   I have sent my "Prometheus Unbound" to
P. ; if you ask him for it he will show it you.   I think
it will please you.

Whilst I went to Florence, Mary wrote, but I did
not see her letter.—Well, good b'ye.   Next Monday I
shall write to you from Florence.   Love to all.

Most affectionately your friend,

P. B. S.

TO MRS. GISBORNE.

Florence, [October 13th or 14th, 1819.]

MY DEAR FRIEND,

THE regret we feel at our absence from you persuades
me that it is a state which cannot last, and which, so
long as it must last, will be interrupted by some intervals, one of which is destined to be, your all coming to
visit us here.   Poor Oscar !   I feel a kind of remorse
to think of the unequal love with which two animated
beings regard each other, when I experience no such
sensations for him, as those which he manifested for
us.   His importunate regret is, however, a type of ours,
as regards you.   Our memory—if you will accept so
humble a metaphor—is for ever scratching at the door
of your absence.

About Henry and the steam-engine † I am in torture

---

* The word here left blank was either illegible in the manuscript ;
or, what is more probable, Mrs. Shelley, for whatever reason, designedly withheld it.—ED.

† Shelley set on foot the building of a steam-boat, to ply between
Marseilles, Genoa, and Leghorn.   Such an enterprise promised
fortune to his friend who undertook to build it, and the anticipation
filled him with delight.   An unforeseen complication of circumstances

until this money comes from London, though I am sure that it will and must come ; unless, indeed, my banker has broke, and then it will be my loss, not Henry's— a little delay will mend the matter. I would then write instantly to London an effectual letter, and by return of post all would be set right—it would then be a thing easily set straight—but if it were not, you know me too well not to know that there is no personal suffering or degradation, or toil, or anything that can be named, with which I do not feel myself bound to support this enterprise of Henry. But all this rhodomontade only shows how correct Mr. Bielby's advice was about the discipline necessary for my imagination. No doubt that all will go on with mercantile and common-place exactness, and that you will be spared the suffering, and I the virtue, incident to some untoward event.

I am anxious to hear of Mr. Gisborne's return, and I anticipate the surprise and pleasure with which he

caused the design to be abandoned, when already far advanced towards completion.—[*Note by Mrs. Shelley.*]

An extract from a letter of Mrs. Gisborne to Mrs. Shelley is perhaps necessary to explain further some portion of Shelley's letter :—

" Now, I will tell you the news of the steam-boat. The contract was drawn and signed the day after your departure ; the vessel to be complete, and launched, fit in every respect for the sea, excepting the finishing of the cabin, for 260 sequins. We have every reason to believe that the work will be well executed, and that it is an excellent bargain. Henry and Frankfort go on not only with vigour, but with fury ; the lower part of the house is filled with models prepared for casting, forging, &c. We have procured the wood for the frame from the shipbuilder on credit, so that Frankfort can go on with his work ; but I am sorry to say, that from this time the general progress of the work will be retarded for want of cash. The boilers might now be going on contemporaneously with the casting, but I know that at present there is no remedy for this evil. Every person concerned is making exertions, and is in a state of anxiety to see the quick result of this undertaking. I have advanced about 140 crowns, but prudence prohibits me from going any farther.

" Henry will write to Mr. Shelley when the works are in a greater state of forwardness : in the mean time, he sends his best love to his good friends, patron and patroness."

will learn that a resolution has been taken which leaves
you nothing to regret in that event.   It is with unspeak-
able satisfaction that I reflect that my entreaties and
persuasions overcame your scruples on this point, and
that whatever advantage shall accrue from it will belong
to you, whilst any reproach due to the imprudence of
such an enterprise, must rest on me.   I shall thus share
the pleasure of success, and bear the blame and loss,
(if such a thing were possible,) of a reverse ; and what
more can a man, who is a friend to another, desire for
himself?   Let us believe in a kind of optimism, in which
we are our own gods.   It is best that Mr. Gisborne
should have returned ; it is best that I should have over-
persuaded you and Henry ; it is best that you should
all live together, without any more solitary attempts ;
it is best that this one attempt should have been made,
otherwise, perhaps, one thing which is best might not
have occurred ; and it is best that we should think
all this for the best, even though it is not; because
Hope, as Coleridge says, is a solemn duty, which we
owe alike to ourselves and to the world—a worship
to the spirit of good within, which requires, before it
sends that inspiration forth, which impresses its likeness upon all that it creates, devoted and disinterested
homage.

A different scene is this from that in which you made
the chief character of our changing drama.   We see no
one, as usual.   Madame M * * * is quiet, and we
only meet her now and then, by chance.   Her daughter,
not so fair, but I fear as cold, as the snowy Florimel in
Spenser, is in and out of love with C—— as the winds
happen to blow ; and C——, who, at the moment I
happen to write, is in a high state of transitory content-
ment, is setting off to Vienna in a day or two.

My £100, from what mistake remains to be explained,
has not yet arrived, and the banker here is going to
advance me £50, on my bill at three months—all addi-

tional facilitation, should any such be needed, for the steam-boat. I have yet seen little of Florence. The gallery I have a design of studying piece-meal; one of my chief objects in Italy being the observing in statuary and painting, the degree in which, and the rules according to which, that ideal beauty, of which we have so intense yet so obscure an apprehension, is realised in external forms.

Adieu—I am anxious for Henry's first letter. Give to him, and take to yourself those sentiments, whatever they may be, with which you know that I cannot cease to regard you.

Most faithfully and affectionately yours,

P. B. S.

I had forgotten to say that I should be very much obliged to you, if you would contrive to send the Cencis, which are at the printer's, to England, by the next ship. I forgot it in the hurry of departure.—I have just heard from Peacock, saying, that he don't think that my tragedy will do, and that he don't much like it. But I ought to say, to blunt the edge of his criticism, that he is a nursling of the exact and superficial school in poetry.

If Mr. G. is returned, send the " Prometheus " with them.

TO HENRY REVELEY.

Florence, Oct. 28, 1819.

MY DEAR HENRY,

So it seems *I* am to begin the correspondence, though I have more to ask than to tell.

You know our bargain; you are to write me *uncorrected* letters, just as the words come, so let me have them—I like coin from the mint—though it may be a little rough at the edges ;—clipping is penal according to our statute.

In the first place listen to a reproach ; you ought to have sent me an acknowledgment of my last billet. I am very happy to hear from Mr. Gisborne, and he knows well enough how to interest me himself, not to need to rob me of an occasion of hearing from you. Let you and I try if we cannot be as punctual and business-like as the best of them. But no clipping and coining, if you please.

Now take this that I say in a light just so serious as not to give you pain. In fact, my dear fellow, my motive in soliciting your correspondence, and that flowing from your own mind, and clothed in your own words, is, that you may begin to accustom to discipline yourself in the only practice of life in which you appear deficient. You know that you are writing to a person persuaded of all the confidence and respect due to your powers in those branches of science to which you have addicted yourself; and you will not permit a false shame with regard to the mere mechanical arrangement of words to over-balance the advantage arising from the free communication of ideas. Thus you will become day by day more skilful in the management of that instrument of their communication, on which the attainment of a person's just rank in society depends. Do not think me arrogant. There are subjects of the highest importance in which you are far better qualified to instruct me, than I am qualified to instruct you on this subject.

Well, how goes on all ? The boilers, the keel of the boat, and the cylinder, and all the other elements of that soul which is to guide our "monstruo de fuego y agua" over the sea ? Let me hear news of their birth, and how they thrive after they are born. And is the money arrived at Mr. Webb's ? Send me an account

of the number of crowns you realise ; as I think we had
better, since it is a transaction in this country, keep our
accounts in money of this country.

We have rains enough to set the mills going, which
are essential to your great iron bar. I suppose it is at
present either made or making.

My health is better so long as the scirocco blows,
and, but for my daily expectation of Mary's confinement,
I should have been half tempted to have come to see
you. As it is, I shall wait till the boat is finished. On
the subject of your actual and your expected progress,
you will certainly allow me to hear from you.

Give my kindest regards to your mother and Mr.
Gisborne—tell the latter, whose billet I have neglected
to answer, that I did so, under the idea of addressing
him in a post or two· on a subject which gives me considerable anxiety about you all. I mean the continuance of your property in the British funds at this crisis
of approaching revolution. It is the business of a friend
to say what he thinks without fear of giving offence ;
and, if I were not a friend, argument is worth its market-
price anywhere.

Believe me, my dear Henry,

Your very faithful friend,

P. B. S.

TO MR. AND MRS. GISBORNE.

Florence, Oct. 28, 1819.

MY DEAR FRIENDS,

I RECEIVE this morning the strange and unexpected
news, that my bill of £200 has been returned to Mr.
Webb protested. Ultimately this can be nothing but
delay, as I have only drawn from my banker's hands so
much as to leave them still in possession of £80, and

this I positively know, and can prove by documents. By return of post, for I have not only written to my banker, but to private friends, no doubt Henry will be enabled to proceed.   Let him meanwhile do all that can be done.

Meanwhile, to save time, could not money be obtained temporarily, at Livorno, from Mr. W——, or Mr. G——, or any of your acquaintance, on my bills at three or six months, indorsed by Mr. Gisborne and Henry, so that he may go on with his work ?   If a month is of consequence, think of this.

Be of good cheer, Madonna mia, all will go well. The inclosed is for Henry, and was written before this news, as he will see ; but it does not, strange as it is, abate one atom of my cheer.

Accept, dear Mr. G., my best regards.

Yours faithfully,

P. B. S.

TO MR. AND MRS. GISBORNE.

Florence, Nov. 6, 1819.

MY DEAR FRIENDS,

I HAVE just finished a letter of five sheets on Carlile's affair,* and am in hourly expectation of Mary's confine-ment, you will imagine an excuse for my silence.

I forbear to address you, as I had designed, on the subject of your income as a public creditor of the English government, as it seems you have not the exclusive management of your funds ; and the peculiar circumstances of the delusion are such that none but a very few persons will ever be brought to see its instabi-lity but by the experience of loss.   If I were to convince

* A letter (to Leigh Hunt) on the Trial of Richard Carlile for publishing Paine's *Age of Reason*, intended for insertion in the *Examiner.*—ED.

you, Henry would probably be unable to convince his
uncle.   In vindication, however, of what I have already
said, allow me to turn your attention to England at this
hour.

In order to meet the national expenses, or rather that
some approach towards meeting them might seem to be
made, a tax of £3,000,000 was imposed. The first
consequence of this has been a *defalcation* in the revenue
at the rate of £3,600,000 a-year. Were the country in
the most tranquil and prosperous state, the minister,
in such a condition of affairs, must reduce the interest
of the national debt, or add to it ; a process which
would only insure the greater ultimate reduction of the
interest. But the people are nearly in a state of insurrection, and the least unpopular noblemen perceive the
necessity of conducting a spirit, which it is no longer
possible to oppose. For submitting to this necessity—
which, be assured, the haughty aristocrats unwillingly
did—Lord Fitzwilliam has been degraded from his
situation of Lord Lieutenant. An additional army of
11,500 men has received orders to be organised. Everything is preparing for a bloody struggle, in which, if
the ministers succeed, they will assuredly diminish the
interest of the national debt, for no combination of the
heaviest tyranny can raise the taxes for its payment.
If the people conquer, the public creditor will equally
suffer ; for it is monstrous to imagine that they will
submit to the perpetual inheritance of a double aristocracy. They will perhaps find some crown and church
lands, and appropriate the tithes to make a kind of
compensation to the public creditor. They will confis-
cate the estates of their political enemies. But all this
will not pay a tenth part of their debt. The existing
government, atrocious as it is, is the surest party to
which a public creditor may attach himself. He may
reason that *it may last my time*, though in the event the
ruin is more complete than in the case of a popular

revolution. I know you too well to believe you capable of arguing in this manner; I only reason on how things stand.

Your income may be reduced from £210 to £150, and then £100, and then by the issue of immense quantities of paper to save the immediate cause of one of the conflicting parties, to any value however small; or the source of it may be cut off at once. The ministers had, I doubt not, long since determined to establish an arbitrary government; and if they had not determined so, they have now entangled themselves in that consequence of their instinct as rulers, and if they recede they must perish. They are, however, not receding, and we are on the eve of great actions.

Kindest regards to Henry. I hope he is not stopped for want of money, as I shall assuredly send him what he wants in a month from the date of my last letter. I received his letter from Pistoia, and have no other criticism to make on it, except the severest—that it is too short. How goes on Portuguese—and Theocritus? I have deserted the odorous gardens of literature, to journey across the great sandy desert of politics; not, as you may imagine, without the hope of finding some enchanted paradise. In all probability, I shall be overwhelmed by one of the tempestuous columns which are forever traversing, with the speed of a storm, and the confusion of a chaos, that pathless wilderness. You meanwhile will be lamenting in some happy oasis that I do not return. This is out-Calderonizing Muley. We have had lightning and rain here in plenty. I like the Cascini very much, where I often walk alone, watching the leaves, and the rising and falling of the Arno. I am full of all kinds of literary plans.

Meanwhile, all yours most faithfully,

P. B. S.

TO MRS. GISBORNE.

Florence, Nov. 16, 1819.

MADONNA,

I HAVE been lately voyaging in a sea without my pilot, and although my sail has often been torn, my boat become leaky, and the log lost, I have yet sailed in a kind of way from island to island ; some of craggy and mountainous magnificence, some clothed with moss and flowers, and radiant with fountains, some barren deserts. *I have been reading Calderon without you.* I have read the " Cisma de Ingalaterra," the " Cabellos de Absolom," and three or four others. These pieces, inferior to those we read, at least to the " Principe Constante," in the splendour of particular passages, are perhaps superior in their satisfying completeness. The " Cabellos de Absolom " is full of the deepest and tenderest touches of nature. Nothing can be more pathetically conceived than the character of old David, and the tender and impartial love, overcoming all insults and all crimes, with which he regards his conflicting and disobedient sons. The incest scene of Amon and Tamar is perfectly tremendous. Well may Calderon say in the person of the former—

> Si sangre sin fuego hiere,
> que fara sangre con fuego?

Incest is, like many other incorrect things, a very poetical circumstance. It may be the excess of love or hate. It may be the defiance of everything for the sake of another, which clothes itself in the glory of the highest heroism, or it may be that cynical rage which, confounding the good and the bad in existing opinions, breaks through them for the purpose of rioting in selfishness and antipathy. Calderon, following the Jewish historians, has represented Amon's action in the basest

II.   U

point of view—he is a prejudiced savage, acting what
he abhors, and abhorring that which is the unwilling
party to his crime.

Adieu, Madonna, yours truly,

P. B. S.

I transcribe you a passage from the Cisma de Ingalaterra—spoken by "Carlos, Embaxador de Francia,
enamorado de Ana Bolena." Is there anything in
Petrarch finer than the second stanza?

Porque apenas el Sol se coronaba
de nueva luz en la estacion primeva,
quando yo en sus umbrales adoraba
segundo Sol en abreviada esfera ;
la noche apenas tremula baxaba,
à solos mis deseos lisonjera,
quando un jardin, republica de flores,
era tercero fiel de mis amores.

Alli, el silencio de la noche fria,
el jazmin, que en las redes se enlazava,
el cristal de la fuente que corria,
el arroyo que à solas murmurava,
El viento que en las hojas se movia,
el Aura que en las flores respirava ;
todo era amor' ; què mucho, si en tal calma
aves, fuentes, y flores tienen alma !

No has visto providente y oficiosa,
mover el ayre iluminada aveja,
que hasta beber la purpura a la rosa
ya se acerca cobarde, y ya se alexa?
No has visto enamorada mariposa,
dar cercos a la luz, hasta que dexa,
en monumento facil abrasadas
las alas de color tornasoladas?

Assi mi amor, cobarde muchos dias,
tornos hizo a la rosa y a la llama ;
temor che ha sido entre cenizas frias,
tantas vezes llorado de quien ama ;
pero el amor, que vence con porfias,
y la ocasion, que con disculpas llama,
me animaron, y aveja y mariposa
quemè las alas, y lleguè a la rosa.

TO MR. JOHN GISBORNE.

MY DEAR SIR,

I ENVY you the first reading of Theocritus. Were not the Greeks a glorious people ? What is there, as Job says of the Leviathan, like unto them ? If the army of Nicias had not been defeated under the walls of Syracuse ; if the Athenians had, acquiring Sicily, held the balance between Rome and Carthage, sent garrisons to the Greek colonies in the south of Italy, Rome might have been all that its intellectual condition entitled it to be, a tributary, not the conqueror of Greece ; the Macedonian power would never have attained to the dictatorship of the civilized states of the world. Who knows whether, under the steady progress which philosophy and social institutions would have made, (for, in the age to which I refer, their progress was both rapid and secure,) among a people of the most perfect physical organization, whether the Christian religion would have arisen, or the barbarians have overwhelmed the wrecks of civilization which had survived the conquest and tyranny of the Romans ? What, then, should we have been ? As it is, all of us who are worth anything, spend our manhood in unlearning the follies, or expiating the mistakes of our youth. We are stuffed full of prejudices ; and our natural passions are so managed, that if we restrain them we grow intolerant and precise, because we restrain them not according to reason, but according to error ; and if we do not restrain them, we do all sorts of mischief to ourselves and others. Our imagination and understanding are alike subjected to rules the most absurd ;—so much for Theocritus and the Greeks.*

* " I subjoin here," says Mrs. Shelley, " a fragment of a letter, I know not to whom addressed :—
" It is probable that you will be earnest to employ the sacred

In spite of all your arguments, I wish your money
were out of the funds. This middle course which you
speak of, and which may probably have place, will
amount to your losing not all your income, nor retaining all, but have the half taken away. I feel intimately
persuaded, whatever political forms may have place in
England, that no party can continue many years, perhaps not many months, in the administration, without
diminishing the interest of the national debt.—And once
having commenced—and having done so safely—where
will it end ?

Give Henry my kindest thanks for his most interesting

talisman of language. To acquire these you are now necessitated
to sacrifice many hours of the time, when, instead of being conversant with particles and verbs, your nature incites you to contemplation and inquiry concerning the objects which they conceal.
You desire to enjoy the beauties of eloquence and poetry—to
sympathise in the original language with the institutors and martyrs
of ancient freedom. The generous and inspiriting examples of
philosophy and virtue you desire intimately to know and feel ; not
as mere facts detailing names, and dates, and motions of the human
body, but clothed in the very language of the actors,—that language
dictated by and expressive of the passions and principles that
governed their conduct. Facts are not what we want to know in
poetry, in history, in the lives of individual men, in satire, or in
panegyric. They are the mere divisions, the arbitrary points on
which we hang, and to which we refer those delicate and evanescent hues of mind, which language delights and instructs us in
precise proportion as it expresses. What is a translation of Homer
into English? A person who is ignorant of Greek need only look
at Paradise Lost or the tragedy of Lear translated into French, to
obtain an analogical conception of its worthless and miserable
inadequacy. Tacitus, or Livius, or Herodotus, are equally un-
delightful and uninstructive in translation. You require to know
and to be intimate with those persons who have acted a distinguished
part to benefit, to enlighten, or even to pervert and injure human-
kind. Before you can do this, four years are yet to be consumed
in the discipline of the ancient languages, and those of modern
Europe, which you only imperfectly know, and which conceal from
your intimacy such names as Ariosto, Tasso, Petrarch, and
Macchiavelli ; or Goethe, Schiller, Wieland, &c. The French
language you, like every other respectable woman, already know ;
and if the great name of Rousseau did not redeem it, it would have
been perhaps as well that you had remained entirely ignorant
of it."

letter, and bid him expect one from me by the next post.

Mary and the babe continue well.—Last night we had a magnificent thunder-storm, with claps that shook the house like an earthquake. Both Mary and C—— unite with me in kindest remembrances to all.

Most faithfully yours obliged,

P. B. S.

TO HENRY REVELEY.

Florence, Nov. 17th, 1819.

MY DEAR HENRY,

I WAS exceedingly interested by your letter, and I cannot but thank you for overcoming the inaptitude of a long disuse at my request, for my pleasure. It is a great thing done, the successful casting of the cylinder —may it be a happy auspice for what is to follow ! I hope, in a few posts, to remit the necessary money for the completion. Meanwhile, are not those portions of the work which can be done without expense, saving time in their progress ? Do you think you lose much money or time by this delay ?

All that you say of the alteration in the form of the boat strikes me, though one of the multitude in this respect, as improvement. I long to get aboard her, and be an unworthy partaker in the glory of the astonishment of the Livornese, when she returns from her cruise round Melloria. When do you think she will be fit for sea ?

Your volcanic description of the birth of the cylinder is very characteristic of you, and of it.* One might

* The passage in Mr. Reveley's letter referred to by Shelley was as follows :—

" *Friday,* 12*th Nov.*

" The event is now past—both the steam cylinder and air-pump were cast at three o'clock this afternoon. At two o'clock this imagine God, when he made the earth, and saw the granite mountains and flinty promontories flow into their craggy forms, and the splendour of their fusion filling millions of miles of the void space, like the tail of a comet, so looking, so delighting in his work. God sees his machine spinning round the sun, and delights in its success, and has taken out patents to supply all the suns in space with the same manufacture. Your boat will be to the ocean of water, what this earth is to the ocean of ether—a prosperous and swift voyager.

When shall we see you all? *You* not, I suppose, till your boat is ready to sail—and then, if not before, I must, of course, come to Livorno. Our plans for the winter are yet scarcely defined; they tend towards our spending February and March at Pisa, where our communications will not be so distant, nor so epistolary. C—— left us a week ago, not without many lamentations, as all true lovers pay on such occasions. He is

morning I repaired to the mill to see that the preliminary operations, upon which the ultimate success of a *fount* greatly depends, were conducted with proper attention. The moulds are buried in a pit, made close, before the mouth of the furnace, so that the melted metal, when the plug is driven in, may run easily into them, and fill up the vacant space left between the core and the shell, in order to form the desired cylinders. The fire was lighted in the furnace at nine, and in three hours the metal was fused. At three o'clock it was ready to cast, the fusion being remarkably rapid, owing to the perfection of the furnace. The metal was also heated to an extreme degree, boiling with fury, and seeming to dance with the pleasure of running into its proper form. The plug was struck, and a massy stream of a bluish dazzling whiteness filled the moulds in the twinkling of a shooting star. The castings will not be cool enough to be drawn up till to-morrow afternoon; but, to judge from all appearances, I expect them to be perfect.

" Saturday, 13th Nov.

" They have been excavated and drawn up. I have examined them and found them really perfect; they are massive and strong to bear any usage and sea-water, *in sæcula sæculorum.* I am now going on gently with the brass-work, which does not require any immediate expenses, and which I attend to entirely myself. I have no workmen about me at present."

to write me an account of the Trieste steam-boat, which
I will transmit to you.

Mrs. Shelley and Miss C—— return you their kindest
salutations, with interest.

Most affectionately yours,

P. B. S.

TO HENRY REVELEY.

Florence, 18th Dec., 1819.

MY DEAR HENRY,

YOU see, as I said, it only amounts to delay, all this
abominable entanglement. I send you 484 dollars, or
ordinary francesconi, I suppose, but you will tell me
what you receive in Tuscan money, if they are not—
the produce of £100. So my heart is a little lightened,
which, I assure you, was heavy enough until this moment,
on your account. I write to Messrs. Ward to pay you.

I have received no satisfactory letter from my bankers,
but I must expect it every week—or, at least, in a month
from this date, when I will not fail to transmit you the
remainder of what may be necessary.

Every body here is talking of a steam-ship which is
building at Leghorn ; one person said, as if he knew
the whole affair, that he was waiting in Tuscany to take
his departure to Naples in it. Your name has not, to
my knowledge, been mentioned. I think you would do
well to encourage this publicity.

I have better health than I have known for a long
time—ready for any stormy cruise. When will the ship
be ready to sail ? We have been feeding ourselves
with the hope that Mr. Gisborne and your mother would
have paid us their promised visit. I did not even hope,
perhaps not even wish, that you should, until the engine
is finished. My regret at this failure has several times
impelled me to go to Leghorn—but I have always

resisted the temptation. Ask them, entreat them, from me, to appoint some early day. We have a bed and room, and every thing prepared.

I write in great haste, as you may see. Ever believe me, my dear Henry, your attached friend,

P. B. S.

TO MR. AND MRS. GISBORNE.

Florence, Dec. 23d, 1819.

MY DEAR FRIENDS,

I SUFFERED more pain than it would be manly to confess, or than you can easily conceive, from that wretched uncertainty about the money. At last, however, it is certain that you will encounter no further check in the receiving supplies, and a weight is taken from my spirits, which, in spite of many other causes of discomfort, makes itself known to have been a heavy load, by the lightness which I now feel in writing to you.

So the steamboat will take three months to finish? The vernal equinox will be over by that time, and the early wakening of the year have paved the Mediterranean with calm. Among other circumstances to regret in this delay, it is so far well that our first cruise will be made in serene weather.

I send you enclosed a mandate for 396 francesconi, which is what M. Torlonia incorrectly designates a hundred pounds—but as we count in the money of the country, that need make no difference to us.

I have just finished an additional act to "Prometheus," which Mary is now transcribing, and which will be enclosed for your inspection before it is transmitted to the bookseller. I am engaged in a political work—I am busy enough, and if the faculties of my

mind were not imprisoned within a mind, whose bars
are daily cares and vulgar difficulties, I might yet do
something—but as it is—

Mary is well—but for this affair in London I think
her spirits would be good. What shall I—what can I—
what ought I to do? You cannot picture to yourself my
perplexity.

Adieu, my dear friends.

Ever yours, faithfully attached,

P. B. S.

TO MR. JOHN GISBORNE.

Florence, Jan. 25th, 1820.

MY DEAR SIR,

WE have suddenly taken the determination to avail
ourselves of this lovely weather to approach you as far
as Pisa. I need not assure you—unless my malady
should violently return—you will see me at Leghorn.

We *embark;* and I promise myself the delight of the
sky, the water, and the mountains. I must suffer at
any rate, but I expect to suffer less in a boat than in a
carriage. I have many things to say, which let me
reserve till we meet.

I sympathise in all your good news, as I have done
in your ill. Let Henry take care of himself, and not,
desiring to combine too many advantages, check the
progress of his recovery, the greatest of all.

Remember me affectionately to him and to Mrs.
Gisborne, and accept for yourself my unalterable
sentiments of regard. Meanwhile, *consider well your
plans*, which I only half understand.

Ever most faithfully yours,

P. B. SHELLEY.

TO MR. AND MRS. GISBORNE.

Pisa, Feb. 9th, 1820.

PRAY let us see you soon, or our threat may cost both us and you something—a visit to Livorno. The stage direction on the present occasion is, " exit Moonshine and enter Wall ; " or rather four walls, who surround and take prisoners the Galan and Dama.

Seriously, pray do not disappoint us. We shall watch the sky, and the death of the Scirocco must be the birth of your arrival.

Mary and I are going to study mathematics. We design to take the most compendious, yet certain methods of arriving at the great results. We believe that your right-angled Triangle will contain the solution of the problem of how to proceed.

Do not write but *come.* Mary is too idle to write, but all that she has to say is *come.* She joins with me in condemning the moonlight plan. Indeed we ought not to be so selfish as to allow you to come at all, if it is to cost you all the fatigue and annoyance of returning the same night. But it will not be—so adieu.

TO MR. AND MRS. GISBORNE.

Pisa, April 23, 1820.

MY DEAR FRIENDS,

WE were much pained to hear of the illness you all seem to have been suffering, and still more at the apparent dejection of your last letter. We are in daily expectation this lovely weather of seeing you, and I think the change of air and scene might be good for your health and spirits, even if *we* cannot enliven you. I shall have

some business at Livorno soon ; and I thought of coming
to fetch you, but I have changed my plan, and mean to
return with you, that I may save myself two journeys.
I have been thinking, and talking, and reading Agriculture this last week. But I am very anxious to see
you, especially now as instead of six hours, you give us
thirty-six, or perhaps more. I shall hear of the steam-
engine, and you will hear of *our* plans, when we meet,
which will be in so short a time that I neither inquire
nor communicate.

Ever affectionately yours,

P. B. SHELLEY.

TO MR. AND MRS. GISBORNE.

(LONDON).

Pisa, May 26th, 1820.

MY DEAR FRIENDS,

I WRITE to you thus early, because I have determined to accept of your kind offer about the correction
of " Prometheus." The bookseller makes difficulties
about sending the proofs to me, and to whom else can
I so well entrust what I am so much interested in having
done well ; and to whom would I prefer to owe the
recollection of an additional kindness done to me ? I
enclose you two little papers of corrections and additions;
—I do not think you will find any difficulty in interpo-
lating them into their proper places.
Well, how do you like London, and your journey;
the Alps in their beauty and their eternity ; Paris in its
slight and transitory colours ; and the wearisome plains
of France—and the *moral* people with whom you drank
tea last night? Above all, *how* are you ? And of the
last question, believe me, we are now most anxiously
waiting for a reply—until which I will say nothing, not

ask anything. I rely on the journal with as much security as if it were already written.

I am just returned from a visit to Leghorn, Casciano, and your old fortress at Sant' Elmo. I bought the vases you saw for about twenty sequins less than Micale asked, and had them packed up, and, by the polite assistance of your friend, Mr. Guebhard, sent them on board. I found your Giuseppe very useful in all this business. He got me tea and breakfast, and I slept in your house, and departed early the next morning for Casciano. Everything seems in excellent order at Casa Ricci— garden, pigeons, tables, chairs, and beds. As I did not find my bed sealed up, I left it as I found it. What a glorious prospect you had from the windows of Sant' Elmo ! The enormous chain of the Apennines, with its many-folded ridges, islanded in the misty distance of the air ; the sea, so immensely distant, appearing as at your feet ; and the prodigious expanse of the plain of Pisa, and the dark green marshes lessened almost to a strip by the height of the blue mountains overhanging them. Then the wild and unreclaimed fertility of the foreground, and the chesnut trees, whose vivid foliage made a sort of resting-place to the sense before it darted itself to the jagged horizon of this prospect. I was altogether delighted. I had a respite from my nervous symptoms, which was compensated to me by a violent cold in the head. There was a tradition about you at Sant' Elmo—*An English family that had lived here in the time of the French.* The doctor, too, at the Bagni, knew you. The house is in a most dilapidated condition, but I suppose all that is curable.

We go to the Bagni next month—but still direct to Pisa as safest. I shall write to you the *ultimates* of my commission in my next letter. I am undergoing a course of the Pisan baths, on which I lay no singular stress—but they soothe. I ought to have peace of mind, leisure, tranquillity ; this I expect soon. Our anxiety about Godwin is very great, and any information that you could give a day or two earlier than he might, respecting any decisive event in his law-suit, would be a great relief. Your impressions about Godwin (I speak especially to Madonna mia, who had known him before,) will especially interest me. You know that added years only add to my admiration of his intellectual powers, and even the moral resources of his character. Of my other friends I say nothing. To see Hunt is to like him ; and there is one other recommendation which he has to you, he is my friend. To know H——, if any one can know him, is to know something very unlike, and inexpressibly superior, to the great mass of men.

Will Henry write me an adamantine letter, flowing, not like the words of Sophocles, with honey, but molten brass and iron, and bristling with wheels and teeth ? I saw his steam-boat asleep under the walls. I was afraid to waken it, and ask it whether it was dreaming of him, for the same reason that I would have refrained from awakening Ariadne, after Theseus had left her—unless I had been Bacchus.

Affectionately and anxiously yours,

P. B. S.

TO MR. AND MRS. GISBORNE

(LONDON).

MY DEAR FRIENDS,

I AM to a certain degree indifferent as to the reply to our last proposal, and, therefore, will not allude to it. Permit me only on subjects of this nature to express one sentiment, which you would have given me credit for, even if not expressed. Let no considerations of *my* interest, or any retrospect to the source from which the funds were supplied, modify your decision as to return-

ing and pursuing or abandoning the adventure of the
steam-engine. My object was solely your true advantage, and it is when I am baffled of this, by any attention
to a mere form, that I shall be ill requited. Nay, more,
I think it for your interest, should you obtain almost
whatever situation for Henry, to accept Clementi's proposal, and remain in England ;—not without accepting
it, for it does no more than balance the difference of
expense between Italy and London ; and if you have
any trust in the justice of my moral sense, and believe
that in what concerns true honour and virtuous conduct
in life, I am an experienced counsellor, you will not
hesitate—these things being equal—to accept this proposal. The opposition I made, while you were in Italy
to the abandonment of the steam-boat project, was
founded, you well know, on the motives which have influenced everything that ever has guided, or ever will
guide, anything that I can do or say respecting you.
I thought it against Henry's interest. I think it now
against his interest that he and you should abandon
your prospects in England. As to us—we are uncertain
people, who are chased by the spirits of our destiny from
purpose to purpose, like clouds by the wind.

There is one thing more to be said. If you decide
to remain in England, assuredly it would be foolish to
return. Your journey would cost you between £100
and £200, a sum far greater than you could expect to
save by the increased price by which you would sell
your things. Remit the matter to me, and I will cast
off my habitual character, and attend to the minutest
points. With Mr. G——'s, devil take his name, I can't
write it—you know who's, assistance, all this might be
accomplished in such a manner as to save a very considerable sum. Though I shall suffer from your decision
in the proportion as your society is delightful to me, I
cannot forbear expressing my persuasion, that the time,
the expense, and the trouble of returning to Italy, if

your ultimate decision be to settle in London, ought
all to be spared. A year, a month, a week, at Henry's
age, and with his purposes, ought not to be unemployed.
It was the depth with which I felt this truth, which
impelled me to incite him to this adventure of the steam-
boat.

TO MRS. SHELLEY

(LEGHORN).

Casa Silva,
Sunday morning, July, 1820.

MY DEAR LOVE,

I BELIEVE I shall have taken a very pleasant and
spacious apartment at the Bagni for three months. It
is as all the others are—dear. I shall give forty or
forty-five sequins for the three months, but as yet I do
not know which. I could get others something cheaper,
and a great deal worse; but if we would write, it is
requisite to have space.

To-morrow evening, or the following morning, you
will probably see me. T—— is planning a journey
to England to secure his property in the event of a
revolution, which, he is persuaded, is on the eve of
exploding. I neither believe that, nor do I fear that
the consequences will be so immediately destructive to
the existing forms of social order. Money will be
delayed, and the exchange reduced very low, and my
annuity and ****, on account of these being *money*,
will be in some danger; but land is quite safe. Besides,
it will not be so rapid. Let us hope we shall have a
reform. T—— will be lulled into security, while the
slow progress of things is still flowing on, after this affair
of the Queen may appear to be blown over. There are
bad news from Palermo : the soldiers resisted the people,

and a terrible slaughter, amounting, it is said, to four thousand men, ensued. The event, however, was as it should be. Sicily, like Naples, is free. By the brief and partial accounts of the Florence paper, it appears that the enthusiasm of the people was prodigious, and that the women fought from the houses, raining down boiling oil on the assailants.

I am promised a bill on Vienna on the 5th, the day on which my note will be paid, and the day on which I purpose to leave Leghorn. *** is very unhappy at the idea of T.'s going to England, though she seems to feel the necessity of it. Some time or other he must go to settle his affairs, and they seem to agree that this is the best opportunity. *I* have no thought of leaving Italy. The best thing we can do is to save money, and, if things take a decided turn, (which I am convinced they will at last, but not perhaps for two or three years,) it will be time for me to assert my rights, and preserve my annuity. Meanwhile, another event may decide us.

Kiss sweet babe, and kiss yourself for me—I love you affectionately.

P. B. S.

Sunday evening.

I have taken the house for forty sequins for three months—a good bargain, and a very good house as things go—this is about thirteen sequins a month. To-morrow I go to look over the inventory ; expect me therefore on Tuesday morning.

TO MRS. SHELLEY

(BAGNI DI SAN GIULIANO).

Casa Ricci [*Leghorn*],
Sept. 1st, 1820.

I AM afraid, my dearest, that I shall not be able to be with you so soon as to-morrow evening, though I shall use every exertion. Del Rosso I have not seen, nor shall until this evening. Jackson I have, and he is to drink tea with us this evening, and bring the *Constitutionnel.*

You will have seen the papers, but I doubt that they will not contain the latest and most important news. It is certain, by private letters from merchants, that a serious insurrection has broken out at Paris, and the *reports* last night are, that an attack made by the populace on the Tuileries still continued when the last accounts came away. At Naples the constitutional party have declared to the Austrian minister, that if the Emperor should make war on them, their first action would be to put to death *all* the members of the royal family—a necessary and most just measure, when the forces of the combatants, as well as the merits of their respective causes, are so unequal. That kings should be everywhere the hostages for liberty were admirable.

What will become of the Gisbornes, or of the English, at Paris? How soon will England itself, and perhaps Italy, be caught by the sacred fire? And what, to come from the solar system to a grain of sand, *shall we do?*

Kiss babe for me, and your own self. I am somewhat better, but my side still vexes me—a little.

Your affectionate S.

TO THE EDITOR OF THE "QUARTERLY REVIEW." *

SIR,

SHOULD you cast your eye on the signature of this letter before you read the contents, you might imagine that they related to a slanderous paper which appeared in your Review some time since. I never notice anonymous attacks. The wretch who wrote it has doubtless the additional reward of a consciousness of his motives, besides the thirty guineas a sheet, or what-ever it is that you pay him. Of course you cannot be answerable for all the writings which you edit, and *I* certainly bear you no ill-will for having edited the abuse to which I allude—indeed, I was too much amused by being compared to Pharaoh, not readily to forgive editor, printer, publisher, stitcher, or any one, except the despicable writer, connected with something so ex-quisitely entertaining. Seriously speaking, I am not in the habit of permitting myself to be disturbed by what is said or written of me, though, I dare say, I may be condemned sometimes justly enough. But I feel, in respect to the writer in question, that "I am there sitting, where he durst not soar."

The case is different with the unfortunate subject of this letter, the author of Endymion, to whose feelings and situation I entreat you to allow me to call your attention. I write considerably in the dark; but if it is Mr. Gifford that I am addressing, I am persuaded that in an appeal to his humanity and justice, he will acknowledge the *fas ab hoste doceri.* I am aware that the first duty of a Reviewer is towards the public, and I am willing to confess that Endymion is a poem con-

* This letter was never sent.—[*Note by Mrs. Shelley.*]

siderably defective, and that, perhaps, it deserved as much censure as the pages of your Review record against it ; but, not to mention that there is a certain contemptuousness of phraseology from which it is difficult for a critic to abstain, in the review of Endymion, I do not think that the writer has given it its due praise. Surely the poem, with all its faults, is a very remarkable production for a man of Keats's age, and the promise of ultimate excellence is such as has rarely been afforded even by such as have afterwards attained high literary eminence. Look at book ii. line 833, &c., and book iii. line 113 to 120—read down that page, and then again from line 193. I could cite many other passages, to convince you that it deserved milder usage. Why it should have been reviewed at all, excepting for the purpose of bringing its excellences into notice, I cannot conceive, for it was very little read, and there was no danger that it should become a model to the age of that false taste, with which I confess that it is replenished.

Poor Keats was thrown into a dreadful state of mind by this review, which, I am persuaded, was not written with any intention of producing the effect, to which it has, at least, greatly contributed, of embittering his existence, and inducing a disease from which there are now but faint hopes of his recovery. The first effects are described to me to have resembled insanity, and it was by assiduous watching that he was restrained from effecting purposes of suicide. The agony of his sufferings at length produced the rupture of a blood-vessel in the lungs, and the usual process of consumption appears to have begun. He is coming to pay me a visit in Italy ; but I fear that unless his mind can be kept tranquil, little is to be hoped from the mere influence of climate.

But let me not extort anything from your pity. I have just seen a second volume, published by him evidently in careless despair. I have desired my book-seller to send you a copy, and allow me to solicit your especial attention to the fragment of a poem entitled "Hyperion," the composition of which was checked by the Review in question. The great proportion of this piece is surely in the very highest style of poetry. I speak impartially, for the canons of taste to which Keats has conformed in his other compositions are the very reverse of my own. I leave you to judge for yourself : it would be an insult to you to suppose that from motives, however honourable, you would lend yourself to a deception of the public.

＊   ＊   ＊   ＊   ＊   ＊   ＊

TO MR. JOHN GISBORNE

(AT LEGHORN).

Pisa, oggi [*November,* 1820].

MY DEAR SIR,

I SEND you the Phædon and Tacitus. I congratu-late you on your conquest of the Iliad. You must have been astonished at the perpetually increasing magnificence of the last seven books. Homer there truly begins to be himself. The battle of the Sca-mander, the funeral of Patroclus, and the high and solemn close of the whole bloody tale in tenderness and inexpiable sorrow, are wrought in a manner incomparable with any thing of the same kind. The Odyssey is sweet, but there is nothing like this.

I am bathing myself in the light and odour of the flowery and starry Autos. I have read them all more than once. Henry will tell you how much I am in love with Pacchiani. I suffer from my disease con-siderably. Henry will also tell you how much, and how whimsically, he alarmed me last night.

My kindest remembrances to Mrs. Gisborne, and best wishes for your health and happiness.

Faithfully yours,

P. B. S.

I have a new Calderon coming from Paris.

TO HENRY REVELEY.

Pisa, Tuesday, 1 *o'clock,*
April 17*th,* 1821.

MY DEAR HENRY,

OUR ducking last night has added fire, instead of quenching the nautical ardour which produced it ; and I consider it a good omen in any enterprise, that it begins in evil : as being more probable that it will end in good. I hope *you* have not suffered from it. I am rather feverish, but very well as to the side, whence I expected the worst consequences. I send you directions for the complete equipment of our boat, since you have so kindly promised to undertake it. In putting into execution, a little more or less expense in so trifling an affair, is to be disregarded. I need not say that the approaching season invites expedition. You can put her in hand immediately, and write the day on which we may come for her.

We expect with impatience the arrival of our false friends, who have so long cheated us with delay ; and Mary unites with me in desiring, that, as *you* participated equally in the crime, you should not be omitted in the expiation.

All good be with you.—Adieu.

Yours faithfully,

S.

Williams desires to be kindly remembered to you, and begs to present his compliments to Mr. and Mrs. G., and—heaven knows what.

TO HENRY REVELEY.

Pisa, April 19*th* [1821].
MY DEAR HENRY,

THE rullock, or place for the oar, ought not to be
placed where the oar-pins are now, but ought to be
nearer to the mast; as near as possible, indeed, so
that the rower has room to sit. In addition let a false
keel be made in this shape, so as to be four inches
deep at the stern, and to decrease towards the prow.
It may be as thin as you please.

Tell Mr. and Mrs. G—— that I have read the
Numancia, and after wading through the singular
stupidity of the first act, began to be greatly delighted,
and, at length, interested in a very high degree, by
the power of the writer in awakening pity and admiration, in which I hardly know by whom he is excelled.
There is little, I allow, in a strict sense, to be called
poetry in this play; but the command of language, and
the harmony of versification, is so great as to deceive
one into an idea that it is poetry.

Adieu.—We shall see you soon.

Yours ever truly,

S.

TO MR. AND MRS. GISBORNE.

Bagni, Tuesday Evening,
(June 5*th,* 1821.)
MY DEAR FRIENDS,

WE anxiously expect your arrival at the Baths; but
as I am persuaded that you will spend as much time
with us as you can save from your necessary occupations before your departure, I will forbear to vex you
with importunity. My health does not permit me to

spend many hours from home. I have been engaged these last days in composing a poem on the death of Keats, which will shortly be finished; and I anticipate the pleasure of reading it to you, as some of the very few persons who will be interested in it and understand it. It is a highly-wrought *piece of art*, and perhaps better, in point of composition, than anything I have written.

I have obtained a purchaser for some of the articles of your three lists, a catalogue of which I subjoin. I shall do my utmost to get more; could you not send me a complete list of your *furniture*, as I have had inquiries made about chests of drawers, &c.

*   *   *   *   *

My unfortunate box! it contained a chaos of the elements of Charles I. If the idea of the *creator* had been packed up with them, it would have shared the same fate; and that, I am afraid, has undergone another sort of shipwreck.

*   *   *   *   *

Very faithfully and affectionately yours,

S.

TO MR. JOHN GISBORNE.

Pisa, Saturday,
(*June* 16, 1821.)

MY DEAR FRIEND,

I HAVE received the heart-rending account of the closing scene of the great genius whom envy and ingratitude scourged out of the world.* I do not think that if I had seen it before, I could have composed my poem. The enthusiasm of the imagination would have overpowered the sentiment.

* John Keats.

As it is, I have finished my Elegy ; * and this day I send it to the press at Pisa. You shall have a copy the moment it is completed. I think it will please you. I have dipped my pen in consuming fire for his destroyers ; otherwise the style is calm and solemn.

Pray, when shall we see you ? Or are the streams of Helicon less salutary than sea-bathing for the nerves? Give us as much as you can before you go to England, and rather divide the term than not come soon.

Mrs. * * * wishes that none of the books, desk, &c., should be packed up with the piano ; but that they should be sent, one by one, by Pepi. Address them to *me* at her house. She desired me to have them addressed to *me*, why I know not.

A droll circumstance has occurred. Queen Mab, a poem written by me when very young, in the most furious style, with long notes against Jesus Christ, and God the Father, and the king, and bishops, and marriage, and the devil knows what, is just published by one of the low booksellers in the Strand, against my wish and consent, and all the people are at loggerheads about it. H. S.† gives me this account. You may imagine how much I am amused. For the sake of a dignified appearance, however, and really because I wish to protest against all the bad poetry in it, I have given orders to say that it is all done against my desire, and have directed my attorney to apply to Chancery for an injunction, which he will not get.

I am pretty ill, I thank you, just now ; but I hope you are better.

Most affectionately yours,

P. B. S.

* Adonais.   † Horace Smith.

TO MR. AND MRS. GISBORNE.

Bagni, Friday Night,
(July 13th, 1821.)

MY DEAR FRIENDS,

I HAVE been expecting every day a writ to attend at
your court at Guebhard's, whence you know it is settled
that I should conduct you hither to spend your last days
in Italy. A thousand thanks for your maps; in return
for which I send you the only copy of Adonais the
printer has yet delivered. I wish I could say, as
Glaucus could, in the exchange for the arms of Diomed,
—ἑκατόμβοι ἐννεαβοίων.

*   *   *   *   *

I will only remind you of Faust; my desire for the
conclusion of which is only exceeded by my desire to
welcome you. Do you observe any traces of him in
the poem I send you? Poets—the best of them, are a
very cameleonic race; they take the colour not only of
what they feed on, but of the very leaves under which
they pass.

Mary is just on the verge of finishing her novel; but
it cannot be in time for you to take to England.—Farewell.

Most faithfully yours,
P. B. S.

TO MR. AND MRS. GISBORNE.

Bagni, July 19th [1821].

MY DEAREST FRIENDS,

I AM fully repaid for the painful emotions from which
some verses of my poem sprung, by your sympathy and
approbation—which is all the reward I expect—and as
much as I desire. It is not for me to judge whether, in

the high praise your feelings assign me, you are right or wrong. The poet and the man are two different natures ; though they exist together, they may be unconscious of each other, and incapable of deciding on each other's powers and efforts by any reflex act. The decision of the cause, whether or no *I* am a poet, is removed from the present time to the hour when our posterity shall assemble ; but the court is a very severe one, and I fear that the verdict will be, " Guilty—death !"

I shall be with you on the first summons. I hope that the time you have reserved for us, " this bank and shoal of time," is not so short as you once talked of.

In haste, most affectionately yours,

P. B. S.

TO MRS. SHELLEY

(BAGNI DI PISA).

Lione Bianco, Florence,
(Tuesday, August 1st, 1821.)

MY DEAREST LOVE,

I SHALL not return this evening ; nor, unless I have better success, to-morrow. I have seen many houses, but very few within the compass of our powers ; and, even in those which seem to suit, nothing is more difficult than to bring the proprietors to terms. I congratulate myself on having taken the season in time, as there is great expectation of Florence being full next winter. I shall do my utmost to return to-morrow evening. You may expect me about ten or eleven o'clock, as I shall purposely be late, to spare myself the excessive heat.

The Gisbornes (four o'clock, Tuesday,) are just set out in a diligence-and-four, for Bologna. They have promised to write from Paris. I spent three hours this morning principally in the contemplation of the Niobe, and of a favourite Apollo ; all worldly thoughts and cares seem to vanish from before the sublime emotions such spectacles create ; and I am deeply impressed with the great difference of happiness enjoyed by those who live at a distance from these incarnations of all that the finest minds have conceived of beauty, and those who can resort to their company at pleasure. What should we think if we were forbidden to read the great writers who have left us their works ? And yet to be forbidden to live at Florence or Rome, is an evil of the same kind, of scarcely less magnitude.

I am delighted to hear that the W.'s are with you. I am convinced that Williams must persevere in the use of the doccia. Give my most affectionate remembrances to them. I shall know all the houses in Florence, and can give W. a good account of them all. You have not sent my passport, and I must get home as I can. I suppose you did not receive my note.

I grudge my sequins for a carriage ; but I have suffered from the sun and the fatigue, and dare not expose myself to that which is necessary for house-hunting.

Kiss little babe, and how is he ? but I hope to see him fast asleep to-morrow night. And pray, dearest Mary, have some of your novel prepared for my return.

Your ever affectionate

S.

TO MRS. SHELLEY

(BAGNI DI PISA).

Bologna, Agosto 6 [1821].

DEAREST MINE,

I AM at Bologna, and the caravella is ordered for Ravenna. I have been detained, by having made an embarrassing and inexplicable arrangement, more than twelve hours ; or I should have arrived at Bologna last night instead of this morning.

Though I have travelled all night at the rate of two miles and a half an hour, in a little open calesso, I am perfectly well in health. One would think that I were the spaniel of Destiny, for the more she knocks me about, the more I fawn on her. I had an overturn about daybreak ; the old horse stumbled, and threw me and the fat vetturino into a slope of meadow, over the hedge. My angular figure stuck where it was pitched ; but my vetturino's spherical form rolled fairly to the bottom of the hill, and that with so few symptoms of reluctance in the life that animated it, that my ridicule (for it was the drollest sight in the world) was suppressed by my fear that the poor devil had been hurt. But he was very well, and we continued our journey with great success.

*   *   *   *   *   *   *

My love to the Williams's. Kiss my pretty one, and accept an affectionate one for yourself from me. The chaise waits. I will write the first night from Ravenna at length.

Yours ever,

S.

TO MRS. SHELLEY.

Ravenna, August 7, 1821.

MY DEAREST MARY,

I ARRIVED last night at ten o'clock, and sat up talking with Lord Byron until five this morning. I then went to sleep, and now awake at eleven, and having despatched my breakfast as quick as possible, mean to devote the interval until twelve, when the post departs, to you.

Lord Byron is very well, and was delighted to see me. He has in fact completely recovered his health, and lives a life totally the reverse of that which he led at Venice. He has a permanent sort of liaison with Contessa Giuccioli, who is now at Florence, and seems from her letters to be a very amiable woman. She is waiting there until something shall be decided as to their emigration to Switzerland or stay in Italy; which · is yet undetermined on either side. She was compelled to escape from the Papal territory in great haste, as measures had already been taken to place her in a convent, where she would have been unrelentingly confined for life. The oppression of the marriage contract, as existing in the laws and opinions of Italy, though less frequently exercised, is far severer than that of England. I tremble to think of what poor Emilia is destined to.

Lord Byron had almost destroyed himself in Venice: his state of debility was such that he was unable to digest any food, he was consumed by hectic fever, and would speedily have perished, but for this attachment, which has reclaimed him from the excesses into which he threw himself from carelessness and pride, rather than taste. Poor fellow! he is now quite well, and immersed in politics and literature. He has given me a number of the most interesting details on the former subject, but we will not speak of them in a letter. Fletcher is here, and as if like a shadow, he waxed and waned with the substance of his master: Fletcher also has recovered his good looks, and from amidst the unseasonable grey hairs, a fresh harvest of flaxen locks put forth.

We talked a great deal of poetry, and such matters last night; and as usual differed, and I think more than ever. He affects to patronize a system of criticism fit for the production of mediocrity, and although all his fine poems and passages have been produced in defiance of this system, yet I recognise the pernicious effects of it in the Doge of Venice; and it will cramp and limit his future efforts however great they may be, unless he gets rid of it. I have read only parts of it, or rather he himself read them to me, and gave me the plan of the whole.

*   *   *   *   *   *   *

Lord Byron has also told me of a circumstance that shocks me exceedingly; because it exhibits a degree of desperate and wicked malice for which I am at a loss to account. When I hear such things my patience and my philosophy are put to a severe proof, whilst I refrain from seeking out some obscure hiding-place, where the countenance of man may never meet me more.

*   *   *   * Imagine my despair of good, imagine how it is possible that one of so weak and sensitive a nature as mine can run further the gauntlet through this hellish society of men. *You* should write to the Hoppners a letter refuting the charge, in case you believe, and know, and can prove that it is false; stating the grounds and proofs of your belief. I need not dictate what you should say; nor, I hope, inspire you with warmth to rebut a charge, which you only can effectually rebut. If you will send the letter to me here, I will forward it to the Hoppners. Lord Byron is not up, I do not know the Hoppners' address, and I am anxious not to lose a post

TO MRS. SHELLEY.

8th August [1821].

MY DEAREST MARY,

I WROTE to you yesterday, and I begin another letter to-day, without knowing exactly when I can send it, as I am told the post only goes once a week. I dare say the subject of the latter half my letter gave you pain, but it was necessary to look the affair in the

face, and the only satisfactory answer to the calumny
must be given by you, and could be given by you
alone. This is evidently the source of the violent
denunciations of the *Literary Gazette*, in themselves
contemptible enough, and only to be regarded as
effects, which show us their cause, which until we put
off our mortal nature, we never despise—that is the
belief of persons who have known and seen you, that
you are guilty of crimes.

*   *   *   *   *

After having sent my letter to the post yesterday, I
went to see some of the antiquities of this place; which
appear to be remarkable. This city was once of vast
extent, and the traces of its remains are to be found
more than four miles from the gate of the modern
town. The sea, which once came close to it, has now
retired to the distance of four miles, leaving a melancholy extent of marshes, interspersed with patches of
cultivation, and towards the sea shore with pine forests,
which have followed the retrocession of the Adriatic,
and the roots of which are actually washed by its
waves. The level of the sea and of this tract of
country correspond so nearly, that a ditch dug to a few
feet in depth is immediately filled up with sea water.
All the ancient buildings have been choked up to the
height of from five to twenty feet by the deposit of the
sea, and of the inundations, which are frequent in the
winter. I went in Lord Byron's carriage, first to the
Chiesa San Vitale, which is certainly one of the most
ancient churches in Italy. It is a rotunda supported
upon buttresses and pilasters of white marble; the ill
effect of which is somewhat relieved by an interior row
of columns. The dome is very high and narrow. The
whole church, in spite of the elevation of the soil, is
very high for its breadth, and is of a very peculiar
and striking construction. In the section of one of the

large tables of marble with which the church is lined,
they showed me the *perfect figure*, as perfect as if it
had been painted, of a capuchin friar, which resulted
merely from the shadings and the position of the stains
in the marble.   This is what may be called a pure
anticipated cognition of a Capuchin.

I then went to the tomb of Theodosius, which has
now been dedicated to the Virgin, without however
any change in its original appearance.   It is about
a mile from the present city.   This building is more
than half overwhelmed by the elevated soil, although
a portion of the lower story has been excavated, and
is filled with brackish and stinking waters, and a sort
of vaporous darkness, and troops of prodigious frogs.
It is a remarkable piece of architecture, and without
belonging to a period when the ancient taste yet survived, bears nevertheless a certain impression of that
taste.   It consists of two stories ; the lower supported
on Doric arches, and pilasters, and a simple entablature.   The other circular within, and polygonal outside, and roofed with one single mass of ponderous
stone, for it is evidently one, and Heaven alone knows
how they contrived to lift it to that height.   It is
a sort of flattish dome, rough-wrought within by the
chisel, from which the Northern conquerors tore the
plates of silver that adorned it, and polished without,
with things like handles appended to it, which were
also wrought out of the solid stone, and to which I
suppose the ropes were applied to draw it up.   You
ascend externally into the second story by a flight of
stone-steps, which are modern.

The next place I went to was a church called *la
Chiesa di Sant' Appollinare*, which is a Basilica, and
built by one, I forget whom, of the Christian Emperors ; it is a long church, with a roof like a barn, and
supported by twenty-four columns of the finest marble,
with an altar of jasper, and four columns of jasper and

giallo antico, supporting the roof of the tabernacle, which are said to be of immense value. It is something like that church (I forget the name of it) we saw at Rome, *fuore delle mure.* I suppose the emperor stole these columns, which seem not at all to belong to the place they occupy. Within the city, near the church of San Vitale, there is to be seen the tomb of the Empress Galla Placidia, daughter of Theodosius the Great, together with those of her husband Constantius, her brother Honorius, and her son Valentinian—all Emperors. The tombs are massy cases of marble, adorned with rude and tasteless sculpture of lambs, and other Christian emblems, with scarcely a trace of the antique. It seems to have been one of the first effects of the Christian religion, to destroy the power of producing beauty in art. These tombs are placed in a sort of vaulted chamber, wrought over with rude mosaic, which is said to have been built in 1300. I have yet seen no more of Ravenna.

Friday.

We ride out in the evening, through the pine forests which divide this city from the sea. Our way of life is this, and I have accommodated myself to it without much difficulty :—Lord Byron gets up at two, breakfasts; we talk, read, &c., until six; then we ride, and dine at eight; and after dinner sit talking till four or five in the morning. I get up at twelve, and am now devoting the interval between my rising and his, to you.

Lord Byron is greatly improved in every respect. In genius, in temper, in moral views, in health, in happiness. The connexion with la Guiccioli has been an inestimable benefit to him. He lives in considerable splendour, but within his income, which is now about £4000 a year, £100 of which he devotes to purposes of charity. He has had mischievous passions, but these he seems to have subdued, and he is becoming, what he should be, a virtuous man. The interest which he took in the politics of Italy, and the actions he performed in consequence of it, are subjects not fit to be *written*, but are such as will delight and surprise you. He is not yet decided to go to Switzerland—a place, indeed, little fitted for him : the gossip and the cabals of those anglicised coteries would torment him, as they did before, and might exasperate him into a relapse of libertinism, which he says he plung·d into not from taste, but despair. La Guiccioli and her brother (who is Lord Byron's friend and confidant, and acquiesces perfectly in her connexion with him) wish to go to Switzerland ; as Lord Byron says, merely from the novelty of the pleasure of travelling. Lord Byron prefers Tuscany or Lucca, and is trying to persuade them to adopt his views. He has made *me* write a long letter to her to engage her to remain—an odd thing enough for an utter stranger to write on subjects of the utmost delicacy to his friend's mistress. But it seems destined that I am always to have some active part in everybody's affairs whom I approach. I have set down in lame Italian the strongest reasons I can think of against the Swiss emigration—to tell you the truth, I should be very glad to accept, as my fee, his establishment in Tuscany. Ravenna is a miserable place ; the people are barbarous and wild, and their language the most infernal patois that you can imagine. He would be, in every respect, better among the Tuscans. I am afraid he would not like Florence, on account of the English there.

*   *   *   *   *

There is Lucca, Florence, Pisa, Siena, and I think nothing more. What think you of Prato, or Pistoia, for him ?—no Englishman approaches those towns ; but I am afraid no house could be found good enough for him in that region.

He has read to me one of the unpublished cantos of Don Juan, which is astonishingly fine. It sets him not

only above, but far above, all the poets of the day—
every word is stamped with immortality.   I despair of
rivalling Lord Byron, as well I may, and there is no
other with whom it is worth contending.   This canto
is in the style, but totally, and sustained with incredible
ease and power, like the end of the second canto.   There
is not a word which the most rigid assertor of the dignity of human nature would desire to be cancelled.   It
fulfils, in a certain degree, what I have long preached
of producing—something wholly new and relative to the
age, and yet surpassingly beautiful.   It may be vanity,
but I think I see the trace of my earnest exhortations
to him to create something wholly new.   He has finished
his *life* up to the present time, and given it to Moore,
with liberty for Moore to sell it for the best price he
can get, with condition that the bookseller should publish it after his death.   Moore has sold it to Murray for
two thousand pounds.   I have spoken to him of Hunt,
but not with a direct view of demanding a contribution ;
and, though I am sure that if asked it would not be
refused—yet, there is something in me that makes it
impossible.   Lord Byron and I are excellent friends,
and were I reduced to poverty, or were I a writer who
had no claims to a higher station than I possess—or did
I possess a higher than I deserve, we should appear in all
things as such, and I would freely ask him any favour.
Such is not the case.   The demon of mistrust and pride
lurks between two persons in our situation, poisoning
the freedom of our intercourse.   This is a tax and a
heavy one, which we must pay for being human.   I
think the fault is not on my side, nor is it likely, I being
the weaker.   I hope that in the next world these things
will be better managed.   What is passing in the heart
of another rarely escapes the observation of one who is
a strict anatomist of his own.

Write to me at Florence, where I shall remain a day
at least, and send me letters, or news of letters.   How

is my little darling? And how are you, and how do
you get on with your book? Be severe in your corrections, and expect severity from me, your sincere admirer.
I flatter myself you have composed something unequalled
in its kind, and that, not content with the honours of
your birth and your hereditary aristocracy, you will add
still higher renown to your name. Expect me at the
end of my appointed time. I do not think I shall be
detained. Is C. with you, or is she coming? Have
you heard anything of my poor Emilia, from whom I
got a letter the day of my departure, saying, that her
marriage was deferred for a *very short* time, on account
of the illness of her sposo. How are the Williamses,
and Williams especially? Give my very kindest love
to them.

Lord Byron has here splendid apartments in the
house of his mistress's husband, who is one of the
richest men in Italy. *She* is divorced, with an allow-
ance of 1200 crowns a-year, a miserable pittance from
a man who has 120,000 a-year.—Here are two monkeys,
five cats, eight dogs, and ten horses, all of whom
(except the horses) walk about the house like the
masters of it. *Tita* the Venetian is here, and operates
as my valet; a fine fellow, with a prodigious black beard,
and who has stabbed two or three people, and is one of
the most good-natured looking fellows I ever saw.

We have good rumours of the Greeks here, and a
Russian war. I hardly wish the Russians to take any
part in it. My maxim is with Æschylus :—τὸ δυσσέβὲς
—μετὰ μὲν πλείονα τίκτει, σφετέρᾳ δ' εἴκοτα γεννᾷ. There
is a Greek exercise for you. How should slaves produce
anything but tyranny—even as the seed produces the
plant?

Adieu, dear Mary,

Yours affectionately,

S.

TO MRS. SHELLEY. XXVI

MY DEAR MARY,

YOU will be surprised to hear that Lord Byron has decided upon coming to *Pisa*, in case he shall be able, with my assistance, to prevail upon his mistress to remain in Italy, of which I think there is little doubt. He wishes for a large and magnificent house, but he has furniture of his own, which he would send from Ravenna. Inquire if any of the large palaces are to be let. We discussed Prato, Pistoia, Lucca, &c., but they would not suit him so well as Pisa, to which, indeed, he shows a decided preference. So let it be! Florence he objects to, on account of the prodigious influx of English.

I don't think this circumstance ought to make any difference in our own plans with respect to this winter in Florence, because we could easily reassume our station, with the spring, at Pugnano or the baths, in order to enjoy the society of the noble lord. But do you consider this point, and write to me your full opinion, at the Florence post-office.

I suffer much to-day from the pain in my side, brought on, I believe, by this accursed water. In other respects, I am pretty well, and my spirits are much improved ; they had been improving, indeed, before I left the baths, after the deep dejection of the early part of the year.

I am reading Anastasius.* One would think that Lord Byron had taken his idea of the three last cantos of Don Juan from this book. That, of course, has nothing to do with the merit of this latter, poetry having

---

* *Memoirs of a Greek* [by Thomas Hope], 3 vols. Murray, 1819. —ED.

nothing to do with the invention of facts. It is a very powerful and very entertaining novel, and a faithful picture, they say, of modern Greek manners. I have read Lord Byron's letter to Bowles—some good things —but he ought not to write prose criticism.

You will receive a long letter, sent with some of Lord Byron's, express to Florence.

I write this in haste.—Yours most affectionately,

S.

TO MRS. SHELLEY.

Ravenna, Tuesday, August 14th, 1821.

MY DEAREST LOVE,

I ACCEPT your kind present of your picture, and wish you would get it prettily framed for me. I will wear, for your sake, upon my heart this image which is ever present to my mind.

I have only two minutes to write, the post is just setting off. I shall leave this place on Thursday or Friday morning. You would forgive me for my longer stay, if you knew the fighting I have had to make it so short. I need not say where my own feelings impel me.

It still remains fixed that Lord Byron should come to Tuscany, and, if possible, Pisa ; but more of that to-morrow,

Your faithful and affectionate

S.

TO MRS. SHELLEY.

Ravenna, Wednesday [Aug. 15, 1821].

MY DEAREST LOVE,

I WRITE, though I doubt whether I shall not arrive before this letter ; as the post only leaves Ravenna once a week, un Saturdays, and as I hope to set out to-morrow evening by the courier. But as I must necessarily stay a day at Florence, and as the natural incidents of travelling may prevent me from taking my intended advantage of the couriers, it is probable that this letter will arrive first. Besides, as I will explain, I am not *yet* quite my own master. But that by and bye. I do not think it necessary to tell you of my impatience to return to you and my little darling, or the disappointment with which I have prolonged my absence from you. I am happy to think that you are not quite alone.

Lord Byron is still decided upon Tuscany; and such is his impatience, that he has desired me—as if I should not arrive in time—to write to you to inquire for the best unfurnished palace in Pisa, and to enter upon a treaty for it. It is better not to be on the Lung' Arno; but, in fact, there is no such hurry, and as I shall see you so soon, it is not worth while to trouble yourself about it.

I told you I had written by Lord Byron's desire to la Guiccioli, to dissuade her and her family from Switzerland. Her answer is this moment arrived, and my representation seems to have reconciled them to the unfitness of that step. At the conclusion of a letter, full of all the fine things she says she has heard of me, is this request, which I transcribe ;—"*Signore—la vostra bontà mi fa ardita di chiedervi un favore—me lo accorderete voi? Non partite da Ravenna senza Milord.*" Of course, being now, by all the laws of knighthood, captive to a lady's request, I shall only be at liberty on *my parole*, until Lord Byron is settled at Pisa. I shall reply, of course, that the *boon* is granted, and that if her lover is reluctant to quit Ravenna, after I have made arrangements for receiving him at Pisa, I am bound to place myself in the same situation as now, to assail him with importunities to rejoin her. Of this there is, fortunately, no need; and I need not tell you

there is no fear that this chivalric submission of mine
to the great general laws of antique courtesy, against
which I never rebel, and which is my religion, should
interfere with my quick returning, and long remaining
with you, dear girl.

I have seen Dante's tomb, and worshipped the sacred
spot. The building and its accessories are comparatively modern, but, the urn itself, and the tablet of
marble, with his portrait in relief, are evidently of equal
antiquity with his death. The countenance has all the
marks of being taken from his own ; the lines are
strongly marked, far more than the portraits, which,
however, it resembles ; except, indeed, the eye, which
is half closed, and reminded me of Pacchiani. It was
probably taken after death. I saw the library, and
some specimens of the earliest illuminated printing from
the press of Fust. They are on vellum, and of an
execution little inferior to that of the present day.

We ride out every evening as usual, and practise
pistol-shooting at a pumpkin ; and I am not sorry to
observe that I approach towards my noble friend's
exactness of aim. The water here is villainous, and I
have suffered tortures ; but I now drink nothing but
alcalescent water, and am much relieved. I have the
greatest trouble to get away ; and Lord Byron, as a
reason for my stay, has urged, that without either me
or the Guiccioli, he will certainly fall into his old habits.
I then talk, and he listens to reason ; and I earnestly
hope that he is too well aware of the terrible and degrading consequences of his former mode of life, to
be in danger from the short interval of temptation
that will be left him. Lord Byron speaks with great
kindness and interest of you, and seems to wish to
see you.

I have received your letter with that to Mrs. Hoppner. I do not wonder, my dearest friend, that you should have been moved. I was at first, but speedily regained the indifference which the opinion of anything, or anybody, except our own consciousness, amply merits ; and day by day shall more receive from me. I have not recopied your letter ; such a measure would destroy its authenticity, but have given it to Lord Byron, who has engaged to send it with his own comments to the Hoppners. People do not hesitate, it seems, to make themselves panders and accomplices to slander, for the Hoppners had exacted from Lord Byron that these accusations should be concealed from *me*. Lord Byron is not a man to keep a secret, good or bad ; but in openly confessing that he has not done so, he must observe a certain delicacy, and therefore he wished to send the letter himself, and indeed this adds weight to your representations. Have you seen the article in the Literary Gazette on me? They evidently allude to some story of this kind—however cautious the Hoppners have been in preventing the calumniated person from asserting his justification, you know too much of the world not to be certain that this was the utmost limit of their caution. So much for nothing.

Lord Byron is immediately coming to Pisa. He will set off the moment I can get him a house. Who would have imagined this ? Our first thought ought to be ——, our second our own plans. The hesitation in your letter about Florence has communicated itself to me ; although I hardly see what we can do about Horace Smith, to whom our attentions are so due, and would be so useful. If I do not arrive before this long scrawl, write something to Florence to decide me. I shall certainly not, without strong reasons, at present *sign* the agreement for the old codger's house ; although the

extreme beauty and fitness of the place, should we
decide on Florence, might well overbalance the objection
of your deaf visitor.   One thing—with Lord Byron and
the people we know at Pisa, we should have a security
and protection, which seems to be more questionable
at Florence.   But I do not think that this consideration
ought to weigh.   What think you of remaining at Pisa ?
The Williamses would probably be induced to stay there
if we did ; Hunt would certainly stay, at least this
winter, near us, should he emigrate at all ; Lord Byron
and his Italian friends would remain quietly there ; and
Lord Byron has certainly a great regard for us—the
regard of such a man is worth—*some* of the tribute we
must pay to the base passions of humanity in any intercourse with those within their circle ; he is better worth
it than those on whom we bestow it from mere custom.
The —— are there, and as far as solid affairs are concerned, are my friends. * * * At Pisa I need not
distil my water—if I *can* distil it anywhere.   Last
winter I suffered less from my painful disorder than the
winter I spent at Florence.   The arguments for Florence
you know, and they are very weighty ; judge (*I know
you like the job*) which scale is overbalanced.

My greatest content would be utterly to desert all
human society.   I would retire with you and our child
to a solitary island in the sea, would build a boat, and
shut upon my retreat the flood-gates of the world.   I
would read no reviews, and talk with no authors.   If I
dared trust my imagination, it would tell me that there
are one or two chosen companions beside yourself
whom I should desire.   But to this I would not listen
—where two or three are gathered together, the devil
is among them.   And good, far more than evil impulses,
love, far more than hatred, has been to me, except as
you have been its object, the source of all sorts of mischief.   So on this plan, I would be *alone*, and would
devote either to oblivion or to future generations, the

overflowings of a mind which, timely withdrawn from the contagion, should be kept fit for no baser object. But this it does not appear that we shall do. The other side of the alternative (for a medium ought not to be adopted) is to form for ourselves a society of our own class, as much as possible in intellect, or in feelings ; and to connect ourselves with the interests of that society. Our roots never struck so deeply as at Pisa, and the transplanted tree flourishes not. People who lead the lives which we led until last winter, are like a family of Wahabee Arabs, pitching their tent in the midst of London. We must do one thing or the other—for yourself, for our child, for our existence. The calumnies, the sources of which are probably deeper than we perceive, have ultimately, for object, the depriving us of the means of security and subsistence. You will easily perceive the gradations by which calumny proceeds to pretext, pretext to persecution, and persecution to the ban of fire and water. It is for this, and not because this or that fool, or the whole court of fools, curse and rail, that calumny is worth refuting or chastising.

TO HORATIO SMITH.

Pisa, Sept. 14th, 1821.

MY DEAR SMITH,

I CANNOT express the pain and disappointment with which I learn the change in your plans, no less than the afflicting cause of it. Florence will no longer have any attractions for me this winter, and I shall contentedly sit down in this humdrum Pisa, and refer to hope and to chance the pleasure I had expected from your society this winter. What shall I do with your packages, which have now, I believe, all arrived at Guebhard's at Leghorn ? Is it not possible that a favourable change

in Mrs. Smith's health might produce a corresponding
change in your determinations, and would it, or would
it not, be premature to forward the packages to your
present residence, or to London ?   I will pay every possible attention to your instructions in this regard.

I had marked down several houses in Florence, and
one especially on the Arno, a most lovely place, though
they asked rather more than perhaps you would have
chosen to pay—yet nothing approaching to an English
price.—I do not yet entirely give you up.—Indeed, I
should be sorry not to hope that Mrs. Smith's state
of health would not soon become such, as to remove
your principal objection to this delightful climate. I
have not, with the exception of three or four days,
suffered in the least from the heat this year.   Though,
it is but fair to confess, that my temperament approaches
to that of the salamander.

We expect Lord Byron here in about a fortnight.   I
have just taken the finest palace in Pisa for him, and
his luggage, and his horses, and all his train, are, I
believe, already on their way hither.   I dare say you
have heard of the life he led at Venice, rivalling the
wise Solomon almost, in the number of his concubines.
Well, he is now quite reformed, and is leading a most
sober and decent life, as *cavaliere servente* to a very
pretty Italian woman, who has already arrived at Pisa,
with her father and her brother (such are the manners
of Italy), as the jackals of the lion.   He is occupied in
forming a new drama, and, with views which I doubt
not will expand as he proceeds, is determined to write
a series of plays, in which he will follow the French
tragedians and Alfieri, rather than those of England and
Spain, and produce something new, at least, to England.
This seems to me the wrong road ; but genius like his
is destined to lead and not to follow.   He will shake off
his shackles as he finds they cramp him.   I believe he
will produce something very great ; and that familiarity

with the dramatic power of human nature will soon
enable him to soften down the severe and unharmonising
traits of his " Marino Faliero." I think you know
Lord Byron personally, or is it your brother? If the
latter, I know that he wished particularly to be introduced
to you, and that he will sympathise, in some degree, in
this great disappointment which I feel in the change, or,
as I yet hope, in the prorogation of your plans.

I am glad you like "Adonais," and, particularly, that
you do not think it metaphysical, which I was afraid it
was. I was resolved to pay some tribute of sympathy
to the unhonoured dead, but I wrote, as usual, with a
total ignorance of the effect that I should produce.—
I have not yet seen your pastoral drama ; if you have
a copy, could you favour me with it? It will be six
months before I shall receive it from England. I have
heard it spoken of with high praise, and I have the
greatest curiosity to see it.

The Gisbornes promised to buy me some books in
Paris, and I had asked you to be kind enough to
advance them what they might want to pay for them.
I cannot conceive why they did not execute this little
commission for me, as they knew how very much I
wished to receive these books by the same conveyance
as the filtering-stone. Dare I ask you to do me the
favour to buy them? *A complete edition of the works
of Calderon*, and the French translation of Kant, a
German Faust, and to add the Nympholept?*—I am
indifferent as to a little more or less expense, so that I
may have them immediately. I will send you an order
on Paris for the amount, together with the thirty-two
francs you were kind enough to pay for me.

All public attention is now centred on the wonderful
revolution in Greece. I dare not, after the events of last
winter hope that slaves can become freemen so cheaply ;

* *Amarynthus the Nympholept,* by Horace Smith.—ED.

yet I know one Greek of the highest qualities, both of courage and conduct, the Prince Mavrocordato, and if the rest be like him, all will go well.—The news of this moment is, that the Russian army has orders to advance.

Mrs. S. unites with me in the most heartfelt regret,
        And I remain, my dear Smith,
                Most faithfully yours,
                        P. B. S.

If you happen to have brought a copy of Clarke's edition of Queen Mab for me, I should like very well to see it.—I really hardly know what this poem is about. I am afraid it is rather rough.

TO MR. JOHN GISBORNE.

Pisa, October 22, 1821.

MY DEAR GISBORNE,

AT length the post brings a welcome letter from you, and I am pleased to be assured of your health and safe arrival. I expect with interest and anxiety the intelligence of your progress in England, and how far the advantages there compensate the loss of Italy. I hear from Hunt that he is determined on emigration, and if I thought the letter would arrive in time, I should beg you to suggest some advice to him. But you ought to be incapable of forgiving me the fact of depriving England of what it must lose when Hunt departs.

Did I tell you that Lord Byron comes to settle at Pisa, and that he has a plan of writing a periodical work in conjunction with Hunt? His house, Madame Felichi's, is already taken and fitted up for him, and he has been expected every day these six weeks. La Guiccioli, who awaits him impatiently, is a very pretty, sentimental, innocent Italian, who has sacrificed an immense fortune for the sake of Lord Byron, and who, if I know any thing of my friend, of her and of human nature, will hereafter have plenty of leisure and opportunity to repent her rashness. Lord Byron is, however, quite cured of his gross habits, as far as habits; the perverse ideas on which they were formed are not yet eradicated.

We have furnished a house at Pisa, and mean to make it our head-quarters. I shall get all my books out, and entrench myself like a spider in a web. If you can assist P. in sending them to Leghorn, you would do me an especial favour; but do not buy me Calderon, Faust, or Kant, as H. S.* promises to send them me from Paris, where I suppose you had not time to procure them. Any other books you or Henry think would accord with my design, Ollier will furnish you with.

I should like very much to hear what is said of my Adonais, and you would oblige me by cutting out, or making Ollier cut out, any respectable criticism on it, and sending it me; you know I do not mind a crown or two in postage. The Epipsychidion is a mystery; as to real flesh and blood, you know that I do not deal in those articles; you might as well go to a gin-shop for a leg of mutton, as expect anything human or earthly from me. I desired Ollier not to circulate this piece except to the συνετοί, and even they, it seems, are inclined to approximate me to the circle of a servant girl and her sweetheart. But I intend to write a Symposium of my own to set all this right.

I am just finishing a dramatic poem, called Hellas, upon the contest now raging in Greece—a sort of imitation of the Persæ of Æschylus, full of lyrical poetry. I try to be what I might have been, but am not successful. I find that (I dare say I shall quote wrong,)

> " Den herrlichsten, den sich der Geist emprängt
> Drängt immer fremd und fremder Stoff sich an."

The Edinburgh Review lies. Godwin's answer to Malthus is victorious and decisive ; and that it should not be generally acknowledged as such, is full evidence of the influence of successful evil and tyranny. What Godwin is, compared to Plato and Bacon, we well know ; but compared with these miserable sciolists, he is a vulture to a worm.

I read the Greek dramatists and Plato for ever. You are right about Antigone ; how sublime a picture of a woman ! and what think you of the choruses, and especially the lyrical complaints of the godlike victim ? and the menaces of Tiresias, and their rapid fulfilment ? Some of us have, in a prior existence, been in love with an Antigone, and that makes us find no full content in any mortal tie. As to books, I advise you to live near the British Museum, and read there. I have read, since I saw you, the " Jungfrau von Orleans " of Schiller,—a fine play, if the fifth act did not fall off. Some Greeks, escaped from the defeat in Wallachia, have passed through Pisa, to re-embark at Leghorn for the Morea ; and the Tuscan Government allowed them, during their stay and passage, three lire each per day and their lodging ; that is good. Remember me and Mary most kindly to Mrs. Gisborne and Henry, and believe me,

Yours most affectionately,

P. B. S.

TO MR. JOHN GISBORNE.

Pisa, April 10, 1822.

MY DEAR GISBORNE,

I HAVE received Hellas, which is prettily printed, and with fewer mistakes than any poem I ever published. Am I to thank you for the revision of the press ? or who acted as midwife to this last of my orphans, introducing it to oblivion, and me to my accustomed failure? May the cause it celebrates be more fortunate than either! Tell me how you like *Hellas*, and give me your opinion freely. It was written without much care, and in one of those few moments of enthusiasm which now seldom visit me, and which make me pay dear for their visits. I know what to think of *Adonais*, but what to think of those who confound it with the many bad poems of the day, I know not.

I have been reading over and over again Faust, and always with sensations which no other composi tion excites. It deepens the gloom and augments the rapidity of ideas, and would therefore seem to me an unfit study for any person who is a prey to the re-proaches of memory, and the delusions of an imagina-tion not to be restrained. And yet the pleasure of sympathising with emotions known only to few, although they derive their sole charm from despair, and the scorn of the narrow good we can attain in our present state, seems more than to ease the pain which belongs to them. Perhaps all discontent with the *less* (to use a Platonic sophism) supposes the sense of a just claim to the *greater*, and that we admirers of Faust are on the right road to Paradise. Such a supposition is not more absurd, and is certainly less demoniacal than that of Wordsworth, where he says—

> " This earth,
> Which is the world of all of us, and where
> *We find our happiness, or not at all.*"

As if, after sixty years' suffering here, we were to be roasted alive for sixty million more in hell, or chari-tably annihilated by a *coup-de-grâce* of the bungler who brought us into existence at first!

Have you read Calderon's *Magico Prodigioso?* I find a striking similarity between Faust and this drama, and if I were to acknowledge Coleridge's distinction,

II.   Z

should say Goethe was the *greatest* philosopher, and Calderon the *greatest* poet. *Cyprian* evidently furnished the *germ* of Faust, as Faust may furnish the germ of other poems; although it is as different from it in structure and plan as the acorn from the oak. I have —imagine my presumption—translated several scenes from both, as the basis of a paper for our journal. I am well content with those from Calderon, which in fact gave me very little trouble; but those from Faust —I feel how imperfect a representation, even with all the licence I assume to figure to myself how Goethe would have written in English, my words convey. No one but Coleridge is capable of this work.

We have seen here a translation of some scenes, and indeed the most remarkable ones, accompanying those astonishing etchings which have been published in England from a German master. It is not bad—and faithful enough—but how weak! how incompetent to represent Faust! I have only attempted the scenes omitted in this translation, and would send you that of the *Walpurgisnacht*, if I thought Ollier would place the postage to my account. What etchings those are! I am never satiated with looking at them; and, I fear, it is the only sort of translation of which Faust is susceptible. I never perfectly understood the Hartz Mountain scene, until I saw the etching; and then, Margaret in the summer-house with Faust! The artist makes one envy his happiness that he can sketch such things with calmness, which I only dared look upon once, and which made my brain swim round only to touch the leaf on the opposite side of which I knew that it was figured. Whether it is that the artist has surpassed Faust, or that the pencil surpasses language in some subjects, I know not, or that I am more affected by a visible image, but the etching certainly excited me far more than the poem it illustrated. Do you remember the fifty-fourth letter of the first part

of the "Nouvelle Héloïse"?   Goethe, in a subsequent
scene, evidently had that letter in his mind, and this
etching is an idealism of it.   So much for the world of
shadows !

  What think you of Lord Byron's last volume?   In
my opinion it contains finer poetry than has appeared
in England since the publication of "Paradise Regained." *Cain* is apocalyptic—it is a revelation not
before communicated to man.   I write nothing but by fits.
I have done some of "Charles the First," but although
the poetry succeeded very well, I cannot seize on the
conception of the subject as a whole, and seldom now
touch the canvas.   You know I don't think much about
Reviews, nor of the fame they give, nor that they take
away.   It is absurd in any Review to criticise *Adonais*,
and still more to pretend that the verses are bad.
"Prometheus" was never intended for more than five or
six persons.

  And how are you getting on?   Do your plans still
want success?   Do you regret Italy? or anything that
Italy contains?   And in case of an entire failure in·
your expectations, do you think of returning here?
You see the first blow has been made at funded-property :
—do you intend to confide and invite a second?   You
would already have saved something per cent., if you
had invested your property in Tuscan land.   The next
best thing would be to invest it in English, and reside
upon it.   I tremble for the consequences, to you personally, from a prolonged confidence in the funds.
Justice, policy, the hopes of the nation and renewed
institutions, demand your ruin, and I, for one, cannot
bring myself to desire what is in itself desirable, till you
are free.   You see how liberal I am of advice ; but you
know the motives that suggest it.   What is Henry about,
and how are his prospects?   Tell him that some ad-
venturers are engaged upon a steam-boat at Leghorn, to
make the *trajet* we projected.   I hope he is charitable

enough to pray that they may succeed better than we did.

Remember me most affectionately to Mrs. Gisborne, to whom, as well as to yourself, I consider that this letter is written. How is she, and. how are you all in health ? And pray tell me, what are your plans of life, and how Henry succeeds, and whether he is married or not ? How can I send you such small sums as you may want for postages, &c., for I do not mean to tax with my unreasonable letters both your purse and your patience? We go this summer to Spezzia ; but direct as ever to Pisa,—Mrs. —— will forward our letters. If you see anything which you think would particularly interest me, pray make Ollier pay for sending it out by post. Give my best and affectionate regards to H——, to whom I do not write at present, imagining that you will give him a piece of this letter.

Ever most faithfully yours,

P. B. S.

TO ——*

Pisa, April 11th, 1822.

My dear ——,

I HAVE, as yet, received neither the * * *, nor his metaphysical companions—*Time, my Lord, has a wallet on his back*, and I suppose he has bagged them by the way. As he has had a good deal of " *alms* for oblivion " out of me, I think he might as well have favoured me this once ;

* For reasons which will appear in the sequel, Mrs. Shelley concealed the name of Shelley's correspondent in this letter and the following one of June 29, 1822, under the initials " To C. T. ; " but it appears from the original autographs, which have been preserved, that these two letters were addressed to Horatio Smith.—ED.

I have, indeed, just dropped another mite into his treasury, called *Hellas*, which I know not how to send to you; but I dare say, some fury of the Hades of authors will bring one to Paris. It is a poem written on the Greek cause last summer—a sort of lyrical, dramatic, nondescript piece of business.

You will have heard of a *row* we have had here, which, I dare say, will grow to a serious size before it arrives at Paris. It was, in fact, a trifling piece of business enough, arising from an insult of a drunken dragoon, offered to one of our party, and only serious, because one of Lord Byron's servants wounded the fellow dangerously with a pitchfork. He is now, however, recovering, and the echo of the affair will be heard long after the original report has ceased.

Lord Byron has read me one or two letters of Moore to him, in which Moore speaks with great kindness of me; and, of course, I cannot but feel flattered by the approbation of a man, my inferiority to whom I am proud to acknowledge.—Amongst other things, however, Moore, after giving Lord Byron much good advice about public opinion, &c., seems to deprecate *my* influence on his mind, on the subject of religion, and to attribute the tone assumed in "Cain" to my suggestions. Moore cautions him against my influence on this particular, with the most friendly zeal; and it is plain that his motive springs from a desire of benefitting Lord Byron, without degrading me. I think you know Moore. Pray assure him that I have not the smallest influence over Lord Byron, in this particular, and if I had, I certainly should employ it to eradicate from his great mind the delusions of Christianity, which, in spite of his reason, seem perpetually to recur, and to lay in ambush for the hours of sickness and distress. "Cain" was *conceived* many years ago, and begun before I saw him last year at Ravenna. How happy should I not be to attribute to myself, however indirectly, any participation in that immortal work !—I differ with Moore in thinking Christianity useful to the world ; no man of sense can think it true ; and the alliance of the monstrous superstitions of the popular worship with the pure doctrines of the Theism of such a man as Moore, turns to the profit of the former, and makes the latter the fountain of its own pollution. I agree with him that the doctrines of the French, and Material Philosophy, are as false as they are pernicious ; but, still, they are better than Christianity, inasmuch as anarchy is better than despotism ; for this reason, that the former is for a season, and that the latter is eternal. My admiration of the character, no less than of the genius of Moore, makes me rather wish that he should not have an ill opinion of me.

Where are you ? We settle this summer near Spezzia ; Lord Byron at Leghorn. May not I hope to see you even for a trip in Italy ? I hope your wife and little ones are well. Mine grows a fine boy, and is quite well.

I have contrived to get my musical coals at Newcastle itself. —My dear ——, believe me,

Faithfully yours,

P. B. S.

TO MRS. SHELLEY

(AT SPEZZIA).

[Lerici, Sunday, April 28th, 1822.]

DEAREST MARY,

I AM this moment arrived at Lerici, where I am necessarily detained, waiting the furniture, which left Pisa last night at midnight ; and as the sea has been calm, and the wind fair, I may expect them every moment. It would not do to leave affairs here in an

impiccio, great as is my anxiety to see you.—How are
you, my best love ?   How have you sustained the trials
of the journey ?   Answer me this question, and how
my little babe and C * * * are.

Now to business :—Is the Magni House taken ? if
not, pray occupy yourself instantly in finishing the
affair, even if you are obliged to go to Sarzana, and
send a messenger to me to tell me of your success.   I,
of course, cannot leave Lerici, to which place the
boats, (for we were obliged to take two,) are directed.
But *you* can come over in the same boat that brings
this letter, and return in the evening.

I ought to say that I do not think that there is
accommodation for you all at this inn ; and that, even
if there were, you would be better off at Spezzia ; but
if the Magni House is taken, then there is no possible
reason why you should not take a row over in the boat
that will bring this—but don't keep the men long.   I
am anxious to hear from you on every account.

Ever yours,

S.

TO HORATIO SMITH

(VERSAILLES).

Lerici, May, 1822.

MY DEAR SMITH,

IT is some time since I have heard from you ; are
you still at Versailles ?   Do you still cling to France,
and prefer the arts and conveniences of that over-
civilised country to the beautiful nature and mighty
remains of Italy ?   As to me, like Anacreon's swallow,
I have left my Nile, and have taken up my summer
quarters here, in a lonely house close by the sea-side,
surrounded by the soft and sublime scenery of the gulf

of Spezzia. I do not write; I have lived too long near Lord Byron, and the sun has extinguished the glow-worm; for I cannot hope, with St. John, that "*the light came into the world, and the world knew it not.*"

The object of my present letter is, however, a request, and as it concerns that most odious of all subjects, money, I will put it in the shortest shape. Godwin's law-suit, he tells us, is decided against him; and he is adjudged to pay 900*l.* He writes, of course, to his daughter in the greatest distress : but we have no money except our income, nor any means of procuring it. My wife has sent him her novel, which is now finished, the copyright of which will probably bring him 3 or 400*l.*—as Ollier offered the former sum for it, but as he required a considerable delay for the payment, she rejected his offer. Now, what I wish to know is, whether you could with convenience lend me the 400*l.* which you once dedicated to this service, and allow Godwin to have it, under the precautions and stipulations which I formerly annexed to its employment. You could not obviously allow this money to lie idle waiting for this event, without interest. I forgot this part of the business till this instant, and now I reflect that I ought to have assured you of the regular payment of interest, which I omitted to mention, considering it a matter of course.

I can easily imagine that circumstances may have arisen to make this loan inconvenient or impossible — in any case, believe me,

My dear Smith,
Yours very gratefully and faithfully,
P. B. SHELLEY.

TO —— *

· MY DEAR ——,

* * * * *

* * * * ✣

PRAY thank Moore for his obliging message. I wish
I could as easily convey my sense of his genius and
character. I should have written to him on the subject
of my late letter, but that I doubted how far I was justi-
fied in doing so; although, indeed, Lord Byron made
no secret of his communication to me. It seems to me
that things have now arrived at such a crisis as requires
every man plainly to utter his sentiments on the inefficacy
of the existing religion, no less than political systems,
for restraining and guiding mankind. Let us see the
truth, whatever that may be. The destiny of man can
scarcely be so degraded, that he was born only to die;
and if such should be the case, delusions, especially the
gross and preposterous ones of the existing religion, can
scarcely be supposed to exalt it. If every man said
what he thought, it could not subsist a day. But all,
more or less, subdue themselves to the element that
surrounds them, and contribute to the evils they lament
by the hypocrisy that springs from them.

England appears to be in a desperate condition,
Ireland still worse; and no class of those who subsist
on the public labour will be persuaded that *their* claims
on it must be diminished. But the government must
content itself with less in taxes, the landholder must
submit to receive less rent, and the fundholder a

---

* To Horatio Smith. The opening paragraph, omitted by Mrs.
Shelley, has been found, on reference to the original autograph, to
refer to the pecuniary embarrassments of her father, William Godwin,
alluded to in the previous letter.—ED.

diminished interest, or they will all get nothing. I once thought to study these affairs, and write or act in them. I am glad that my good genius said, *refrain.* I see little public virtue, and I foresee that the contest will be one of blood and gold, two elements which, however much to my taste in my pockets and my veins, I have an objection to out of them.

Lord Byron continues at Leghorn, and has just received from Genoa a most beautiful little yacht, which he caused to be built there. He has written two new cantos of "Don Juan," but I have not seen them. I have just received a letter from Hunt, who has arrived at Genoa. As soon as I hear that he has sailed, I shall weigh anchor in my little schooner, and give him chase to Leghorn, when I must occupy myself in some arrangements for him with Lord Byron. Between ourselves, I greatly fear that this alliance will not succeed ; for I, who could never have been regarded as more than the link of the two thunderbolts, cannot now consent to be even that ; and how long the alliance may continue, I will not prophesy. Pray do not hint my doubts on the subject to any one, or they might do harm to Hunt ; and they *may* be groundless.

I still inhabit this divine bay, reading Spanish dramas, and sailing, and listening to the most enchanting music. We have some friends on a visit to us, and my only regret is that the summer must ever pass, or that Mary has not the same predilection for this place that I have, which would induce me never to shift my quarters.

Farewell.—Believe me ever your

Affectionate friend,

P. B. SHELLEY.

TO MRS. WILLIAMS

(CASA MAGNI).

Pisa, July 4, 1822.

YOU will probably see Williams before I can disen-
tangle myself from the affairs with which I am now
surrounded. I return to Leghorn to-night, and shall
urge him to sail with the first fair wind, without expecting me. I have thus the pleasure of contributing to
your happiness when deprived of every other, and of
leaving you no other subject of regret, but the absence
of one scarcely worth regretting. I fear you are solitary and melancholy at Villa Magni, and, in the intervals
of the greater and more serious distress in which I am
compelled to sympathise here, I figure to myself the
countenance which had been the source of such consola-
tion to me, shadowed by a veil of sorrow.

How soon those hours passed, and how slowly they
return, to pass so soon again, perhaps for ever, in
which we have lived together so intimately, so happily !
Adieu, my dearest friend ! I only write these lines for
the pleasure of tracing what will meet your eyes. Mary
will tell you all the news.   S.

TO MRS. SHELLEY

(CASA MAGNI).

Pisa, July 4, 1822.

MY DEAREST MARY,

I HAVE received both your letters, and shall attend
to the instructions they convey. I did not think of
buying the Bolivar; Lord Byron wishes to sell her, but I
imagine would prefer ready money. I have as yet made
no inquiries about houses near Pugnano—I have no

moment of time to spare from Hunt's affairs ; I am
detained unwillingly here, and you will probably see
Williams in the boat before me,—but that will be
decided to-morrow.

Things are in the worst possible situation with
respect to poor Hunt. I find Marianne in a desperate
state of health, and on our arrival at Pisa sent for
Vaccà. He decides that her case is hopeless, and that
although it will be lingering, must inevitably end fatally.
This decision he thought proper to communicate to
Hunt, indicating at the same time, with great judgment
and precision, the treatment necessary to be observed
for availing himself of the chance of his being deceived.
This intelligence has extinguished the last spark of poor
Hunt's spirits, low enough before. The children are
well and much improved.

Lord Byron is at this moment on the point of leaving Tuscany. The Gambas have been exiled, and he
declares his intention of following their fortunes. His
first idea was to sail to America, which was changed to
Switzerland, then to Genoa, and last to Lucca. Everybody is in despair, and everything in confusion.
Trelawny was on the point of sailing to Genoa for the
purpose of transporting the Bolivar overland to the lake
of Geneva, and had already whispered in my ear his
desire that I should not influence Lord Byron against
this terrestrial navigation. He next received *orders* to
weigh anchor and set sail for Lerici. He is now without instructions, moody and disappointed. But it is the
worst for poor Hunt, unless the present storm should
blow over. He places his whole dependence upon the
scheme of a journal, for which every arrangement has
been made. Lord Byron must of course furnish the
requisite funds at present, as I cannot ; but he seems
inclined to depart without the necessary explanations
and arrangements due to such a situation as Hunt's.
These, in spite of delicacy, I must procure ; he offers

him the copyright of the Vision of Judgment for the first number. This offer, if sincere, is *more* than enough to set up the journal, and, if sincere, will set everything right.

How are you, my best Mary? Write especially how is your health, and how your spirits are, and whether you are not more reconciled to staying at Lerici, at least during the summer.

You have no idea how I am hurried and occupied; I have not a moment's leisure, but will write by next post.

Ever, dearest Mary,

Yours affectionately,

S.

I have found the translation of the Symposium.

MISCELLANEOUS
ESSAYS AND LETTERS.

A LETTER

TO

LORD ELLENBOROUGH,

Occasioned by the Sentence which he passed on

MR D. I. EATON,

As Publisher of

The THIRD PART of PAINE'S AGE OF REASON

———◆———

Deorum offensa, Diis curæ.

— It is contrary to the mild spirit of the Christian Religion, for no sanction can be found under that dispensation which will warrant a Government to impose disabilities and penalties upon any man, on account of his religious opinions. [*Hear, Hear.*]
Marquis Wellesley's Speech. Globe, July 2.

ADVERTISEMENT.

—⋈—

I have waited impatiently for these last four months, in the hopes that some pen, fitter for the important task, would have spared me the perilous pleasure of becoming the champion of an innocent man.—This may serve as an excuse for delay, to those who think that I have let pass the aptest opportunity, but it is not to be supposed that in four short months the public indignation, raised by Mr. Eaton's unmerited suffering, can have subsided.

LETTER.

MY LORD,

As the station to which you have been called by your country is important, so much the more awful is your responsibility, so much the more does it become you to watch lest you inadvertently punish the virtuous and reward the vicious.

You preside over a court which is instituted for the suppression of crime, and to whose authority the people submit on no other conditions than that its decrees should be conformable to justice.

If it should be demonstrated that a judge had condemned an innocent man, the bare existence of laws in conformity to which the accused is punished, would but little extenuate his offence. The inquisitor when he burns an obstinate heretic may set up a similar plea, yet few are sufficiently blinded by intolerance to acknowledge its validity. It will less avail such a judge to assert the policy of punishing one who has committed no crime. Policy and morality ought to be deemed synonymous in a court of justice, and he whose conduct has been regulated by the latter principle, is not justly amenable to any penal law for a supposed violation of the former. It is true, my Lord, laws exist which suffice to screen you from the animadversions of any constituted power, in consequence of the unmerited sentence which you have passed upon Mr. Eaton ; but there are no laws which screen you from the reproof of a nation's disgust, none which ward off the just judgment of posterity, if that posterity will deign to recollect you.

By what right do you punish Mr. Eaton? What but antiquated precedents, gathered from times of priestly and tyrannical domination, can be adduced in palliation of an outrage so insulting to humanity and justice? Whom has he injured? What crime has he committed? Wherefore may he not walk abroad like other men and follow his accustomed pursuits? What end is proposed in confining this man, charged with the commission of no dishonourable action? Wherefore did his aggressor avail himself of popular prejudice, and return no answer but one of common place contempt to a defence of plain and simple sincerity? Lastly, when the prejudices of the jury, as Christians, were strongly and unfairly inflamed * against this injured man as a Deist, wherefore did not you, my Lord, check such unconstitutional pleading, and desire the jury to pronounce the accused innocent or criminal † without reference to the particular faith which he professed?

In the name of justice, what answer is there to these questions? The answer which Heathen Athens made to Socrates, is the same with which Christian England must attempt to silence the advocates of this injured man—" He has questioned established opinions."— Alas! the crime of enquiry is one which religion never has forgiven. Implicit faith and fearless enquiry have in all ages been irreconcileable enemies. Unrestrained philosophy has in every age opposed itself to the reveries of credulity and fanaticism.—The truths of astronomy demonstrated by Newton have superseded astrology; since the modern discoveries in chemistry the philosopher's stone has no longer been deemed attainable. Miracles of every kind have become rare, in proportion to the hidden principles which those who study nature have developed. That which is false will

---

* See the Attorney General's speech.
† By Mr. Fox's bill (1791) Juries are, in cases of libel, judges both of the law and the fact.

ultimately be controverted by its own falsehood. That which is true needs but publicity to be acknowledged. It is ever a proof that the falsehood of a proposition is felt by those who use power and coercion, not reasoning and persuasion, to procure its admission.—Falsehood skulks in holes and corners, "it lets I dare not wait upon I would, like the poor cat in the adage,"* except when it has power, and then, as it was a coward, it is a tyrant; but the eagle-eye of truth darts through the undazzling sunbeam of the immutable and just, gathering thence wherewith to vivify and illuminate a universe !

Wherefore, I repeat, is Mr. Eaton punished?—Because he is a Deist?—And what are you, my Lord? —A Christian. Ha then I the mask is fallen off; you persecute him because his faith differs from yours. You copy the persecutors of Christianity in your actions, and are an additional proof that your religion is as bloody, barbarous, and intolerant as theirs.—If some deistical Bigot in power (supposing such a character for the sake of illustration) should in dark and barbarous ages have enacted a statute making the profession of christianity criminal, if you my Lord were a christian bookseller, and Mr. Eaton a judge, those arguments which you consider adequate to justify yourself for the sentence which you have passed must likewise suffice, in this suppositionary case to justify Mr. Eaton, in sentencing you to Newgate and the pillory for being a christian. Whence is any right derived but that which power confers for persecution? Do you think to convert Mr. Eaton to your religion by embittering his existence? You might force him by torture to profess your tenets, but he could not believe them, except you should make them credible, which perhaps exceeds your power. Do you think to please the God you worship by this exhibition of your zeal?

* Shakespeare.

If so, the Demon to whom some nations offer human hecatombs is less barbarous than the Deity of civilized society.

You consider man as an accountable being—but he can only be accountable for those actions which are influenced by his will.

Belief and disbelief are utterly distinct from and unconnected with volition. They are the apprehension of the agreement or disagreement of the ideas which compose any proposition. Belief is an involuntary operation of the mind, and, like other passions, its intensity is precisely proportionate to the degrees of excitement. Volition is essential to merit or demerit. How then can merit or demerit be attached to what is distinct from that faculty of the mind whose presence is essential to their being? I am aware that religion is founded on the voluntariness of belief, as it makes it a subject of reward and punishment; but before we extinguish the steady ray of reason and common sense, it is fit that we should discover, which we cannot do without their assistance, whether or no there be any other which may suffice to guide us through the labyrinth of life.

If the law 'de heretico comburendo' has not been formally repealed, I conceive that, from the promise held out by your Lordship's zeal, we need not despair of beholding the flames of persecution rekindled in Smithfield. Even now the lash that drove Descartes and Voltaire from their native country, the chains which bound Galileo, the flames which burned Vanini, again resound:—And where? in a nation that presumptuously calls itself the sanctuary of freedom. Under a government which, whilst it infringes the very right of thought and speech, boasts of permitting the liberty of the press; in a civilized and enlightened country, a man is pilloried and imprisoned because he is a Deist, and no one raises his voice in the indignation of outraged humanity. Does the Christian God, whom his followers eulogize as the Deity of humility and peace ; he, the regenerator of the world, the meek reformer, authorize one man to rise against another, and because lictors are at his beck, to chain and torture him as an Infidel ?

When the Apostles went abroad to convert the nations, were they enjoined to stab and poison all who disbelieved the divinity of Christ's mission ; assuredly, they would have been no more justifiable in this case than he is at present who puts into execution the law which inflicts pillory and imprisonment on the Deist.

Has not Mr. Eaton an equal right to call your Lordship an Infidel, as you have to imprison him for promulgating a different doctrine from that which you profess ?—What do I say !—Has he not even a stronger plea ?—The word *Infidel* can only mean any thing when applied to a person who professes that which he disbelieves. The test of truth is an undivided reliance on its inclusive powers ;—the test of conscious falsehood is the variety of the forms under which it presents itself, and its tendency towards employing whatever coercive means may be within its command, in order to procure the admission of what is unsusceptible of support from reason or persuasion. A dispassionate observer would feel himself more powerfully interested in favor of a man, who depending on the truth of his opinions, simply stated his reasons for entertaining them, than in that of his aggressor, who daringly avowing his unwillingness to answer them by argument, proceeded to repress the activity and break the spirit of their promulgator, by that torture and imprisonment whose infliction he could command.

I hesitate not to affirm that the opinions which Mr. Eaton sustained, when undergoing that mockery of a trial at which your Lordship presided, appear to me more true and good than those of his accuser ;—but

were they false as the visions of a Calvinist, it still would
be the duty of those who love liberty and virtue, to raise
their voice indignantly against a reviving system of persecution, against the coercively repressing any opinion,
which, if false, needs but the opposition of truth ; which,
if true, in spite of force, must ultimately prevail.

Mr. Eaton asserted that the scriptures were, from
beginning to end, a fable and imposture,* that the
Apostles were liars and deceivers.   He denied the
miracles, resurrection, and ascension of Jesus Christ.—
He did so, and the Attorney General denied the pro-
positions which he asserted, and asserted those which
he denied.   What singular conclusion is deducible from
this fact ?   None, but that the Attorney General and
Mr. Eaton sustained two opposite opinions.   The
Attorney General puts some obsolete and tyrannical
laws in force against Mr. Eaton, because he publishes
a book tending to prove that certain supernatural events,
which are supposed to have taken place eighteen centuries ago, in a remote corner of the world, did not
actually take place.   But how are the truth or falsehood
of the facts in dispute relevant to the merit or demerit
attachable to the advocates of the two opinions ?   No
man is accountable for his belief, because no man is
capable of directing it.   Mr. Eaton is therefore totally
blameless.   What are we to think of the justice of a
sentence, which punishes an individual against whom it
is not even attempted to attach the slightest stain of
criminality ?

It is asserted that Mr. Eaton's opinions are calculated
to subvert morality—How ?   What moral truth is
spoken of with irreverence or ridicule in the book which
he published ?   Morality, or the duty of a man and a
citizen, is founded on the relations which arise from the
association of human beings, and which vary with the
circumstances produced by the different states of this

* See the Attorney General's Speech.

association.—This duty in similar situations must be precisely the same in all ages and nations.—The opinion contrary to this has arisen from a supposition that the will of God is the source or criterion of morality : it is plain that the utmost exertion of Omnipotence could not cause that to be virtuous which actually is vicious. An all-powerful Demon might, indubitably, annex punishments to virtue and rewards to vice, but could not by these means effect the slightest change in their abstract and immutable natures.—Omnipotence could vary, by a providential interposition, the relations of human society ;—in this latter case, what before was virtuous would become vicious, according to the necessary and natural result of the alteration ; but the abstract natures of the opposite principles would have sustained not the slightest change ; for instance, the punishment with which society restrains the robber, the assassin, and the ravisher is just, laudable, and requisite. We admire and respect the institutions which curb those who would defeat the ends for which society was established ;—but, should a precisely similar coercion be exercised against one who merely expressed his disbelief of a system admitted by those entrusted with the executive power, using at the same time no methods of promulgation but those afforded by reason, certainly this coercion would be eminently inhuman and immoral ; and the supposition that any revelation from an unknown power avails to palliate a persecution so senseless, unprovoked, and indefensible, is at once to destroy the barrier which reason places between vice and virtue, and leave to unprincipled fanaticism a plea whereby it may excuse every act of frenzy, which its own wild passions, not the inspirations of the Deity, have engendered.   ·

Moral qualities are such as only a human being can possess. To attribute them to the Spirit of the Universe, or to suppose that it is capable of altering them, is to degrade God into man, and to annex to this incomprehensible being qualities incompatible with any *possible* definition of his nature. It may here be objected— Ought not the Creator to possess the perfections of the creature ? No. To attribute to God the moral qualities of man, is to suppose him susceptible of passions which, arising out of corporeal organisation, it is plain that a pure spirit cannot possess. A bear is not perfect except he is rough, a tyger is not perfect if he be not voracious, an elephant is not perfect if otherwise than docile. How *deep* an argument must that not be which proves that the Deity is as rough as a bear, as voracious as a tyger, and as docile as an elephant ! But even suppose with the vulgar, that God is a venerable old man, seated on a throne of clouds, his breast the theatre of various passions, analogous to those of humanity, his will changeable and uncertain as that of an earthly king,— still goodness and justice are qualities seldom nominally denied him, and it will be admitted that he disapproves of any action incompatible with these qualities. Persecution for opinion is unjust. With what consistency, then, can the worshippers of a Deity whose benevolence they boast, embitter the existence of their fellow being, because his ideas of that Deity are different from those which they entertain.—Alas ! there is no consistency in those persecutors who worship a benevolent Deity ; those who worship a Demon would alone act consonantly to these principles, by imprisoning and torturing in his name.

Persecution is the only name applicable to punishment inflicted on an individual in consequence of his opinions. —What end is persecution designed to answer ? Can it convince him whom it injures ? Can it prove to the people the falsehood of his opinions ? It may make *him* a hypocrite, and them cowards, but bad means can promote no good end. The unprejudiced mind looks with suspicion on a doctrine that needs the sustaining hand of power.

Socrates was poisoned because he dared to combat the degrading superstitions in which his countrymen were educated. Not long after his death, Athens recognized the injustice of his sentence ; his accuser Melitus was condemned, and Socrates became a demigod.

Jesus Christ was crucified because he attempted to supersede the ritual of Moses with regulations more moral and humane—his very judge made public acknowledgment of his innocence, but a bigotted and ignorant mob demanded the deed of horror.—Barabbas the murderer and traitor was released. The meek reformer Jesus was immolated to the sanguinary Deity of the Jews. Time rolled on, time changed the situations, and with them, the opinions of men.

The vulgar, ever in extremes, became persuaded that the crucifixion of Jesus was a supernatural event, and testimonies of miracles, so frequent in unenlightened ages, were not wanting to prove that he was something divine. This belief, rolling through the lapse of ages, acquired force and extent, until the divinity of Jesus became a dogma, which to dispute was death, which to doubt was infamy.

Christianity is now the established religion ; he who attempts to disprove it, must behold murderers and traitors take precedence of him in public opinion, though, if his genius be equal to his courage, and assisted by a peculiar coalition of circumstances, future ages may exalt him to a divinity, and persecute others in his name, as he was persecuted in the name of his predecessor, in the homage of the world.

The same means that have supported every other popular belief, have supported Christianity. War, imprisonment, murder, and falsehood; deeds of unexampled and incomparable atrocity have made it what it is. We derive from our ancestors a belief thus fostered and supported.—We quarrel, persecute, and hate for its maintenance.—Does not analogy favour the opinion that, as like other systems it has arisen and augmented, so like them it will decay and perish ; that, as violence and falsehood, not reasoning and persuasion, have procured its admission among mankind ; so, when enthusiasm has subsided, and time, that infallible con- troverter of false opinions, has involved its pretended evidences in the darkness of antiquity, it will become obsolete, and that men will then laugh as heartily at grace, faith, redemption, and original sin, as they now do at the metamorphoses of Jupiter, the miracles of Romish saints, the efficacy of witchcraft, and the appearance of departed spirits.

Had the christian religion commenced and continued by the mere force of reasoning and persuasion, by its self-evident excellence and fitness, the preceding analogy would be inadmissible. We should never speculate upon the future obsoleteness of a system perfectly con- formable to nature and reason. It would endure so long as they endured, it would be a truth as indisputable as the light of the sun, the criminality of murder, and other facts, physical and moral, which, depending on our organization, and relative situations, must remain ac- knowledged so long as man is man.—It is an incon- trovertible fact, the consideration of which ought to repress the hasty conclusions of credulity, or moderate its obstinacy in maintaining them, that, had the Jews not been a barbarous and fanatical race of men, had even the resolution of Pontius Pilate been equal to his candour, the christian religion never could have prevailed, it could not even have existed. Man ! the very existence of whose most cherished opinions de- pends from a thread so feeble, arises out of a source so equivocal, learn at least humility ; own at least that it is possible for thyself also to have been seduced by education and circumstance into the admission of tenets destitute of rational proof, and the truth of which has not yet been satisfactorily demonstrated. Acknowledge at least that the falsehood of thy brother's opinions is no sufficient reason for his meriting thy hatred.—What ! because a fellow being disputes the reasonableness of thy faith, wilt thou punish him with torture and imprisonment ? If persecution for religious opinions were admitted by the moralist, how wide a door would not be opened by which convulsionists of every kind might make inroads on the peace of society ! How many deeds of barbarism and blood would not receive a sanction !—But I will demand, if that man is not rather entitled to the respect than the discountenance of society, who, by disputing a received doctrine, either proves its falsehood and inutility, thereby aiming at the abolition of what is false and useless, or giving to its adherents an opportunity of establishing its excellence and truth.—Surely this can be no crime. Surely the individual who devotes his time to fearless and unrestricted inquiry into the grand questions arising out of our moral nature, ought rather to receive the patronage, than encounter the vengeance, of an enlightened legislature. I would have you to know, my Lord, that fetters of iron cannot bind or subdue the soul of virtue. From the damps and solitude of its dungeon it ascends free and undaunted, whither thine, from the pompous seat of judgment, dare not soar. I do not warn you to beware lest your profession as a Christian, should make you forget that you are a man ;—but I warn you against festinating that period, which, under the present coercive system, is too rapidly maturing, when the seats of justice shall be the seats of venality and slavishness, and the cells of Newgate become the abode of all that is honorable and true.

I mean not to compare Mr. Eaton with Socrates or Jesus ; he is a man of blameless and respectable character, he is a citizen unimpeached with crime; if, therefore, his rights as a citizen and a man have been infringed, they have been infringed by illegal and immoral violence.

But I will assert that, should a second Jesus arise among men ; should such a one as Socrates again enlighten the earth, lengthened imprisonment and infamous punishment (according to the regimen of persecution revived by your Lordship) would effect, what hemlock and the cross have heretofore effected, and the stain on the national character, like that on Athens and Judea, would remain indelible, but by the destruction of the history in which it is recorded. When the Christian Religion shall have faded from the earth, when its memory like that of Polytheism now shall remain, but remain only as the subject of ridicule and wonder, indignant posterity would attach immortal infamy to such an outrage ; like the murder of Socrates, it would secure the execration of every age.

The horrible and wide-wasting enormities which gleam like comets through the darkness of gothic and superstitious ages, are regarded by the moralist as no more than the necessary effects of known causes ; but, when an enlightened age and nation signalizes itself by a deed, becoming none but barbarians and fanatics, Philosophy itself is even induced to doubt whether human nature will ever emerge from the pettishness and imbecility of its childhood. The system of persecution at whose new birth, you, my Lord, are one of the presiding midwives, is not more impotent and wicked than inconsistent. The press is loaded with what are called (ironically, I should conceive) *proofs* of the Christian Religion : these books are replete with invective and calumny against Infidels, they presuppose that he who rejects Christianity must be utterly divested of reason and feeling. They advance the most unsupported assertions, and take as first principles the most revolting dogmas. The inferences drawn from these assumed premises are imposingly logical and correct ; but if a foundation is weak, no architect is needed to foretell the instability of the superstructure.—If the truth of Chris-

tianity is not disputable, for what purpose are these
books written ? If they are sufficient to prove it, what
further need of controversy ? *If God has spoken, why
is not the universe convinced?* If the Christian Religion
needs deeper learning, more painful investigation, to
establish its genuineness, wherefore attempt to accomplish that by force, which the human mind can alone
effect with satisfaction to itself? If, lastly, its truth
cannot be demonstrated, wherefore impotently attempt
to snatch from God the government of his creation, and
impiously assert that the Spirit of Benevolence has left
that knowledge most essential to the well being of man,
the only one which, since its promulgation, has been the
subject of unceasing cavil, the cause of irreconcileable
hatred?—Either the Christian Religion is true, or it is
not. If true, it comes from God, and its authenticity
can admit of doubt and dispute no further than its
Omnipotent Author is willing to allow;—if true, it
admits of rational proof, and is capable of being placed
equally beyond controversy, as the principles which have
been established concerning matter and mind, by Locke
and Newton ; and in proportion to the usefulness of the
fact in dispute, so must it be supposed that a benevolent
being is anxious to procure the diffusion of its knowledge
on the earth.—If false, surely no enlightened legislature
would punish the reasoner, who opposes a system so
much the more fatal and pernicious as it is extensively
admitted ; so much the more productive of absurd and
ruinous consequences, as it is entwined by education,
with the prejudices and affections of the human heart,
in the shape of a popular belief.

Let us suppose that some half-witted philosopher
should assert that the earth was the centre of the universe,
or that ideas could enter the human mind independently
of sensation or reflection. This man would assert what
is demonstrably incorrect ;—he would promulgate a
false opinion. Yet, would he therefore deserve pillory

and imprisonment ?   By no means ; probably few would discharge more correctly the duties of a citizen and a man.   I admit that the case above stated is not precisely in point.   The thinking part of the community has not received as indisputable the truth of Christianity, as they have that of the Newtonian system.   A very large portion of society, and that powerfully and extensively connected, derives its sole emolument from the belief of Christianity, as a popular faith.

To torture and imprison the asserter of a dogma, however ridiculous and false, is highly barbarous and impolitic :—How, then, does not the cruelty of persecution become aggravated when it is directed against the opposer of an opinion *yet under dispute,* and which men of unrivalled acquirements, penetrating genius, and stainless virtue, have spent, and at last sacrificed, their lives in combating.

The time is rapidly approaching, I hope, that you, my Lord, may live to behold its arrival, when the Mahometan, the Jew, the Christian, the Deist, and the Atheist, will live together in one community, equally sharing the benefits which arise from its association, and united in the bonds of charity and brotherly love.—My Lord, you have condemned an innocent man—no crime was imputed to him—and you sentenced him to torture and imprisonment.   I have not addressed this letter to you with the hopes of convincing you that you have acted wrong.   The most unprincipled and barbarous of men are not unprepared with sophisms, to prove that they would have acted in no other manner, and to show that vice is virtue.   But I raise my solitary voice, to express my disapprobation, so far as it goes, of the cruel and unjust sentence you passed upon Mr. Eaton ; to assert, so far as I am capable of influencing, those rights of humanity, which you have wantonly and unlawfully infringed.   My Lord,

Yours, &c.

PRINCE ALEXY HAIMATOFF.*

[*Memoirs of Prince Alexy Haimatoff.* Translated from the original
Latin MSS. under the immediate inspection of the Prince. By
JOHN BROWN, Esq. Pp. 236, 12mo. Hookham, 1814.]†

S the suffrage of mankind the legitimate criterion
of intellectual energy? Are complaints of the
aspirants to literary fame to be considered as
the honourable disappointment of neglected genius, or
the sickly impatience of a dreamer miserably self deceived? the most illustrious ornaments of the annals
of the human race have been stigmatised by the contempt and abhorrence of entire communities of man;
but this injustice arose out of some temporary superstition, some partial interest, some national doctrine : a
glorious redemption awaited their remembrance. There
is indeed, nothing so remarkable in the contempt of the
ignorant for the enlightened : the vulgar pride of folly
delights to triumph upon mind. This is an intelligible
process : the infamy or ingloriousness that can be thus

---

* From *The Critical Review*, December 1814, vol. vi. pp. 566-
574.
† This pseudonymous romance, as wild in its conception and
execution as Shelley's own romances of *Zastrozzi* and *St. Irvyne*,
was the work of Shelley's college-friend and biographer, Thomas
Jefferson Hogg. To Professor Dowden cf Dublin, Shelley's latest
biographer, is due the credit of disinterring and drawing public
attention to Shelley's curious critical notice of it.—ED.

explained detracts nothing from the beauty of virtue or
the sublimity of genius. But what does utter obscurity
express? if the public do not advert even in censure to a
performance, has that performance already received its
condemnation?

The result of this controversy is important to the
ingenuous critic. His labours are indeed miserably
worthless if their objects may invariably be attained
before their application. He should know the limits of
his prerogative. He should not be ignorant, whether it
is his duty to promulgate the decisions of others, or to
cultivate his taste and judgment, that he may be enabled
to render a reason for his own.

Circumstances the least connected with intellectual
nature have contributed, for a certain period, to retain
in obscurity the most memorable specimens of human
genius. The author refrains perhaps from introducing
his production to the world with all the pomp of
empirical bibliopolism. A sudden tide in the affairs of
men may make the neglect or contradiction of some
insignificant doctrine a badge of obscurity and discredit:
those even who are exempt from the action of these
absurd predilections are necessarily in an indirect
manner affected by their influence. It is perhaps the
product of an imagination daring and undisciplined:
the majority of readers ignorant and disdaining tolera-
tion refuse to pardon a neglect of common rules; their
canons of criticism are carelessly infringed, it is less
religious than a charity sermon, less methodical and
cold than a French tragedy, where all the unities are
preserved : no excellencies, where prudish cant and dull
regularity are absent, can preserve it from the contempt
and abhorrence of the multitude. It is evidently not
difficult to imagine an instance in which the most
elevated genius shall be recompensed with neglect.
Mediocrity alone seems unvaryingly to escape rebuke
and obloquy, it accommodates its attempts to the spirit

of the age which has produced it, and adopts with mimic effrontery the cant of the day and hour for which alone it lives.

We think that "the Memoirs of Prince Alexy Haimatoff" deserves to be regarded as an example of the fact by the frequency of which criticism is vindicated from the imputation of futility and impertinence. We do not hesitate to consider this fiction as the product of a bold and original mind. We hardly remember ever to have seen surpassed the subtle delicacy of imagination, by which the manifest distinctions of character and form are seized and pictured in colours that almost make nature more beautiful than herself. The vulgar observe no resemblances or discrepancies, but such as are gross and glaring. The science of mind to which history, poetry, biography serve as the materials, consists in the discernment of shades and distinctions where the unenlightened discover nothing but a shapeless and unmeaning mass. The faculty for this discernment distinguishes genius from dulness. There are passages in the production before us which afford instances of just and rapid intuition belonging only to intelligences that possess this faculty in no ordinary degree. As a composition the book is far from faultless. Its abruptness and angularities do not appear to have received the slightest polish or correction. The author has written with fervour, but has disdained to revise at leisure. These errors are the errors of youth and genius and the fervid impatience of sensibilities impetuously disburthening their fulness. The author is proudly negligent of connecting the incidents of his tale. It appears more like the recorded day dream of a poet, not unvisited by the sublimest and most lovely visions, than the tissue of a romance skilfully interwoven for the purpose of maintaining the interest of the reader, and conducting his sympathies by dramatic gradations to the denoûment. It is, what it professes to be, a memoir, not a novel.

Yet its claims to the former appellation are established, only by the impatience and inexperience of the author, who, possessing in an eminent degree, the higher qualifications of a a novelist, we had almost said a poet, has neglected the number by which that success would probably have been secured, which, in this instance, merits of a far nobler stamp have unfortunately failed to acquire. Prince Alexy is by no means an unnatural, although no common character. We think we can discern his counterpart in Alfieri's delineation of himself. The same propensities, the same ardent devotion to his purposes, the same chivalric and unproductive attachment to unbounded liberty, characterises both. We are inclined to doubt whether the author has not attributed to his hero the doctrines of universal philanthropy in a spirit of profound and almost unsearchable irony : at least he appears biassed by no peculiar principles, and it were perhaps an insoluble inquiry whether any, and if any, what moral truth he designed to illustrate by his tale. Bruhle, the tutor of Alexy, is a character delineated with consummate skill ; the power of intelligence and virtue over external deficiencies is forcibly exemplified. The calmness, patience and magnanimity of this singular man, are truly rare and admirable : his disinterestedness, his equanimity, his irresistible gentleness, form a finished and delightful portrait. But we cannot regard his commendation to his pupil to indulge in promiscuous concubinage without horror and detestation. The author appears to deem the loveless intercourse of brutal appetite a venial offence against delicacy and virtue ! he asserts that a transient connexion with a cultivated female may contribute to form the heart without essentially vitiating the sensibilities. It is our duty to protest against so pernicious and disgusting an opinion. No man can rise pure from the poisonous embraces of a prostitute, or sinless from the desolated hopes of a confiding heart. Whatever may be the

claims of chastity, whatever the advantages of simple
and pure affections, these ties, these benefits, are of
equal obligation to either sex. Domestic relations
depend for their integrity upon a complete reciprocity of
duties. But the author himself has in the adventure of
the Sultana, Debesh-Sheptuti, afforded a most impressive
and tremendous allegory of the cold-blooded and malignant selfishness of sensuality.

We are incapacitated by the unconnected and vague
narrative from forming an analysis of the incidents:
they would consist indeed, simply of a catalogue of
events, and which, divested of the aërial tinge of
genius, might appear trivial and common. We shall
content ourselves, therefore, with selecting some passages calculated to exemplify the peculiar powers of
the author. The following description of the simple
and interesting Rosalie is in the highest style of delineation :—

" Her hair was unusually black, she truly had raven locks, the
same glossiness, the same varying shade, the same mixture of
purple and sable for which the plumage of the raven is remarkable, were found in the long elastic tresses depending from her
head and covering her shoulders. Her complexion was dark
and clear : the colours which composed the brown that dyed
her smooth skin, were so well mixed, that not one blot, not one
varied tinge, injured its brightness, and when the blush of
animation or of modesty flushed her cheek, the tint was so rare,
that could a painter have dipped his pencil in it, that single
shade would have rendered him immortal. The bone above
her eye was sharp, and beautifully curved ; much as I have
admired the wonderful properties of curves, I am convinced
that their most stupendous properties collected would fall far
short of that magic line. The eyebrow was pencilled with
extreme nicety ; in the centre it consisted of the deepest shade
of black, at the edges it was hardly perceptible, and no man
could have been hardy enough to have attempted to define the
precise spot at which it ceased : in short the velvet drapery of
the eyebrow was only to be rivalled by the purple of the long
black eyelashes that terminated the ample curtain. Rosalie's
eyes were large and full ; they appeared at a distance uniformly

dark, but upon close inspection the innumerable strokes of various hues of infinite fineness and endless variety, drawn in concentric circles behind the pellucid crystal, filled the mind with wonder and admiration, and could only be the work of infinite power directed by infinite wisdom."

Alexy's union with Aür-Ahebeh the Circassian slave is marked by circumstances of deep pathos, and the sweetest tenderness of sentiment. The description of his misery and madness at her death deserves to be remarked as affording evidence of an imagination vast, profound and full of energy.

"Alexy, who gained the friendship, perhaps the love of the native Rosalie: the handsome Haimatoff, the philosophic Haimatoff, the haughty Haimatoff, Haimatoff the gay, the witty, the accomplished, the bold hunter, the friend of liberty, the chivalric lover of all that is feminine, the hero, the enthusiast : see him now, that is he, mark him ! he appears in the shades of evening, he stalks as a spectre, he has just risen from the damps of the charnel-house ; see, the dews still hang on his forehead. He will vanish at cock-crowing, he never heard the song of the lark, nor the busy hum of men ; the sun's rays never warmed him, the pale moonbeam alone shows his unearthly figure, which is fanned by the wing of the owl, which scarce obstructs the slow flight of the droning beetle, or of the drowsy bat. Mark him ! he stops, his lean arms are crossed on his bosom ; he is bowed to the earth, his sunken eye gazes from its deep cavity on vacuity, as the toad skulking in the corner of a sepulchre, peeps with malignity through the circumambient gloom. His cheek is hollow ; the glowing tints of his complexion, which once resembled the autumnal sunbeam on the autumnal beech, are gone, the cadaverous yellow, the livid hue, have usurped their place, the sable honours of his head have perished, they once waved in the wind like the jetty pinions of the raven, the skull is only covered by the shrivelled skin, which the rook views wistfully, and calls to her young ones. His gaunt bones start from his wrinkled garments, his voice is deep, hollow, sepulchral ; it is the voice which wakes the dead, he has long held converse with the departed. He attempts to walk he knows not whither, his legs totter under him, he falls, the boys hoot him, the dogs bark at him, he hears them not, he sees them not.—Rest there, Alexy, it beseemeth thee, thy bed is the grave, thy bride is the worm, yet once thou stoodest erect, thy cheek was flushed with joyful ardour, thy eye blazing told what thy head conceived, what thy heart felt, thy limbs were vigour and activity, thy bosom expanded with pride, ambition, and desire, every nerve thrilled to feel, every muscle swelled to execute.

"Haimatoff, the blight has tainted thee, thou ample roomy web of life, whereon were traced the gaudy characters, the gay embroidery of pleasure, how has the moth battened on thee; Haimatoff, how has the devouring flame scorched the plains, once yellow with the harvest! the simoon, the parching breath of the desert, has swept over the laughing plains, the carpet of verdure rolled away at its approach, and has bared amid desolation. Thou stricken deer, thy leather coat, thy dappled hide hangs loose upon thee, it was a deadly arrow, how has it wasted thee, thou scathed oak, how has the red lightning drank thy sap: Haimatoff, Haimatoff, eat thy soul with vexation. Let the immeasurable ocean roll between thee and pride: you must not dwell together," p. 129.

The episode of Viola is affecting, natural, and beautiful. We do not ever remember to have seen the unforgiving fastidiousness of family honour more awfully illustrated. After the death of her lover, Viola still expects that he will esteem, still cherishes the delusion that he is not lost to her for ever.

"She used frequently to go to the window to look for him, or walk in the Park to meet him, but without the least impatience, at his delay. She learnt a new tune, or a new song to amuse him, she stood behind the door to startle him as he entered, or disguised herself to surprise him."

The character of Mary, deserves, we think, to be considered as the only complete failure in the book. Every other female whom the author has attempted to describe is designated by an individuality peculiarly marked and true. They constitute finished portraits of whatever is eminently simple, graceful, gentle, or disgustingly atrocious and vile. Mary alone is the miserable parasite of fashion, the tame slave of drivelling and drunken folly, the cold-hearted coquette. the lying

and meretricious prude. The means employed to gain
this worthless prize corresponds exactly with its worth-
lessness. Sir Fulke Hildebrand is a strenuous Tory,
Alexy, on his arrival in England professes himself
inclined to the principles of the Whig party, finding
that the Baronet had sworn that his daughter should
never marry a Whig, he sacrifices his principles and
with inconceivable effrontery thus palliates his apostasy
and falsehood.

" The prejudices of the Baronet were strong in proportion as
they were irrational.   I resolved rather to humour than to thwart
them.   I contrived to be invited to dine in company with him ;
I always proposed the health of the minister, I introduced
politics and defended the Tory party in long speeches, I attended
clubs and public dinners of that interest.   I do not know whether
this conduct was justifiable ; it may certainly be excused when
the circumstances of my case are duly considered.   I would tear
myself in pieces if I suspected that I could be guilty of the
slightest falsehood or prevarication ; (see Lord Chesterfield's
Letters for the courtier-like distinction between simulation and
dissimulation,) but there was nothing of that sort here.   I was
of no party, consequently, I could not be accused of deserting
any one.   I did not defend the injustice of any body of men, I
did not detract from the merits of any virtuous character.   I
praised what was laudable in the Tory party, and blamed what
was reprehensible in the Whigs : I was silent with regard to
whatever was culpable in the former or praiseworthy in the
latter.   The stratagem was innocent which injured no one, and
which promoted the happiness of two individuals, especially of
the most amiable woman the world ever knew."

An instance of more deplorable perversity of the human
understanding we do not recollect ever to have witnessed.
It almost persuades us to believe that scepticism or indifference concerning certain sacred truths may occasionally produce a subtlety of sophism, by which the
conscience of the criminal may be bribed to overlook
his crime.

Towards the conclusion of this strange and powerful
performance it must be confessed that *aliquando bonus*

dormitat Homerus. The adventure of the Eleutheri,* although the sketch of a profounder project, is introduced and concluded with unintelligible abruptness. Bruhle dies, purposely as it should seem that his pupil may renounce the romantic sublimity of his nature, and that his inauspicious union and prostituted character might be exempt from the censure of violated friendship. Numerous indications of profound and vigorous thought are scattered over even the most negligently compacted portions of the narrative. It is an unweeded garden where nightshade is interwoven with sweet jessamine, and the most delicate spices of the east peep over struggling stalks of rank and poisonous hemlock.

In the delineation of the more evanescent feelings and uncommon instances of strong and delicate passion we conceive the author to have exhibited new and unparalleled powers. He has noticed some peculiarities of female character with a delicacy and truth singularly exquisite. We think that the interesting subject of sexual relations requires for its successful development the application of a mind thus organised and endowed. Yet even here how great the deficiencies ; this mind must be pure from the fashionable superstitions of gallantry, must be exempt from the sordid feelings which with blind idolatry worship the image and blaspheme the deity, reverence the type, and degrade the reality of which it is an emblem.

We do not hesitate to assert that the author of this volume is a man of ability. His great though indisciplinable energies and fervid rapidity of conception

---

* From Edinburgh, Nov. 26, 1813. Shelley had written to Hogg: —" Your novel is now printed. Write more like this. Delight us again with a character so natural and energetic as Alexy : but do not persevere in writing after you grow weary of your toil. *Aliquando bonus dormitat Homerus ;* and the swans and the Eleutherarchs are proofs that you were a little sleepy." (See Hogg's Life of Shelley, vol. ii. p. 481.)—ED.

embody scenes and situations, and passions affording
inexhaustible food for wonder and delight. The interest
is deep and irresistible. A moral enchanter seems to
have conjured up the shapes of all that is beautiful
and strange to suspend the faculties in fascination and
astonishment.

BIBLIOGRAPHY

ARRANGED IN CHRONOLOGICAL ORDER

OF THE PUBLISHED WRITINGS IN VERSE AND PROSE

OF

PERCY BYSSHE SHELLEY.

THE BIBLIOGRAPHY OF SHELLEY.

1810.

ZASTROZZI. A Romance. By P. B. S. London : Printed for G. Wilkie and J. Robinson, 57 Paternoster Row. 1810. 12mo, pp. 252.

> ——That their God
> May prove their foe, and with repenting hand
> Abolish his own works—This would surpass
> Common revenge.—*Paradise Lost.*

POSTHUMOUS FRAGMENTS OF MARGARET NICHOLSON. Being Poems found amongst the Papers of that noted Female, who attempted the Life of the King in 1786. Edited by John Fitzvictor. Oxford : Printed and sold by J. Munday. 1810. 4to, pp. 29.

1811.

ST. IRVYNE; or, The Rosicrucian. A Romance. By a Gentleman of the University of Oxford. London : Printed for J. J. Stockdale, 41 Pall Mall. 1811. 12mo, pp. 236.

A POETICAL ESSAY ON THE EXISTING STATE OF THINGS. By a Gentleman of the University of Oxford. For assisting to maintain in prison Mr. Peter Finnerty, imprisoned for a libel. London : Sold by B. Crosby & Co., and all other Booksellers. 1811.

> And Famine at her bidding wasted wide
> The Wretched Land, till in the Public way,
> Promiscuous where the dead and dying lay,
> Dogs fed on human bones in the open light of day.
> —*Curse of Kehama.*

THE NECESSITY OF ATHEISM. Worthing : Printed by E. & W. Phillips. Sold in London and Oxford. [1811.] 8vo, pp. 13.

> Quod clarâ et perspicuâ demonstratione careat
> pro vero habere mens omnino nequis humana.
> —*Bacon de Augment. Scient.*

ORIGINAL POETRY. By Victor and Cazire. London : J. J. Stockdale, 41 Pall Mall. 1811. Royal 8vo, pp. 64.

1812.

A LETTER TO LORD ELLENBOROUGH. Occasioned by the Sentence which he passed on Mr. D. I. Eaton, as Publisher of the Third Part of Paine's Age of Reason. [1812.] Small 8vo, pp. 23.

Deorum offensa, Diis curæ.

—It is contrary to the mild spirit of the Christian Religion, for no sanction can be found under that dispensation which will warrant a Government to impose disabilities and penalties upon any man, on account of his religious opinions. [*Hear, Hear.*]—*Marquis Wellesley's Speech. Globe, July* 2.

AN ADDRESS TO THE IRISH PEOPLE. By Percy Bysshe Shelley. Dublin. 1812. Price 5d. 8vo, pp. 22.

ADVERTISEMENT.—The lowest possible price is set on this publication, because it is the intention of the author to awaken in the minds of the Irish poor, a knowledge of their real state, summarily pointing out the evils of that state, and suggesting rational means of remedy.—Catholic Emancipation, and a Repeal of the Union Act, (the latter, the most successful engine that England ever wielded over the misery of fallen Ireland,) being treated of in the following address, as grievances which unanimity and resolution may remove and associations conducted with peaceable firmness, being earnestly recommended, as means for embodying that unanimity and firmness, which must finally be successful.

PROPOSALS FOR AN ASSOCIATION OF THOSE PHILANTHROPISTS, who convinced of the inadequacy of the moral and political state of Ireland to produce benefits which are nevertheless attainable are willing to unite to accomplish its regeneration. By Percy Bysshe Shelley. Dublin : Printed by I. Eton, Winetavern Street. [1812.] 8vo, pp. 18.

1813.

QUEEN MAB. A Philosophical Poem. With Notes. By Percy Bysshe Shelley. London : Printed by P. B. Shelley, 23 Chapel Street, Grosvenor Square. 1813. Crown 8vo pp. 240.

ECRASEZ L'INFAME !
Correspondance de Voltaire.

Avia Pieridum peragro loca, nullius ante
Trita solo ; juvat integros accedere fonteis;
Atque haurire : juratque novos decerpere flores.
*   *   *   *   *
Unde prius nulli velarint tempora musæ.
Primum quod magnis doceo de rebus ; et arctis
Religionum animos nodio exsolvere pergo.—*Lucret.* lib. iv

Δος του στῶ, καὶ κοσμος κινησω.—*Archimedes.*

A VINDICATION OF NATURAL DIET. Being one in a Series of
Notes to Queen Mab, a Philosophical Poem. London :
Printed for J. Callow, Medical Bookseller, Crown Court,
Princes Street, Soho, by Smith & Davy, Queen Street,
Seven Dials. 1813. Price 1s. 6d. 12mo, pp. 43.

Ιαπετιονιδη, παντων περι μηδεα ειδωσ,
Χαιρεισ μεν πυρ κλεψασ, και εμασ φρενασ ηπεροπευσασ ;
Σοιτ' αυτω μεγα πημα και ανδρασιν εσσομενοισι.
Τοισ δ'εγω αντι πυροσ δωσω κακον, ω κεν απαντεσ
Τερπωνται κατα θυμον, εον κακον αμφαγαπωντεσ.
—ΗΣΙΩΔ. *Op. et Dies.* i. 54.

1814.

A REFUTATION OF DEISM. In a Dialogue. London : Printed
by Schulze & Dean, 13 Poland Street. 1814. 8vo, pp. v.
101.

ΣΥΝΕΤΟΙΣΙΝ.

1816.

ALASTOR; or, The Spirit of Solitude, and other Poems. By
Percy Bysshe Shelley. London : Printed for Baldwin,
Cradock, & Joy, Paternoster Row, and Carpenter & Son,
Old Bond Street, by S. Hamilton, Weybridge, Surrey.
1816. Fcp. 8vo, pp. 101.

1817.

A PROPOSAL FOR PUTTING REFORM TO THE VOTE THROUGH-
OUT THE KINGDOM. By the Hermit of Marlow. London :
Printed for C. & J. Ollier, 3 Welbeck Street, Cavendish
Square, by C. H. Reynell, 21 Piccadilly. 1817. 8vo,
pp. 13.

AN ADDRESS TO THE PEOPLE ON THE DEATH OF THE PRIN-
CESS CHARLOTTE. By the Hermit of Marlow. [1817.]

" We Pity the Plumage, but forget the Dying Bird."

No copy of the original edition, apparently limited to twenty copies, is
known to exist. A facsimile reprint, reprinted for Thomas Rodd, 2 Great
Newport Street, 8vo, pp. 16, was issued not later than 1843, and is still
procurable.

HISTORY OF A SIX WEEKS' TOUR THROUGH A PART OF
FRANCE, SWITZERLAND, GERMANY, AND HOLLAND.
With Letters descriptive of a Sail round the Lake of Geneva,
and of the Glaciers of Chamouni. London : Published by

II. 2 C

T. Hookham, Jun., Old Bond Street, and C. & J. Ollier, Welbeck Street. 1817. Fcp. 8vo, pp. vi. 183.

1818.

LAON AND CYTHNA; or, The Revolution of the Golden City. A Vision of the Nineteenth Century. In the Stanza of Spenser. By Percy B. Shelley. London: Printed for Sherwood, Neely, & Jones, Paternoster Row, and C. & J. Ollier, Welbeck Street, by B. M'Millan, Bow Street, Covent Garden. 1818. 8vo, pp. xxxii. 270.

ΔΟΣ ΠΟΥ ΣΤΩ ΚΑΙ ΚΟΣΜΟΝ ΚΙΝΗΣΩ.—*Archimedes.*

THE REVOLT OF ISLAM. A Poem, in Twelve Cantos. By Percy Bysshe Shelley. London : Printed for C. & J. Ollier, Welbeck Street, by B. M'Millan, Bow Street, Covent Garden. 1818. 8vo, pp. xxxii. 270.

1819.

ROSALIND AND HELEN. A Modern Eclogue; with other Poems. By Percy Bysshe Shelley. London : Printed for C. & J. Ollier, Vere Street, Bond Street. 1819. 8vo, pp. 92.

THE CENCI. A Tragedy, in Five Acts. By Percy B. Shelley. Italy: Printed for C. & J. Ollier, Vere Street, Bond Street, London. 1819. 8vo, pp. xiv. 104.

THE CENCI. A Tragedy in Five Acts. By Percy Bysshe Shelley. Second edition. London : C. & J. Ollier, Vere Street, Bond Street. 1821. 8vo, pp. xviii. 104.

1820.

PROMETHEUS UNBOUND. A Lyrical Drama in Four Acts, with other Poems. By Percy Bysshe Shelley. London : C. & J. Ollier, Vere Street, Bond Street. 1820. 8vo, pp. 222.

Audisne hæc, amphiaræ, sub terram abdite?

ŒDIPUS TYRANNUS; or, Swellfoot the Tyrant. A Tragedy in Two Acts. Translated from the Original Doric. London : Published for the Author, by J. Johnston, 98 Cheapside, and sold by all Booksellers. 1820. 8vo, pp. 39.

——— Choose Reform or civil-war,
When thro' thy streets, instead of hare with dogs,
A CONSORT-QUEEN shall hunt a KING with hogs,
Riding on the IONIAN MINOTAUR.

1821.

ADONAIS. An Elegy on the Death of John Keats, Author of Endymion, Hyperion, &c. By Percy B. Shelley. Pisa : With the types of Didot. 1821. 4to, pp. 25.

Αστήρ πρὶν μὲν ἔλαμπες ἐνι ζῶοισιν ἐῶος.
Νῦν δε θανὼν, λαμπεις ἔσπερος εν φθίμενοις.—*Plato.*

EPIPSYCHIDION. Verses addressed to the Noble and Unfortunate Lady Emilia V——, now imprisoned in the Convent of ——. London : C. & J. Ollier, Vere Street, Bond Street. 1821. 8vo, pp. 31.

L'anima amante si slancia fuori del creato, e si crea nel infinito un Mondo tutto per essa, diverso assai da questo oscuro e pauroso baratro.
HER OWN WORDS.

1822.

HELLAS. A Lyrical Drama. By Percy B. Shelley. London : Charles and James Ollier, Vere Street, Bond Street. 1822. 8vo, pp. xii. 60.

ΜΑΝΤΙΣ ΕΙΜ' ΕΣΘΛΩΝ 'ΑΓΩΝΩΝ.—*Odip. Colon.*

The last work published by Shelley himself. The remainder are posthumous publications.

POSTHUMOUS PUBLICATIONS.

POSTHUMOUS POEMS OF PERCY BYSSHE SHELLEY. London : Printed for John and Henry L. Hunt, Tavistock Street, Covent Garden. 1824. 8vo, pp. xii. 415.

In nobil sangue vita umile e queta,
Ed in alto intelletto un puro core ;
Frutto senile in sul giovenil fiore,
E in aspetto pensoso anima lieta.—*Petrarca.*

THE MASQUE OF ANARCHY. A Poem. By Percy Bysshe Shelley. Now first published, with a Preface by Leigh Hunt. London : Edward Moxon, 64 New Bond Street. 1832. Fcp. 8vo, pp. xxx. 47.

Hope is strong :
Justice and Truth their winged child have found.—*Revolt of Islam*

THE SHELLEY PAPERS. Memoir of Percy Bysshe Shelley, by T. Medwin, Esq., and Original Poems and Papers, by Percy Bysshe Shelley. Now first collected. London : Whittaker, Treacher, & Co. 1833. 18mo, pp. viii. 180.

ESSAYS, LETTERS FROM ABROAD, TRANSLATIONS AND FRAG- MENTS. By Percy Bysshe Shelley. Edited by Mrs. Shelley. In two volumes. London : Edward Moxon, Dover Street. 1840. Crown 8vo, pp. xxxii. 320, viii. 360.

RELICS OF SHELLEY. Edited by Richard Garnett. London : Edward Moxon & Co., Dover Street. 1862. Fcp. 8vo, pp. xvi. 191.

> "Sing again, with your dear voice revealing
> A tone
> Of some world far from ours,
> Where music and moonlight and feeling
> Are one."

CONTENTS.—(Preface)—Prologue to Hellas (with note)—The Magic Plant (with note)—Orpheus (with note)—Scene from Tasso (with note)—Fiordi- spina (with note)—To his Genius—Love, Hope, Desire, and Fear—Lines ("We meet not as we parted")—Lines written in the Bay of Lerici—Frag- ments of the Adonais (with notes)—Translation of the First Canzone of Dante's Convito.

INDEX.

THE END.

www.ingramcontent.com/pod-product-compliance
Lightning Source LLC
Chambersburg PA
CBHW032312280326

41932CB00009B/788